Remembering Margaret Thatcher

REMEMBERING
MARGARET THATCHER

Commemorations, Tributes and Assessments

EDITED AND ANNOTATED BY JOHN BLUNDELL
INTRODUCTION BY THE RT HON DAVID DAVIS MP

Extracts from
the House of Commons Official Report
(Volume 560 No. 138) Wednesday 10 April 2013
and from
the House of Lords Official Report
(Volume 744 No. 134) Wednesday 10 April 2013

Algora Publishing
New York

TABLE OF CONTENTS

FOREWORD

John Blundell

Margaret Thatcher died in her suite at the Ritz Hotel on Piccadilly in central London Monday, 8 April 2013. She was 87 years old and since a series of minor strokes in 2001 had been in decline.

She was the longest serving UK Prime Minister of the 20th century; she was the first female Prime Minister of any major Western country; but she was most of all proud of being the first (and still only) scientist to serve in that role.

Two days later on Wednesday, 10 April the House of Commons and the House of Lords, the UK's lower and upper chambers, were recalled to hear tributes to her remarkable life.

The Commons heard 78 such tributes while the Lords heard 50 for a total of 128.

This book starts with an Introduction by the Rt Hon David Davis MP, a parliamentarian of over 25 years standing. As an ardent admirer of Margaret Thatcher, one might have expected him to speak in the Commons. However, on seeing the very long list of those wanting to do so, he decided to approach the day differently. Privy Counsellors, of which he is one, are allowed to enter the Lords and listen to the speeches therein, sitting on the steps to the throne of HM Queen Elizabeth II. So David, quite probably uniquely, flitted between both chambers listening to key speeches and absorbing the atmosphere in both Houses. His Introduction very much sets the scene.

And what a scene! It was unprecedented for Parliament, which was not sitting, to be recalled except for national emergency. Normal practice would be to have, say, 45 to 75 minutes of tributes at the start of business the next day each House was scheduled to sit. Instead, each House sat for a combined total of nearly 13 hours and in the Commons it was technically a debate.

Next, following my Biographical Essay, comes all or at least part of all 128 speeches, first those from the House of Commons and then those from the House of Lords, in the order they were delivered. Each speaker is briefly described by me, within square brackets, and references to idiosyncratic matters such as broken cricket bats are explained. Anything else in square brackets is part of the official record. I have added a few clarifications in italics, within parentheses.

A few explanatory notes are in order:

- Virtually every speech contained condolences to the family; most of these have, after the opening speeches, been removed.

- I have not changed the official British spelling, punctuation or style, so Downing Street (as one would write in America) is Downing street. Likewise Berlin Wall is Berlin wall. Also the times given as the speeches unfold follow two different conventions. One minute past three in the Commons is 3.1pm while in the Lords it is 3:01pm; these have not been changed.

- I struggled with clear factual errors and just noted them. The Clitheroe by-election was surely 1 March 1979 and not February 1974; likewise Margaret surely worked for Robert Carr, not the other way around.

- When it came to unusual locutions, I was tempted to re-write some of them for clarity but resisted, in order to preserve the unique voice and perspective of each commentator.

- For party affiliation, the House of Commons transcript gives the relevant information, unlike the House of Lords, where I inserted such names if I felt it necessary.

- In the House of Lords we hear from many Crossbenchers. These are not people who are angry but rather Peers with no formal affiliation. In American English, they are Independents.

Finally, this book concludes with a section of quotes from world leaders and newspapers which reflect the global impact of Margaret Thatcher. After all it was the President, the Pope, and the Prime Minister who tore down that wall and destroyed an evil empire without a shot being fired, and her policy of privatizing the commanding heights of the economy has been copied everywhere except Cuba and North Korea.

INTRODUCTION

The Rt Hon David Davis MP

The day that Parliament was recalled to recognize the passing of Lady Thatcher was memorable in many ways. Margaret Thatcher was as controversial in death as she was in life.

The plans for her funeral had been published — drawn up under Prime Minister Tony Blair, approved by Prime Minister Gordon Brown, and implemented under Prime Minister David Cameron — and they came under immediate attack as being too costly. Technically not a state funeral, it was that in all but name, attended by the Queen and all living Prime Ministers.

Similarly criticised was the recall of the House of Commons this day. Normally only done under conditions of national emergency, it was unheard of for Parliament to be recalled for the death of an erstwhile Prime Minister. Some of the carping was from the extreme left, but not all. Some was from the cash-strapped lower middle classes who were hit hardest by the government's austerity measures, from that part of middle England that she herself represented so well.

So, ironically, I think Mrs. Thatcher herself would have agreed with the critics of spending so much in austere times. I can just see her now, furrowed brow, shaking her head and saying "The cost, my dear. The cost!"

But history would not be denied, and neither should it have been. This was a celebration of a lady of enormous personal and political greatness. Not only did she defeat the Marxist dogma of her day, she was the living proof that, contrary to Marx, individuals could make a difference.

People tend to assume that past history was inevitable. In fact, the world was incredibly lucky that we had the triumvirate of Reagan, Gorbachev, and

Thatcher in place at precisely the time when we needed them. It was a time for heroes, and unusually it was a time when the heroes were politicians.

I remember once sitting across from Margaret at a function in Phoenix, Arizona. She started her speech with "I come from a place where we produce more history than we locally consume." It was a good joke, but also a subtle reminder to her American audience that a great deal of the modern world had been effectively created by Great Britain.

It was a tradition that, with Reagan and Gorbachev, she was determined to continue. In a single decade she was the catalyst for the turnaround of the British economy, the resounding defeat of the socialist conventional wisdom in the United Kingdom, and with Reagan and Gorbachev, the liberation of hundreds of millions of souls from Communist oppression. These, of course, are just the headlines. As by-blows of her efforts, she also created the conditions for a range of changes in her opposition from the reform of the Labour Party under Tony Blair to the embrace of property rights by the Chinese leadership. That she dominated the age, there is no doubt.

This was reflected in the debates in the House of Commons and House of Lords on that momentous day, the Commons reflecting on the history and outcomes of her premiership, the Lords informing us with contemporaneous accounts of her style and personality.

It was notable that in the Commons and the Lords she was praised by both her own Party and her opponents, albeit in somewhat nuanced terms by the latter. They had all learned from experience that the things she believed in and fought for had worked, that to a very large extent her often tough solutions to the problems of the day had delivered results.

Take as perhaps the best example Paddy Ashdown, past leader of the Liberal Democrats, previous UN High Representative in Bosnia, and erstwhile Special Forces warrior:

> In my view, three qualities set her apart as something different but each of them had its drawbacks. The first was a passionate commitment to freedom. As a Liberal, needless to say, I mostly welcomed that, although perhaps not as much as I should have at the time. Later, in Bosnia, when I tried to get a stagnant economy moving, I found myself putting into practice many of the very things that I had opposed when she introduced them: aggressive liberalisation of the markets, stripping down the barriers to business and lowering taxation. In these things she was right at the time....Our challenge today is to find a kinder, less destructive, more balanced way of shaping our economy, but that is today. At the time when she did those things, they needed to be done.

> Her second defining quality was her patriotism. David Cameron, the present Prime Minister, recently called her the "patriot Prime Minister". It is a good phrase and an apposite one. However, her patriotism too, though so powerfully held and expressed, was more about the preservation and restoration of Britain's past position than it was about preparing us for the chal-

lenges of what came next. She used her formidable talents to give our country a few more years of glory, and for that we should be eternally grateful....

Her final triumphant quality was of course her courage. This, I think, is the pre-eminent quality of leadership and she had it in abundance. Yet this, too — her greatest asset — had its dangers....She could see the risks but she ignored them if she believed she was right, and paradoxically this, in the final analysis, was what ended her long term as Prime Minister.

What also came across in those contemporaneous comments was the difference between Margaret Thatcher the public figure and Margaret the private person. It is a comforting simplicity for many of us who supported her to think of her as fearless. She was anything but. However, like all great historical figures she mastered those fears because she knew she had to, if she was going to achieve great things.

Someone who saw this at closer range than most was Richard Butler, her Principal Private Secretary between 1982 and 1985, arguably the time when she transformed Britain the most.

Inside No. 10, having the privilege of seeing her in that intimate setting, we of course saw a very different person from the one that the public saw outside. The public saw the bravura performances and the confidence. She has been charged with being overconfident, even arrogant, but you saw a very different picture, before the great public appearances, inside No. 10. Somebody whose motivation and force was not built on overconfidence but was in fact built on lack of self-confidence. I say that because I heard her say it herself publicly, after she left office. She said it was something that the media never really realised about her. I believe that that was the driving force behind her perfectionism in her appearance, in her dress, in her speeches and in her grip on her briefing. All those things had to be perfect before she would appear in public. [Before] the conference speech after the Brighton bomb [she was] sitting in the green room, saying, "I am not sure I can go through with this". Gordon Reece said, "Of course you can go through with it". I am absolutely certain that she was always going to go through with it. Many times, I saw her say beforehand that she was not sure she could do something and then go out and give a bravura performance.

That understandable nervousness was the reason that she managed to combine such strategic boldness with tactical caution, and it was the tactical caution that made the bold strategies work. History is full of figures who started out bold, but had to abandon their strategies because they could not make them work. She was never one of those.

I suspect that this combination of caution and confidence was most important when she was carrying out those policies, from council house sales to trades union reforms that, paradoxically, were most attacked by the Left, but which were explicitly designed to help the ordinary British working family.

Lord Bhattacharyya, the great professor of manufacturing and engineering, understood this only too well:

Baroness Thatcher was never anti-worker, as people think she was. She certainly hated restrictive practices, barriers and compulsion, but she truly wanted to give workers a chance to achieve and improve their lives. That is why she came to encourage us to connect with industry, support advanced technology and give industrial workers new skills and opportunities, which we did.

What is Baroness Thatcher's legacy to British manufacturers? Through some very tough times, and despite much criticism, she built a framework for prosperity by giving British businesses the freedoms they needed to manage, invest and trade. The removing of the shackles made a huge difference. What we did not do, after she left, was capitalise on this.

The British working classes understood this much better than their supposed intellectual superiors, which is why more of them voted for Mrs. Thatcher than any other modern Tory Prime Minister.

Many of her opponents never saw beyond the protective carapace of self confidence and certainty that she projected around her. I sometimes think that it was entirely appropriate that the Russians saw that certainty of purpose and dubbed her the "Iron Lady", because she wore that certainty like a suit of metal armour, to cover the softer person underneath.

That softer person, almost unknown to the public, was also enormously kindly and generous. This was reflected in both Lords and Commons in innumerable anecdotes about numerous acts of kindness, that touch on the arm, that gentle inquiry after a sick loved one. But the story that stands out was a remarkable one told by Maurice Saatchi, one of the architects of her electoral victories. He is explaining to Margaret at a Party Conference where he had been dining the night before.

"We went to a lovely restaurant, but a funny thing happened". She asked what. I explained that we were upstairs; the downstairs was absolutely packed, as all restaurants in Blackpool are during party conference week. Upstairs, there was only our table for two and the rest of the room was empty. A long table was laid out for dinner for about 16 people. [My guest] and I had the room to ourselves. When it came to pay the bill, I asked the woman who owned the restaurant: "What happened to those people?" It was a shocking moment and I remember it vividly. She said, "You did this. Your party did this. Don't you realise that my husband and I can't keep this place running. Party conference week is the most important week of our lives. Without the money from party conference week, this restaurant would close". I said that I was very sorry; I paid the bill and we left. It was very upsetting. She was in tears.

I explained all that to Margaret and then she said, "Maurice, pass me my handbag"....I passed her handbag to her and she started to rummage inside and took out her pen. She continued to rummage inside and took out a cheque book. She said, "Maurice, what was the name of the restaurant you went to last night?" I said, "I think it was the Blackpool Brasserie". She wrote the words Blackpool Brasserie on the cheque and said, "How much do you think they lost as a result of those people not coming?" I said, "I don't know, £300 or £350". She made out the cheque; she signed it "Margaret Thatcher". She tore it out of her cheque book, gave it to me and said, "I want you, Maurice, to take this cheque to the restaurant, give it to the man or the woman who owns it and tell them: 'Conservatives don't behave like that'".

Other Lords recounted other kindnesses. Lord Young spoke of how when his brother died he received a three-page handwritten letter of condolence from her the same day — as did his brother's wife and their mother. She did the same for every soldier who fell in the Falklands war, when the casualty lists came in every night.

This is, of course, the mark of a kind and good person. But I think it had an even greater influence in her dealings with other great statesmen. Lord Thomas, who headed the Centre for Policy Studies, a think tank she established in 1974 with Sir Keith Joseph, said this:

> It was remarkable that by the late 1980s, she was on the closest possible terms with Mr Gorbachev, the secretary general of the Soviet Union and at the same time a great personal friend and ally of President Reagan. To have been great friends with the Soviet Union and the United States was a remarkable and unique achievement. I do not think that we ever had that, even in the days of Sir Winston Churchill, when the doubts about Stalin were always present and lurking behind.

Only someone who simultaneously had her strength of character and generosity of spirit could have bridged that gap.

This ability to bridge great differences with people that she dealt with was less obvious at home, but it was there. Like Lincoln, she was able to manage a "Team of Rivals" in her Cabinet, and she loved to challenge her own thinking with a wide range of expert opinion. Lord Thomas recounted how she summoned a whole range of Russian historians prior to her first visit to Russia. John Selwyn Gummer, her famously Europhile environment Secretary, tells of how she used to pick an argument with him to test out and crystallise her own views on Europe. It was all part of the process of challenge that was such a fundamental part of her policy making.

This process of policy formation was intellectually exacting and sometimes very testing for the people who took part in it. Lord Burns was her Chief Economic Adviser and famously someone who had changed his mind when the facts changed (he was a Keynesian when he taught me, but I think not when he worked for her!) His comments were very informative:

> Of course, those people who did not work with Mrs. Thatcher assume that by her very nature she began and ended with an entrenched position and refused to listen.... That that is not at all how the process took place. Part of her enormous talent was her ability to question, challenge and press you on issues as a way of trying to find whether the views that she held herself could stand that stress-testing. I always felt that she was trying to test her own ideas and your ideas to see how they stood up to this process of questioning.

Like all very great leaders, she had a strong set of principles and values and a clear sense of what she wanted to achieve. But... the issues that we dealt with were looked at in enormous depth. The notion that these ideas were pulled off in a casual way and immediately pursued could not be further from the truth. They were issues that we went through time and time again, very often at meeting after meeting until all the aspects of the problem had been identified and she was satisfied that we had covered the issues. I often think that it was as a result of the extent of that process and the argument and debate that she gained strength in the end to make decisions and stick to them in the way that is well known.

...She was not always right. She often changed her position on issues. But whatever view you take of individual parts of it, I join with many others in thinking that her contribution in terms of the transformation of the British economy was enormous. I have little doubt that it came about by this combination of a very clear strategic mind and the ability to concentrate and look at issues in depth, stress-test them and go through them at great length before finally coming to a conclusion.

From what I saw of the process, I rather think that some of the people who took part felt that they were being "stress-tested" every bit as much as the policy was.

So she was a master of detail and a commander of strategy; she was brave in the true sense of the word; she had depth as a human being both domestically and dealing with other great leaders; but all this would not have mattered if it were not for that final passage, because that ensured one other thing: that what she did was right. Right for the country, right for the time, and as it turned out, right for the world.

But not everybody thought so. There were one or two discordant notes that day, most notably from the Hollywood actress and now MP for Hampstead, Glenda Jackson.

When she first came to the House, I asked her what she thought of her colleague's performances. She answered in a single phrase. "Under rehearsed."

Glenda Jackson's comments on this day were sharp:

When I made my maiden speech in this Chamber, a little over two decades ago, Margaret Thatcher had been elevated to the other place but Thatcherism was still wreaking, and had wrought for the previous decade, the most heinous social, economic and spiritual damage upon this country, upon my constituency and upon my constituents.

In coming to the basis of Thatcherism, I come to the spiritual part of what I regard as the desperately wrong track down which Thatcherism took this country. We were told that everything I had been taught to regard as a vice — and I still regard them as vices — was, in fact, under Thatcherism, a virtue: greed, selfishness, no care for the weaker, sharp elbows, sharp knees, all these were the way forward.

To pay tribute to the first Prime Minister denoted by female gender, okay; but a woman? Not on my terms.

This was the formulaic response of the small minority up and down the country of those who celebrated Lady Thatcher's death rather than her life. I guess that they had to have their views represented in Parliament, but I am afraid it all sounded a little too prepared to me. In a phrase, over rehearsed.

But the general tenor of the day was not that. It was a heartfelt and widespread recognition of great public service from a great Englishwoman.

And that public service was recognised just as much outside her home country as it was here. Many referred to her international standing, but it was perhaps summarised best by George Robertson, a Labour opponent and subsequent Secretary General of NATO:

> She was a remarkable person. As I travelled both as Defence Secretary and Secretary-General of NATO, I realised that she was a very significant figure outside the country. As her popularity declined in this country and indeed in her own party, there was absolutely no doubt that the pioneering instinct that she had had, especially in central and eastern Europe, was well registered and recorded, and will be there for a long time to come. I have had a lot to do with Russia. I was the first chairman of the NATO-Russia Council. I recognise that the Russians saw in her somebody who was strong in her beliefs and in what she stood for. They respect strength. The collapse of the Soviet Union that occurred — I remind the House — 30 months after its exit from Afghanistan was a seminal moment in world politics. However much we disagree with her in other areas, we cannot underestimate the role that she played in that tectonic shift.

I started with one of her opponents, Paddy Ashdown, so I could conclude with his summary of her.

> She was complex, extraordinary, magnificent, fallible, flawed and infuriating. One thing, however, is certain and cannot be denied except by those so sunk in bitterness that they will not see: she won great victories for what she stood for at home and huge respect for our country abroad. If politics is defined — and I think it can be — by principles, the courage to hold to them and the ability to drive them through to success, then she was without a doubt the commanding politician and the greatest Prime Minister of our age.

Or if we want to finish with a larger than life quote about a larger than life character, we could take this quote from Lord King, who had been her Defence Secretary:

> I suppose this is the ultimate endorsement. Some may remember the interview that she did in the United States with Walter Cronkite, which showed that the standing of Britain under Margaret Thatcher had changed completely. At the end, Walter Cronkite turned to her and said, "Mrs Thatcher, will you accept a nomination for the presidency of the United States?"'

But I want to reserve the last word for myself. It will, incidentally, be the only time in my entire history with Margaret that I ever had the last word.

Sometimes in the heat of political battle, when your thoughts are dominated by the immediate tactical issues, a vote, a debate, winning a critical policy, resolving a pressing crisis, perhaps even just surviving to fight another day, you can overlook that you are living alongside real human greatness.

Some months before Margaret Thatcher won the leadership of the Conservative Party, I wrote an article in *The Daily Telegraph* [a leading London newspaper] that argued that it was time for centre right political parties to stop seeing their role as simply mitigating the onward march of socialist ideas. Virtually all Conservative leaders up to this point had in effect surrendered to the intellectual dominance of the Left, both in national and international terms, and acted as though their task in life was simply to slow down the inevitable drift to the left. This defeatist attitude in British politics coexisted with a mindset that said our role was to manage an inevitable decline in the power and standing of the United Kingdom, as we withdrew from Empire and our economy struggled to compete.

My argument was that this decline was not inevitable, that there was no socialist ratchet at work, and that the role of the centre Right in politics was to challenge that world view and offer a more optimistic alternative future. Now it is one thing as a noisy twenty-something student to talk about reversing the trend of history, it is quite another thing to do it. And I was wholly unaware that my Party was about to elect the very person to do that job.

Yet that was exactly what happened. She fought against the prevailing intellectual tide of the time. She faced down critic after critic. She battled vested interest after vested interest. She overcame astonishing snobbery and prejudice. There was never any certainty of victory, and always the immediate risk of humiliating failure, a failure that many at the time would have celebrated, including some of those that she was trying to help.

Yet she pressed on, and reversed the ratchet of history. As this extraordinary day in Parliament showed, for the rest of us, it was a privilege to be there to witness it.

Biographical Essay

John Blundell

Margaret Hilda Roberts was born on 13th October 1925, over her father's grocer's shop on North Parade, Grantham, Lincolnshire, a county on the east side of England. Self-employment dominated both sides of her family tree, and her origins were modest. Provincial Methodist-raised daughters of small town grocers are not meant to become great world leaders.

She was the second daughter of Alf Roberts of Northampton and Beatrice Ethel Stephenson of Lincolnshire and had a sister Muriel born four years earlier.

Father Alf was a true pillar of the local community and held possibly every conceivable civic post from councilman and alderman to mayor and even Air Raid Precaution Warden during World War II. As home to a munitions factory Grantham was targeted by the German Luftwaffe, so trains on the line to the north could often be delayed. He was known to bring wounded servicemen stranded in the local station home for the night to enjoy breakfast served by Margaret.

Alf Roberts was not formally well educated, having left school aged 12, but he was known as the most learned man in town and every week he and Margaret brought home an armful or two of books from the local public library to devour.

Their apartment above the shop had no indoor bathroom; no running hot water; and no radio or TV; but it did have lots of books and adult conversation was the order of the day at breakfast, lunch, tea, and supper.

The local movie house opened Margaret's eyes to the outside world and a particular favorite was James Stewart's role in *Mr Smith Goes to Washington*, a classic, often rated in the top 100 movies ever made. It was a primer in how government works.

US entry into World War II brought air force bases to Margaret's neighborhood for two reasons: first, it was flat, and second, it was closer to enemy territory than, say, the west or north of England. But this led to the kind of problem she grew up hearing Dad discuss. Some servicemen on rotation would have their day off on a Sunday, but Sundays were sacrosanct, with everything closed. What to do?

"Should we unlock the park or let the movie house open?" wondered Alf. He decided the latter would be less disruptive to the peace.

Margaret walked to school in the morning, back for lunch as that was cheaper, and back for the afternoon, going past the dole queues of the 1930s and the bombing attacks of the early 1940s on that local munitions factory.

She was so bright she skipped a grade at school and set her sights on a degree in chemistry at the University of Oxford. This was an incredible reach: provincial small town girl with parents not formally educated tries for a man's subject at an Ivy League School! It was a bigger leap than shadow Cabinet to Prime Minister decades later.

A real problem reared its head. She needed Latin to study at Oxford and of course her school had not trained her in that subject. It did not even have a Latin teacher (unlike the local boys' school), so Alf dipped into his savings, hired the boys' school Latin teacher privately, and Margaret did seven years of Latin in six months on top of all her other studies and duties.

Her initial application to Somerville College, Oxford, failed and she went back to school for another attempt, but within just a few days a telegram arrived: a student ahead of her had dropped out, and aged 17, Margaret was on her way to a four-year program in chemistry.

At university she shunned the famous debating society, the Oxford Union, because while women could watch from high above, in "the Gods" as it was called, they could not participate on the actual floor. This did not change until the 1960s.

Instead she volunteered two nights a week bussing tables for American aviators at a nearby base and threw herself into the choir, her Methodist Church, and the Oxford University Conservative Association (OUCA).

She became the second ever female President of OUCA but the first to win the job purely on merit. The only woman who preceded her, Rachel Willink, had a father close to the party leaders and could guarantee the participation of great speakers. Margaret took its membership over the 1,000 mark for the first time since the 1920s. She was already demanding and achieving results.

On graduating, she worked in industry but was soon adopted to fight the 1950 and later 1951 general elections in Dartford, Kent, a heavily socialist area just south east of London.

It was a very daring move by the Dartford conservatives but they thought, "we're never going to win, so let's have some fun with this very bright, pretty, vivacious young lady", and being close to London she drew a lot of press attention, national and even international. And she made serious inroads into the socialist majority.

The young Margaret was already grounded in classical liberal ideas from her father. She knew her Rudyard Kipling and Walt Whitman as well as C S Lewis, F A Hayek, Colm Brogan, Arthur Koestler, and Karl Popper. Dicey followed later as did Milton Friedman.

As early as 1950, as a warm up speaker at a public rally, she proclaimed: "We believe in the democratic way of life. If we serve the idea faithfully, with tenacity of purpose, we have nothing to fear from Russian communism." The Russians gave her the nickname Iron Lady in 1976 but it was already clearly there over 25 years earlier.

It was during her two campaigns in Dartford that she met the well-established local businessman Denis Thatcher, and after careful consideration she agreed to his offer of marriage. She made him sweat a little.

Twins Mark and Carol followed on 15 August 1953 by Cesarean operation as Denis blithely watched England beat Australia at cricket for the first time in two decades. He was over the moon: twins and an England win over Australia!

While recovering in hospital for some two weeks, Margaret decided to train as an attorney, and sitting in her bed signed the relevant papers. Her first thought was to aim for the patent bar so as to combine her science training with her new passion for law. But the pickings were slim there and she ended up at the tax bar, a fortuitous happenstance — see below.

As the heavily predicted 1959 General Election approached she, having fought in 1950 and 1951 and having sat out 1955 with twin babies to care for, felt she deserved a safe seat, and the hierarchy of her party agreed. But time and again she'd come second, and always to a man, because the women on the local selection committees wanted a nice young gentleman who'd had a good war, wore a few medals and had a pretty stay-at-home wife with 2.5 kids and not some well-off (because of Denis) chemist turned attorney with ornery views who worked all day.

She finally was selected by a slender margin to fight Finchley in north London, although since her death a story has emerged that the person in charge that evening conveniently lost some ballots cast for the man who came second. Even after she "won", the traditional adoption vote of "unanimous" failed to materialize and was merely "overwhelming" in the press release, but she did win the Finchley seat and held it 1959–1992.

Between 1959 and 1979 she worked hard to climb to power. She had to give a maiden speech and her first thought was monetary policy. Astonishing! Who else in 1959 except for a handful of academics had even heard of monetary policy?

Then she entered the annual draw for time to present a Private Member's Bill and came so high (3rd out of 310) she had a very good chance of a reasonable bill becoming an Act of Parliament.

So, quite possibly uniquely in Parliamentary history, her maiden speech was not 15 minutes from the backbenches but 30 minutes from the front bench or Dispatch Box. She did it without a note and people began to take notice. It was widely said to be the best speech of the new intake of MPs.

She first wanted to put through a bill to reform trade unions. "Oh no", said her Chief Whip in horror. So instead she settled on a bill — which did pass into law — to increase the rights of the press to scrutinize public expenditures, in US terms a strengthening of the 1st Amendment.

So by 1959 we can already see a Margaret Thatcher who has no fear of Russian communism, is interested in monetary policy, wants trade union reform, and is keen on extra oversight of taxpayers' money. It's all there by 1959.

She was soon promoted — after all, there were very few women of talent available — and the promotions continued as her party went into opposition 1964–1970. It was during this period that she made two six-week long tours of the United States, the first at the behest of the talent scouts in the US State Department who, on paper, touted her as a future Prime Minister, and the second on behalf of the London-based English Speaking Union (ESU). One branch Chair in Florida wrote back to ESU: "She came. She saw. She conquered."

Those two coast-to-coast, North-to-South tours of the US were very important. When Prime Minister, later, her staff would say that on setting foot on American soil she lost 10 years and gained a new spring in her step. She loved America and America loved her back, and still does.

In 1970, her party returned to power and new Prime Minister Ted Heath appointed her Education Secretary as his "statutory woman" and then placed her where he could not see her, on his side at the end of the very long Cabinet table.

Her record in that job is often questioned, but unfairly so in my view. She cut frivolous expenditures, she eased the way for the UK's first new private university, and most importantly she slowed the tsunami of socialization of good grammar schools that had been building for decades, thus saving many fine establishments.

Her party lost twice in 1974 after a confrontation with the National Union of Mineworkers and her Leader, Ted Heath, was now batting one and three. A challenge was inevitable, but one by one, men such as Keith Joseph and Edward du Cann dropped away, leaving only Margaret. Heath first had made her shadow environment spokesperson, then number two shadow treasury spokesperson — and here her time at the tax bar came into play.

A big Finance Bill was going through Parliament and her leadership campaign chief, Airey Neave MP, told her to just do her stuff on the floor and in committee while he and his officers rounded up the troops. She did just that, weighing into the Labour Government's plans with biting comments. For the first time in a long while, Conservative backbenchers were on their feet in the Commons, cheering.

She won and became Leader of the Opposition, Prime Minister in Waiting.

All kinds of folk dropped by to visit over the next four years, including Ronald Reagan, who twice had one-hour appointments — both times they talked for over three hours. Denis Thatcher had spotted him as a potential ally.

Margaret became Prime Minister at the end of what the press called "The Winter of Discontent", namely January through March 1979, inspired by the opening line of William Shakespeare's *Richard III*: "Now is the winter of our discontent."

She faced a truly appalling situation. The UK had enjoyed double-digit inflation rising to all but 30% in the previous six years. Gas supplies were uncertain. There were pickets all over the landscape. Millions were unemployed or laid off. There were food shortages in the shops. Hospital trade union leaders — not nurses or doctors — were deciding whom to admit, and if folk died, "so be it", as one socialist organizer commented. Trolleys of food destined for old folks' homes were smashed. And British Rail — then still nationalized — issued the shortest press release in history: "There are no trains today."

But that was not all, by any means.

There were mountains of trash everywhere as the garbage collectors were on strike. Every corner and square in London, for example, was a rat fest as enormous piles of household and commercial refuse just rotted away.

The gravediggers were on strike and corpses in coffins were stacked high in disused factories as Medical Officers pondered over mass burials at sea.

Possibly the most egregious event was the strike by ambulance drivers. Imagine living in a country where emergency calls are not answered! Indeed, Dr Madsen Pirie of the UK's Adam Smith Institute tells the story of the ambulance driver and his co-worker who, on being told over their radio that the strike is "now on", pulled to the side of the road and together deposited their charge on his gurney! And in the winter!

The French Ambassador used the term "degringolade", meaning the UK economy was collapsing.

The West German Ambassador (Germany had yet to be reunited) said the economy reminded him of East Germany.

Said economy was ranked 19th of 22 by the OECD.

And otherwise sensible folk opined, "What a pity we had not been bombed like the Germans and thus forced to replace our capital!"

My great mentor F A Hayek responded: "I do not think the solution to an economic problem is to destroy our capital!"

So what did she do?

In no particular order:

- She confronted the whole trade union movement, brought it back under the rule of law, took leadership away from extremists and gave it back to ordinary members;

- She privatized the commanding heights of the economy and transformed over-staffed, slow-moving, tax subsidy-seeking behemoths into slim, nimble, profit-making and thus tax-paying world class companies which in turn started a worldwide trend;

- She taught us the need for monetary continence if we wish to enjoy low inflation;

- She enfranchised millions of local authority serfs by giving them a statutory right to buy their unit of public housing — millions did and immediately replaced the black metal government door with a much nicer wooden one; same for the windows;

- She cut overall debt;

- She cut the annual budget deficit; and

- She slashed marginal tax rates from as high as 98% which stopped and even reversed the "fame drain" and the "brain drain";

- She transformed the nation's view of the benefits of private enterprise and made sure all future governments had to be much friendlier toward capitalism;

- She modernized the Labour Party making it realize it was unelectable as a far Left organization;

- She made the British walk tall again with a firm and robust approach to foreign affairs based on the rule of law;

- She supported F W de Klerk on dismantling apartheid, for which Nelson Mandela thanked her;

- She started the process which has now led to peace in Northern Ireland;

- And with the President and the Pope, the Prime Minister helped tremendously to tear down the Berlin Wall and hasten the break-up of the Soviet Union without a shot being fired.

Not bad! So what were the results? Here are some numbers:

- The UK jumped from 19th to 2nd on the OECD ladder;

- Self-employment, a measure of entrepreneurship, doubled from 7% to 14% of all workers;

- The UK venture capital industry, close to not existing before 1979, was by 1985 twice the size of its counterparts in the entire rest of the EU;

- The middle class jumped from 33% to 50%;

- Home ownership soared from 53% to 71%;

- Ownership of shares quoted on the stock exchange rocketed from 7% to 23% among the general population and even more dramatically among trade union members from 6% to 29%. The massive privatizations allowed trade union members to go from just below average to well above average in stock ownership;

- Days lost to strikes went from the tens of millions a year, to under one million, to under a quarter of a million;

- And membership of a trade union dropped from just a fraction over 50% to 18%.

- A major, quite palpable result was the coverage of business and entrepreneurship in the media which went from negligible to significant. After all, we were all capitalists now!

In my book *Margaret Thatcher: A Portrait of the Iron Lady*, I draw ten lessons from her fifteen years as a party leader and her eleven years in power:

1. Above all else she had a strong moral and political compass — as she once said:

    "Disciplining yourself to do what you know is right and important, although difficult, is the high road to pride, self-esteem, and personal satisfaction."

2. She was clever but unlike many if not most clever people, she cut through the fancy embellishments and spoke plainly — no "at this moment in time" but rather "now". Short, clear words.

3. She did lead and expected a great deal from those around her but she also listened to all sides and worried that some of her policies might have gone too far, too quickly;

4. She championed policies that went with, rather than against the grain of, human nature such as privatization and the sale of public housing units, once saying:

   "Popular capitalism is nothing less than a crusade to enfranchise the many in the economic life of the nation. We conservatives are returning power to the people."

5. She thought about the strategy of policy implementation years ahead of time on matters such as coal reserves and suspending exchange controls;

6. She transformed her party from "the stupid party" into a rather smart bunch;

7. She used the sense of her country being in the Last Chance Saloon, brilliantly stating...

   "There can have been few in Britain who did not feel, with mounting alarm, that our society was sick — morally, socially and economically. Trade Union leader Mr Bill Dunn seemed to express the spirit of January 1979 when he said, of the ambulance men's pay demands, if 'lives must be lost, that is the way it must be'."

8. She worked very closely with the Pope and the US President;

9. She prepared between 1975 and 1979 assiduously; and

10. She did not try to do it all at once, as she privatized a few companies every year and hacked away at the legal immunities of the trade unions every two years. She was patient.

To achieve a status like hers, say, a decade from now, a UK Prime Minister would need to:

- Renegotiate the UK's position with the EU;
- Deregulate and stop the landslide of new laws;
- Reform health care;
- Increase educational standards;
- Reduce welfare;
- Cut crime;
- Simplify and cut taxes; and
- Balance the books.

Any takers?

Before she passed on, Margaret was often called, with all due respect to Her Majesty Queen Elizabeth II, the "greatest living English woman", and even the left-leaning BBC made her the 16th greatest ever Briton. But in his rankings on the 20 prime ministers of the 20th century, historian Francis Beckett rates her number one. So do I, peacetime or wartime.

HOUSE OF COMMONS

Wednesday 10 April 2013
The House met at half-past Two o'clock
PRAYERS
[Mr Speaker in the Chair]
Tributes to Baroness Thatcher

[The Rt Hon David Cameron was born 9 October 1966 and attended Eton and Brasenose College, Oxford. After working for the Conservative Party and Carlton Communications, he entered Parliament as MP for Witney (Oxfordshire) in 2002, became leader of his party in 2005 and Prime Minister 12 May 2010, the youngest in nearly 200 years and the first to head a Coalition government since World War II.]

2.35 pm

The Prime Minister (Mr David Cameron)

I beg to move,
That this House has considered the matter of tributes to the right hon. Baroness Thatcher of Kesteven LG OM.

In the long history of this Parliament, Margaret Thatcher was our first — and, so far, our only — woman Prime Minister. She won three elections in a row, serving this country for a longer continuous period than any Prime Minister for more than 150 years. She defined, and she overcame, the great challenges of her age, and it is right that Parliament has been recalled to mark our respect. It is also right that next Wednesday Lady Thatcher's coffin will be draped with the flag that she loved, placed on a gun carriage and taken to St Paul's cathedral, and members of all three services will line the route. This will be a fitting salute to a great Prime Minister.

Today, we in the House of Commons are here to pay our own tributes to an extraordinary leader and an extraordinary woman. What she achieved — even before her three terms in office — was remarkable. Those of us who grew up when Margaret Thatcher was already in Downing street can sometimes fail to appreciate the thickness of the glass ceiling that she broke through — from a grocer's shop in Grantham to the highest office in the land. At a time when it was difficult for a woman to become a Member of Parliament, almost inconceivable that one could lead the Conservative party and, by her own reckoning, virtually impossible that a woman could become Prime Minister, she did all three. [*In the early 1970s Margaret was interviewed as Secretary of State for Education and Science and said that in her lifetime no woman would hold any of the top jobs: Prime Minister, Chancellor of the Exchequer, Secretary of State for Foreign Affairs, or Home Secretary, but she lived to see all but Chancellor of the Exchequer so occupied.*] It is also right to remember that she spent her whole premiership, and indeed much of her life, under direct personal threat from the IRA. She lost two of her closest friends and closest parliamentary colleagues, Airey Neave and Ian Gow, to terrorism. [*Airey Neave was murdered by the IRA on 30 March 1979, and Ian Gow on 30 July 1990, both by car bombs; both were very close indeed to Margaret Thatcher.*] And, of course, she herself was only inches away from death in the Brighton bomb attack of 1984. Yet it was the measure of her leadership that she shook off the dust from that attack and just a few hours later gave an outstanding conference speech reminding us all why democracy must never give in to terror.

Margaret Thatcher was a woman of great contrasts. She could be incredibly formidable in argument yet wonderfully kind in private. In No. 10 Downing street today there are still people who worked with her as Prime Minister, and they talk of her fondly. One assistant tells of how when she got drenched in a downpour on a trip to Cornwall, Margaret Thatcher personally made sure she was looked after and found her a set of dry clothes — of course, she did always prefer dries to wets. [Laughter.] [*Dries are with Margaret on the right of her party while wets are on the left.*] On another occasion, one assistant had put in a hand-written note to Mrs Thatcher to say, "Please can you re-sign this minute [*memo*]?" Unfortunately she had left off the hyphen, leaving a note that actually read, "Please can you resign this minute?" — to which the Prime Minister politely replied, "Thank you dear, but I'd rather not."

Margaret Thatcher was faultlessly kind to her staff and utterly devoted to her family. For more than 50 years, Denis was always at her side, an invaluable confidant and friend. Of her, he said this:

"I have been married to one of the greatest women the world has ever produced. All I could produce — small as it may be — was love and loyalty."

We know just how important the support of her family and friends was to Margaret, and I know that today everyone in this House will wish to send our most heartfelt condolences to her children, Carol and Mark, to her grandchildren and to her many, many loyal friends. She was always incredibly kind to me, and it was a huge honour to welcome her to Downing street shortly after I became

Prime Minister — something that, when I started working for her in 1988, I never dreamed I would do.

As this day of tributes begins, I would like to acknowledge that there are Members in the House today from all parties who profoundly disagreed with Mrs Thatcher but who have come here today willing to pay their respects. Let me say this to those hon. Members: your generosity of spirit does you great credit and speaks more eloquently than any one person can of the strength and spirit of British statesmanship and British democracy.

Margaret Thatcher was a remarkable type of leader. She said very clearly, "I am not a consensus politician, but a conviction politician." She could sum up those convictions, which were linked profoundly with her upbringing and values, in just a few short phrases: sound money; strong defence; liberty under the rule of law; you should not spend what you have not earned; Governments do not create wealth, but businesses do. The clarity of those convictions was applied with great courage to the problems of the age.

The scale of her achievements is only apparent when we look back to Britain in the 1970s. [*The UK was then called "the sick man of Europe".*] Successive Governments had failed to deal with what was beginning to be called the British disease: appalling industrial relations, poor productivity and persistently high inflation. Although it seems absurd today, the state had got so big that it owned our airports and airline, the phones in our houses, trucks on our roads, and even a removal company. The air was thick with defeatism. There was a sense that the role of Government was simply to manage decline. Margaret Thatcher rejected this defeatism. She had a clear view about what needed to change. Inflation was to be controlled not by incomes policies, but by monetary and fiscal discipline; industries were to be set free into the private sector; trade unions should be handed back to their members; and people should be able to buy their own council homes. Success in these endeavours was never assured. Her political story was one of a perpetual battle, in the country, in this place and sometimes even in her own Cabinet.

Of course, her career could have taken an entirely different path. In the late 1940s, before she entered politics, the then Margaret Roberts went for a job at ICI [*a major chemical company.*] The personnel department rejected her application and afterwards wrote:

"This woman is headstrong, obstinate and dangerously self-opinionated."

Even her closest friends would agree that she could be all those things, but the point is this: she used that conviction and resolve in the service of her country, and we are all the better for that.

Margaret Thatcher was also a great parliamentarian. She loved and respected this place and was for many years its finest debater. She was utterly fastidious in her preparations. I was a junior party researcher in the 1980s, and the trauma of preparation for Prime Minister's Questions is still seared into my memory. Twice a week it was as if the arms of a giant octopus shook every building in Whitehall for every analysis of every problem and every answer to every question. Her respect for Parliament was instilled in others. Early in her first Government, a junior Minister was seen running through the Lobby. His hair was dishevelled and he was carrying a heavy box and a full tray of papers under his arm. Another Member cried out, "Slow down. Rome wasn't built in a day." The Minister replied, "Yes, but Margaret Thatcher wasn't the foreman on that job." [*David Davis comments: This anecdote provoked the loudest laughter of the Prime Minister's speech. The story is in fact apochryphal. I know. I wrote it, or more accurately I modified an American story with a similar punch line. The reason it is such a successful story, however, is that although it is not true, it is so close to character it should have been.*]

As Tony Blair said this week — rightly, in my view — Margaret Thatcher was one of the very few leaders who changed the political landscape not only in their own country, but in the rest of the world. She was no starry-eyed internationalist, but again her approach was rooted in some simple and clear principles: strength abroad begins with strength at home; deterrence, not appeasement; and the importance of national sovereignty, which is why she fought so passionately for Britain's interests in Europe and always believed that Britain should keep its own currency.

Above all, she believed to the core of her being that Britain stood for something in the world: for democracy, for the rule of law, for right over might. She loathed communism and believed in the invincible power of the human spirit to resist and ultimately defeat tyranny. She never forgot that Warsaw, Prague and Budapest were great European cities, capitals of free nations temporarily trapped behind the iron curtain.

Today, in different corners of the world, millions of people know that they owe their freedom, in part, to Margaret Thatcher — in Kuwait, which she helped free from Saddam's jackboot; across eastern and central Europe; and, of course, in the Falkland Islands. A week from now, as people gather in London to lay Margaret Thatcher to rest, the sun will be rising over the Falklands, and because of her courage and because of the skill, bravery and sacrifice of our armed forces, it will rise again for freedom.

Much has been said about the battles that Margaret Thatcher fought. She certainly did not shy from the fight and that led to arguments, to conflict and, yes, even to division, but what is remarkable, looking back now, is how many of those arguments are no longer arguments at all. No one wants to return to strikes without a ballot. No one believes that large industrial companies should be owned by the state. The nuclear deterrent, NATO and the special relationship are widely accepted as the cornerstones of our security and defence policies. We argue — sometimes very passionately — in this House about tax, but none of us is arguing for a return to tax rates of 98%. So many of the principles that Lady Thatcher fought for are now part of the accepted political landscape of our country. As Winston Churchill once put it, there are some politicians who "make the weather", and Margaret Thatcher was undoubtedly one of them.

In the Members' Lobby of the House of Commons there are rightly four principal statues: Lloyd George, who gave us the beginnings of the welfare state; Winston Churchill, who gave us victory in war; Clement Attlee, who gave us the NHS; and Margaret Thatcher, who rescued our country from post-war decline. They say that cometh the hour, cometh the man. Well, in 1979 came the hour, and came the lady. She made the political weather. She made history. And let this be her epitaph: she made our country great again. I commend the motion to the House.

[The Rt Hon Edward (Ed) Miliband was born 24 December 1969 and attended Corpus Christi College, Oxford, and the London School of Economics. After working in the media and for the Labour Party he was elected MP for Doncaster North 5 May 2005 and defeated his brother David to become Leader of the Labour Party 25 September 2010. His father was the famous Marxist scholar Ralph Miliband.]

2.47 pm

Edward Miliband (Doncaster North) (Lab)

I join the Prime Minister in commemorating the extraordinary life and unique contribution of Margaret Thatcher. I join him, too, in sending my deepest condolences to her children, Carol and Mark, the whole family and her many, many close friends.

Today is an opportunity for us to reflect on Margaret Thatcher's personal achievements, her style of politics and her political legacy. As the Prime Minister said, the journey from being the child of a grocer to Downing street is an unlikely one, and it is particularly remarkable because she was the daughter, not the son, of a grocer. At each stage of her life, she broke the mould: a woman at Oxford when not a single woman in the university held a full professorship; a woman chemist when most people assumed scientists had to be men; a woman candidate for Parliament in 1950, against the opposition of some in her local party in Dartford, at the age of only 24 [*possibly so, but they knew they could not win the seat and thought 'let's have some fun here' — and indeed they got a lot of attention from the media. The opposition to her adoption by women in Finchley a decade later is much better known and documented*]; a woman MP in 1959 when just 4% of MPs in the whole of this House were women; the only woman in the Cabinet when she was appointed in 1970; and, of course, the first woman Prime Minister. It is no wonder she remarked as early as 1965 in a speech to the National Union of Townswomen's Guilds conference:

"In politics if you want anything said, ask a man. If you want anything done, ask a woman."

I am sure some people in this House — and no doubt many more in the country — will agree with that sentiment.

Having broken so many conventions as a woman, it cannot be a coincidence that she was someone who, in so many other areas of life, was willing to take on the established orthodoxies. Margaret Thatcher's ability to overcome every obstacle in her path was just one measure of her personal strength, and that takes me to her style of politics. We can disagree with Margaret Thatcher, but it is important to understand the kind of political leader she was. What was unusual was that she sought to be rooted in people's daily lives, but she also believed that ideology mattered. Not for her the contempt sometimes heaped on ideas and new thinking in political life, and while she never would have claimed to be, or wanted to be seen as, an intellectual, she believed and showed that ideas matter in politics.

In 1945, before the end of the war, she bought a copy of Friedrich Hayek's *The Road to Serfdom*. [*In the TV series* The Commanding Heights, *the actress who plays her plucks a copy off the shelf in her college library*]. There is even a story that she suggested that Conservative central office distribute it in the 1945 general election campaign. [*She was still a student and was in no position to do that. The Conservative Central Office did use part of its war-rationed paper supply to print extra copies, as it was known as the book nobody could get because it sold out so fast.*]

She said, "It left a permanent mark on my own political character", and nobody can grasp Margaret Thatcher's achievements, and Thatcherism, without also appreciating the ideas that were its foundation and the way in which they departed from the prevailing consensus of the time. In typical homespun-style on breakfast TV she said in 1995:

"Consensus doesn't give you any direction. It is like mixing all the constituent ingredients together and not coming out with a cake...Democracy is about the people being given a choice."

It was that approach which enabled her to define the politics of a whole generation, and influence the politics of generations to come.

The Prime Minister, the Deputy Prime Minister and I all came of age in the 1980s, when people defined their politics by being for or against what she was doing. It is fair to say that we took different paths. Thirty years on, the people of Britain still argue about her legacy. She was right to understand the sense of aspiration felt by people across the country, and she was right to recognise that our economy needed to change. She said in 1982, "How absurd it will seem in a few years' time that the state ran Pickfords removals and the Gleneagles Hotel."

She was right. In foreign policy, she was right to defend the Falklands and bravely reach out to new leadership in the Soviet Union, and something often forgotten is that she was the first political leader in any major country to warn of the dangers of climate change, long before anyone thought of hugging a husky. [*She later came to a much different conclusion.*]

But it would be dishonest and not in keeping with the principles that Margaret Thatcher stood for not to be open with the House, even on this day, about the strong opinions and deep divisions there were, and are, over what she did. In mining areas such as the one I represent, communities felt angry and abandoned. Gay and lesbian people felt stigmatised by measures such as section 28, which today's Conservative party has rightly repudiated. It was no accident that when the right hon. Member for Chingford and Woodford Green (Mr Duncan Smith) became leader of the Conservative party, he wrote a pamphlet called, "There is Such a Thing as Society." On the world stage, as the Prime Minister rightly said in 2006 when he was Leader of the Opposition, Margaret Thatcher made the wrong judgment about Nelson Mandela and about sanctions in South Africa.

Debates about Margaret Thatcher and what she represented will continue for many years to come, which is a mark of her significance as a political leader.

She was someone with deep convictions and was willing to act on them. As she put it:

"Politics is more when you have convictions than a matter of multiple manoeuvrings to get through the problems of the day".

As a person, nothing became her so much as the manner of her final years, which saw the loss of her beloved husband, Denis, and her struggle with illness. She bore both with the utmost dignity and courage — the same courage that she showed decades earlier after the atrocity of the Brighton bombing. I will always remember seeing her at the Cenotaph in frail health but determined to pay her respect to our troops and do her duty by the country.

Whatever one's view of her, Margaret Thatcher was a unique and towering figure. I disagree with much of what she did, but I respect what her death means to the many, many people who admired her, and I honour her personal achievements. On previous occasions, we have come to this House to remember the extraordinary Prime Ministers who have served our nation. Today, we also remember a Prime Minister who defined her age.

[The Rt Hon John Redwood MP was born 15 June 1951 and was educated at Kent College, Canterbury before attending Magdalen College and St Antony's College, both at Oxford. Before becoming MP for Wokingham 11 June 1987, he worked in banking. He has served in Cabinet and Shadow Cabinet most notably as Secretary of State for Wales, 1993–1995 when he was criticized for returning home to his wife in England every night. He famously responded that he must be the only Conservative MP to be criticized for sleeping with his wife.]

2.54 pm

Mr John Redwood (Wokingham) (Con)

I wish to be brief, but I would like to put on record that Margaret Thatcher was the best boss I ever worked for. I was her chief policy adviser in the middle years and was subsequently able to advise and help her a bit as a Member of Parliament and a junior Minister.

Margaret Thatcher was that great figure because her private side was so different from her public side. Yes, many people beyond the House remember the woman who was so powerful in argument and so fierce in conviction, but those who worked with her closely saw someone who worked incredibly long hours with great energy and diligence because she was so keen to get it right.

Margaret Thatcher took a very wide range of advice. When people worked with her and put an idea to her, not only did they need to produce all the evidence and the facts and go over it many times, but they knew that person after person going to Downing street would be given it as a kind of test. They did not know that they were part of a running focus group, but one's idea was in front of the guests, who were asked to shoot it down, because she was so desperately concerned never to use the power of the great office without proper thought. She was also keen to ensure that, before she did anything, she knew what the criticisms would be and what might go wrong with it, because she had tested it to destruction. There is a lot to recommend that approach to those who are making mighty decisions — they should spend time and take trouble, go to a wide range of advice, and ensure that something works well before it is put out there.

Margaret Thatcher came, in the middle of her period in office, to be the champion of wider ownership and wider participation. To me, that was her at her best — when she could reach out beyond the confines of the Conservative party, which she led so well in those days, and beyond the confines of her fairly solid 40% voting support, much more widely in the county. A Prime Minister can become a great national leader when their ideas resonate more widely, and when their ideas become popular with, or are taken up by, those who would normally oppose them.

That spirit of Margaret Thatcher — she had fought her way as a schoolgirl to Oxford, as an Oxford graduate to Parliament, and as a parliamentarian to the Cabinet — made her feel that opportunity was there for people. However, she recognised that it was very difficult, particularly for women and people from certain backgrounds, and always told us that it did not matter where people came from or who their mother and father were, and that what mattered was what people could contribute. That, surely, is a message that goes way beyond the confines of the Conservative party or the years of her supremacy in Parliament. We should all remember that.

When we tried to produce policies to reflect that more generally, we came up with an idea. Owning a home had been the privilege of the richer part of society, but we wondered why everyone or practically everyone should not aspire to it. That is when the council house sale idea [*the statutory right to purchase your unit of public housing from your city at a steep discount off fair market value to reflect years of rent paid*] gathered momentum. Many Labour Members in the early days were very unhappy — debates on the policy remain — but an awful lot of Labour voters and even some Labour councillors decided it was a really good policy and joined us on it. It was one of those policies that reached out so much more widely.

We tried to extend the idea to the ownership of big and small businesses with a big programme of wider share ownership, and with the employee and public elements in the great privatisations. Margaret Thatcher was determined to try to get Britain to break out of the debilitating cycle of decline that we had witnessed under Labour and Conservative Governments in the post-war years.

I have just one fact that the House and those who are worried by the depressing number of jobs lost in the 1980s in the pits and steel industry might like to bear in mind. The newly nationalised coal industry in the early 1950s had 700,000 employees; by the time Margaret Thatcher came to office in 1979, only 235,000 of those jobs were left. There had been a massive haemorrhage of jobs throughout the post-war period. Similar figures could be adduced for rail, steel and the other commanding heights. It was that which drove her to say that there must be a better answer and a way of modernising the old industries and bringing in the new industries. One of her legacies is the modernisation of the car industry, which gathered momentum under the Labour Government and, more recently, under the coalition.

Margaret Thatcher's other great triumph, as the Prime Minister mentioned, was to extend her argument to a much wider audience around the world. The ideas of empowerment, enfranchisement, participation, breaking up industries, allowing competition and new ideas, and allowing the public to be part of the process were exported and took off around the world. That lay behind much of the spirit of revolution in Eastern Europe which led to the bringing down of the Berlin wall. If there is a single picture of the Thatcher legacy that I will remember, it is the tumbling of the Berlin wall and the realisation that the path of enterprise and freedom that has been adopted by all the democratic parties in this House is the right approach, and that tyranny and communism do not work.

We are discussing a great lady, a great stateswoman, a huge personal achievement and a very big achievement politically. At its best, it was an achievement that broke free from conservatism and party dogma, and which showed the world that there is a better way, a democratic way, a freedom-loving way.

[The Rt Hon Nicholas (Nick) Clegg was born 7 January 1967 and later graduated from Robinson College, Cambridge. He held a wide range of jobs in the media and lobbying before becoming a Member of the European Parliament, 1999-2004 and later MP for Sheffield Hallam on 5 May 2005. He became Leader of the Liberal Democrats on 18 December 2007 and Deputy Prime Minister 11 May 2010.]

3.1 pm

The Deputy Prime Minister (Mr Nick Clegg)

I am a Sheffield MP — a city where the mere mention of her name even now elicits strong reactions. I would like to think that she would be pleased that she still provokes trepidation and uncertainty among the leaders of other parties, even when she is not here, eyeballing us across the House. That those of us who are not from her party can shun the tenets of Thatcherism and yet respect Margaret Thatcher is part of what was so remarkable about her. It is in that spirit that I would like to make three short observations.

First, whether people liked or disliked her, it is impossible to deny the indelible imprint that Margaret Thatcher made on the nation and the wider world. She was among those very rare leaders who become a towering historical figure not as written in the history books, but while still in the prime of their political life. Whatever else is said about her, Margaret Thatcher created a paradigm. She set the parameters of economic, political and social debate for decades to come. She drew the lines on the political map that we are still navigating today.

Secondly, Margaret Thatcher was one of the most caricatured figures in modern British politics, yet she was easily one of the most complex. On the one hand, she is remembered as the eponymous ideologue, responsible for her own "-ism". In reality, much of her politics was subtle and pragmatic, and she was sometimes driven by events. Margaret Thatcher was a staunch patriot who was much more comfortable reaching out across the Atlantic than across the channel. However, she participated in one of the most profound periods of European integration and was herself an architect of the single market. Although she was a Conservative to her core, leading a party that traditionally likes to conserve things, she held a deep aversion to the status quo. She was restive about the future, determined to use politics as a force for reform and never feared short-term disruption in pursuit of long-term change. In many ways a traditionalist, she was one of the most iconoclastic politicians of our age.

Margaret Thatcher was therefore far from the cardboard cut-out that is sometimes imagined. For me, the best tribute to her is not to consign her to being a simplified heroine or villain, but to remember her with all the nuance, unresolved complexity and paradox that she possessed.

Finally, there was an extraordinary, even unsettling directness about her political presence. I remember vividly, aged 20, reading that Margaret Thatcher had said that there was no such thing as society. I was dismayed. It was not the kind of thing that a wide-eyed, idealistic social anthropology undergraduate wanted to hear. With hindsight, what strikes me is that although I disagreed with the untempered individualism that those words implied, I never for a second thought that she was being cynical, striking a pose or taking a position for short-term effect.

You always knew, with Margaret Thatcher, that she believed what she said. It is interesting to reflect on how she would have reacted to today's political culture of 24-hour news, pollsters and focus groups. She seemed blissfully indifferent to the popularity of what she said, entirely driven instead by the conviction of what she said. Somehow, her directness made you feel as if she were arguing directly with you — as if it were a clash of her convictions against yours. As a result, you somehow felt as if you knew her, even if you did not.

Whether she inspired or confronted, led or attacked, she did it all with uncluttered clarity. Her memory will no doubt continue to divide opinion and stir deep emotion, but as we as a nation say farewell to a figure who loomed so large, one thing is for sure: the memory of her will continue undimmed, strong and clear for years to come, in keeping with the unusual, unique character of Margaret Thatcher herself.

[The Rt Hon Nigel Dodds was born 20 August 1958 and educated at St John's College, Cambridge. He is an attorney, MP for Belfast North since 7 June 2001, and Deputy Leader of the Democratic Unionist Party.]

3.5 pm

Mr Nigel Dodds (Belfast North) (DUP)

Of course, there were many who disagreed with her. Even within her own party and among those of us who are Unionists in Northern Ireland there were those who disagreed with her on occasion, particularly in relation to the Anglo-Irish agreement. But whatever our views, people today, by and large, must accept, acknowledge and admire her as a politician and statesperson of conviction. The days of focus groups, the amorphous middle, the soft imaging — none of that would have suited her. How many times have we heard it said, during her lifetime and since, that, like her or loathe her, at least you knew where Maggie stood? People admire that in their politicians. It is something that people want to see.

Part of her attraction was that she was seen as taking on the vested interests and the political establishment. She was impatient of the old brigade, and prepared to shake things up. However, like all great human beings and all great politicians, she was a person of contradictions. Very often her rhetoric did not match her actions, and her instincts were blunted. She did become persuaded, on some issues, against her better judgment. On Europe, she is rightly lauded for the actions that she took in relation to, for instance, securing our rebate, for her stance against European federalism, for her Bruges speech, and for her stance in defence of our currency; yet she signed and implemented the Single European Act, which many see as the forerunner of the Maastricht agreement.

On Northern Ireland, again, she was full of contradictions. We in the Democratic Unionist party, and indeed the entire Unionist community in Northern Ireland in the 1980s, opposed the Anglo-Irish agreement, and many Conservative Members and others opposed it too. Once she had said that Ulster was as British as Finchley; once she had said, rightly, that it was "out, out, out" to a united Ireland, a federal Ireland or joint authority. Yet a year later, in 1985, she signed the Anglo-Irish agreement without any consultation with the Unionist community, and without its consent.

The reason why many Unionists felt and spoke so strongly at that time, and why there remain many strong feelings about that era, is that they remembered her strong stance during the hunger strikes, when she had stood up in defence of democracy and against terrorism; they remembered how, as the Prime Minister and others mentioned, she had suffered the loss of close colleagues to terrorism; and they remembered how she herself, just a year before, had survived an IRA assassination attempt. Despite that, she was persuaded to the sign the Anglo-Irish agreement.

I am glad that in her later life, Margaret Thatcher came to recognise that the agreement was a mistake. Lord Powell, her former close adviser, said the other night on "Newsnight" that, as it is said of Mary Queen of Scots that the word "Calais" was inscribed on her heart, so he believed that the words "the Anglo-Irish agreement" would be inscribed on the heart of Margaret Thatcher, because she had become increasingly disillusioned with it. People say, "But was it not the template for what we now have in Ulster?" I say it was not, because we cannot base a future on exclusion. I say that as a Unionist in Northern Ireland, with all our history, because we must go forward with the inclusion of all communities. Today, there is little of the Anglo-Irish agreement left and instead we have a settlement that has been consulted on and has the consent and agreement of both communities in Northern Ireland. I am glad that we have that, as opposed to the previous approach.

I want to close by saying, yes, we had our disagreements with Margaret Thatcher, but she was, fundamentally, instinctively and truly, a great patriot, a great Unionist and a great Briton, and that is why we are right to pay tribute to her today, while recognising her faults and the divisions that exist — of course, there are divisions, but there were divisions long before Margaret Thatcher, and there will be divisions long after her in other eras. She is not unique in that sense. I heard today Gerry Adams and others talk about the legacy of Margaret Thatcher as if she and the British Government and the British state had created the violence in Northern Ireland. The fact is, of course, that the hunger strikers were in jail and had been convicted for terrorist acts long before she came to office.

Those on our streets in Belfast and elsewhere in the United Kingdom — in Glasgow, Bristol or wherever — engaging in the sort of ghoulish celebrations and obscene acts that appall the entire nation should think again of her words: she once said that she took great solace in those who hated her so much because she knew then that she was doing what was right and that they hated her for it.

We — especially those of us in Ulster — must remember Margaret Thatcher for the great things she did for our country, while not remembering her through rose-tinted spectacles. It is right, however, that we mark her life and period in office. Hers was an enormous contribution and an ever-lasting memorial to democracy and freedom in this country and across the world.

[Rt Hon Sir Malcolm Rifkind was born 21 June 1946 and studied law at the University of Edinburgh. He was an MP first for Edinburgh Pentlands 1974–1997 and later Kensington and Chelsea 2005–2010 and then Kensington 2010-today. He served Margaret Thatcher 1986–1990 as Secretary of State for Scotland and continued in Cabinet under John Major as Secretary of State for Transport 1990–1992, Secretary of State for Defence 1992–1995 and Foreign Secretary 1995–1997.]

3.13 pm

Sir Malcolm Rifkind (Kensington) (Con)

I was privileged to serve in Margaret Thatcher's Government for the full 11 years of her term of office and to be in her Cabinet for almost half that time. It was never dull. Each day we saw political leadership and statesmanship of the highest order and a Prime Minister with remarkable personal qualities. It was sometimes said that she did not have a sense of humour, and it was true that there was very little wit in many of her speeches, but I recall on one occasion that she was asked, "Mrs Thatcher, do you believe in consensus?" To our surprise, we heard her saying, "Yes, I do believe in consensus; there should be a consensus behind my convictions." I thought at the time that this was an extraordinary example of wit, but as the years have gone by I have realised that she was actually being deadly serious.

It was also said that Margaret Thatcher could be very intolerant of those who did not agree with her. That was also a parody of the truth. She was intolerant of people who were woolly and who argued that things could not be done because they would be unpopular or that it was too difficult, but when she met someone able to argue from a point of fact and whom she respected, she not only listened, but could change her mind. I was moved to the Foreign Office at the time of the

Falklands, and she recalled Sir Anthony Parsons, our ambassador at the Security Council, to ask him how it was going at the United Nations. He had never met her before; he was a rather grand diplomat. When he started trying to report to her, she, not uncharacteristically, kept interrupting him, and he was not used to this. After the fourth interruption, he stopped and said, "Prime Minister, if you didn't interrupt me so often, you might find that you didn't need to." She not only kept quiet but six months later appointed him her foreign policy adviser.

Of course she was a great leader of the Conservative party, but people are entitled to ask, "Was she actually a Conservative? Does not the word "Conservative" normally mean someone who is rather wedded to tradition, cautious of change, and unwilling to act too precipitately?" Yet she was the most radical Prime Minister of the past few generations. There is nevertheless a consistency between those two statements, because she had recognised that Britain had gone the wrong way — that it had taken the wrong path for 20 or 30 years, and that needed change. That is what made her a radical. Many hon. Members will know the great novel, *The Leopard*, by Giuseppe di Lampedusa, in which the hero says, "If you want things to stay the same, things will have to change." That was very much her belief.

Having spent a lot of my time in the Foreign Office, I am conscious of the fact that diplomats in the Foreign Office were not her favourite Department. I went to see her when I was Defence Secretary some years later, after she had retired, and she said to me, "You know, Ministry of Defence, your problem is you've got no allies. The Foreign Office aren't wet — they're drenched." (*See above for this distinction between dries and wets*).When it came to the Foreign Office and to diplomats, she sometimes had a remarkable capacity to distance herself from the Government of which she was Prime Minister.

On one glorious occasion in which I was personally involved, we had a difficult negotiation getting a package of sanctions against South Africa. They did not include economic sanctions, but she was very unhappy that one of the proposals at the European Community Council was that we should withdraw our defence attachés. The Ministry of Defence did not mind, but it took an awful long time for Geoffrey Howe to persuade her to go along with this, and she was basically unconvinced but did go along with it. Some weeks later, we had a visit from the President of Mozambique, and I was asked to sit in on the meeting at Downing street. The President rebuked her for not doing enough against apartheid in South Africa. I will never forget her response. She bridled and said,

"Mr President, that is simply not the case. We are refusing to sell arms to South Africa. We have initiated the Gleneagles agreement whereby we don't have any sporting contact with South Africa. We're using all diplomatic means to try and bring down apartheid." "We, we, we", she said — and then suddenly she stopped, pointed at me, and said, "They've decided to withdraw our defence attachés", adding, "I don't know what good that will do." The President of Mozambique was rather bemused by what seemed to be happening.

Although she may have had mixed feelings about the Foreign Office (*she famously called its staff 'the traitors'*), she actually owed it a great debt of gratitude, because one of her greatest triumphs — her relationship with Mr Gorbachev and what flowed from that — was a result of the diplomats in the Foreign Office spotting at a very early stage that the youngest new member of the politburo, Mikhail Gorbachev, was a man to try to cultivate, and she had the wisdom to accept their advice. We should not underestimate what followed from that, which was her persuading Ronald Reagan to accept her view that Gorbachev was a man with whom we could do business. Reagan would not have accepted that advice from most people, but coming from the Iron Lady, he said, "Well, if she believes that, then I can proceed on that basis." The result was not only a remarkable set of initiatives but the end of the cold war and the liberation of Eastern Europe without a shot being fired — a remarkable epitaph.

I do not intend to speak for too long, but I want to make one other point. One of the big issues that is relevant to the debates we have today is whether, in the relationship with the United States, British Prime Ministers always have to agree with the President or otherwise we risk that relationship. All I can say is that Margaret Thatcher had no doubt that the answer was, "No, you don't have to." On several occasions she had deep disagreements with Ronald Reagan, one of her closest friends. For example, when British companies had got contracts to help to build a Soviet oil pipeline in the early 1980s, the Americans threatened sanctions against those British companies, and Margaret Thatcher bitterly criticised them. I was sent off to Washington as a junior Minister to have meetings with Mr Kenneth Dam, the American deputy Secretary of State. We reached a compromise. The only thing we could not agree on was whether the compromise would be known as the Rifkind-Dam agreement or the Dam-Rifkind agreement.

Margaret Thatcher had openly and publicly disagreed with Reagan on the Reykjavik summit, when she felt that he was surrendering too many nuclear weapons without getting enough in return, but most important of all, she bitterly resented the invasion of Grenada. The House will recall that Grenada was invaded by the United States, which had forgotten, unfortunately, that Her Majesty was the Head of State of Grenada, and had not even informed the British Government of what it was about to do. (*Reagan apologized for not warning Thatcher. He was told not to do so because of fears her own Foreign Office would leak and US Marines would die*). Margaret Thatcher not only criticised it, but she went on the BBC World Service attacking the United States and saying that it could not behave like that. Some days later, Reagan recorded in his memoirs (*her autobiography claims it took her only 20 minutes*) that he was sitting in the Oval office with some of his aides and he was told that the British Prime Minister was on the phone and would he take a call. Yes, he said, of course he would. She started berating him in a rather strident way down the telephone. It went on for only about a minute, but some of us who have been on the receiving end know how long that can feel. When she was in full flight, Reagan put his hand over the receiver so that she could not hear, turned to his aides and said, "Gee, isn't she marvelous?" Far from resenting it, they appreciated that sometimes they got it wrong and even their closest allies were entitled to point it out.

I conclude by saying that Margaret Thatcher was someone who did not worry, as has already been remarked, about people being rude about her. The term "Iron Lady" was first coined by the Soviets as an insult. She, of course, took it on as a badge of pride. Denis Healey referred to her and the lips of Marilyn Monroe. She took them all as compliments because she asked for no quarter and she certainly gave none.

[Angus Robertson MP was born in Wimbledon, London 28 September 1969 but grew up in Edinburgh, graduating from the University of Aberdeen. He has been the Scottish National Party MP for Moray since 7 June 2001 and is its Parliamentary Group Leader. He formerly worked as a journalist.]

3.22 pm

Angus Robertson (Moray) (SNP)

Thank you, Mr Speaker, for the opportunity to make a brief contribution. It is right to acknowledge that Margaret Thatcher was one of the most formidable politicians of recent times. To her family, to her friends, to her colleagues, to her supporters, I extend the condolences of the Scottish National party and Plaid Cymru.

It would be wrong, however, not to put on record our profound disagreement with her socially and economically divisive policies, which were particularly opposed in Scotland and Wales. We will never forget, we will never forgive the poll tax being imposed on Scots a year before the rest of the UK. No country should have such policies imposed on it when they were rejected at the ballot box. The existence of the Scottish Parliament and the Welsh National Assembly follows this experience.

Margaret Thatcher will be remembered for a long time in Scotland and Wales. She helped remind us that we have a national consensus that values society, values solidarity and values community. For that at least, we can be grateful.

[Rt Hon Peter Lilley MP was born 23 August 1943 and was educated at Dulwich College and Clare College, Cambridge. Following a career in the City (London's financial district) he entered Parliament 9 June 1983 as MP for St Albans later redistricted to become Hitchin and Harpenden which he has held since 1 May 1997. He served both Margaret Thatcher and John Major as Economic Secretary 1987–1989, Financial Secretary 1989–1990, Secretary of State for Trade and Industry 1990–1992, and Secretary of State for Social Security 1992–1997. On taking his seat in Cabinet he famously said to Margaret that since he had gone up to Cambridge to study physics, she was no longer the only scientist in the room. She glared at him! (Probably rightly so, as his final degree was in economics).]

3.23 pm

Mr Peter Lilley (Hitchin and Harpenden) (Con)

For those of us who worked with, loved and admired Mrs Thatcher, her death is immensely sad, but there is one small compensation: she leaves immensely vivid memories. So vigorous, energetic and decisive was her personality that she is unforgettable not just to those of us who worked with her, but to everybody in the country who was there at the time.

I first worked for Mrs Thatcher as a humble speech writer, long before I entered Parliament or became a Minister and eventually joined her Cabinet. My most personal memories conflict with the caricature that has been built up over time, as much by her friends as by her opponents. First, she was immensely kind. The less important someone was, the kinder she was to them. She gave her Ministers a pretty hard time, and quite right too. I remember an occasion on which she had returned from three days, having had little sleep. I had been summoned, in my role as a minor cog in her speech-writing machine, to help with some speech. She tore a strip off the Chancellor of the Exchequer before noticing me. She saw that I was wearing a black tie and deduced that I had been to a funeral, and was immediately full of solicitude for me — in marked contrast to her tearing a strip off her senior Minister.

Mrs Thatcher could also be remarkably diplomatic, not least in how she handled those who worked for her. As a junior Treasury Minister, I once ventured to disagree with a policy of a Secretary of State, and we were both summoned to appear before her to argue our respective cases. I thought my arguments were overwhelmingly the better ones, but she summed up in favour of the Secretary of State. Subsequently, she sent me a private message saying, "Peter, I was impressed by your arguments but it would have been quite wrong for me to overrule a senior Minister in favour of a junior Minister on a matter that was not of paramount importance." She was right.

Mrs Thatcher was also very cautious, again in contrast to the legend that she recklessly took on all comers. At the expense of a humiliating settlement with Arthur Scargill in her first Parliament, she deferred a confrontation in order to allow Nigel Lawson (*Minister for Energy*) to build up coal stocks (*enough to last a full year*) so that, should another confrontation arise — as indeed it did — the nation would not be held to ransom. Her trade union reforms were implemented progressively, step by step, and whenever she felt that she had bitten off enough for one Parliament, she would politely reject proposals for further reform, however much they appealed to her. However, once she was convinced that a policy was right in principle and workable in practice, and that it had been elaborated in detail — of which she had a masterly grasp while maintaining a focus on the central issues — she would push it through with unswerving tenacity.

It is probably not done on these occasions to face up to the criticisms that have been made of Mrs Thatcher, but she was never one to be limited by what was the done thing. I want to respond to the comments, made more in the media and also by the hon. Member for Moray (Angus Robertson), that she was deliberately harsh and divisive. It is said that she was harsh, but she made us face reality, and reality was harsh. Those who did not like facing reality projected their hatred of reality on to her. The human cost of facing up to reality would have been much less if previous Governments of both parties had not, for reasons of false analysis and cowardice, failed to deal with those realities earlier. If blame is due for the fact that any harshness materialised, it is due to her predecessors rather than to her. Those who hated reality, who hated being proved wrong and who hated seeing their illusions shattered transferred their hatred to her. Fortunately, she was big and strong enough to act as a lightning rod for their feelings.

A second adjective, "divisive", was used of Margaret Thatcher this morning by the BBC in its headline news, which probably tells us more about the BBC than it does about her. She was described as a divisive leader. That is a strange epithet, because for any division to exist, there have to be two sides, yet no mention was made of those who opposed the changes that proved so necessary. It is stranger still when we consider that her greatest success was, by her own admission, to convert her opponents to her way of seeing things. Not a single one of the major measures she introduced was subsequently repealed or reversed by those who followed her. Indeed, she has the extraordinary achievement of uniting all parties in this House behind a new paradigm: before she came along the assumption was that all problems could best be solved by top-down direction and control of the state. She introduced the idea that quality and efficiency are most likely to follow if people are free to choose between alternatives. That is now, I am happy to say, a model adopted by other parties and, after a faltering start, was implemented by Tony Blair, even in the public services where she had to feared to step. Far from being harsh or divisive, she leaves a legacy that unites us all. It behooves us, on a day such as this, to remember that.

[Alasdair McDonnell MP was born 1 September 1949 and has been Leader of the Social Democratic and Labour Party since 2011 as well as being both the MP and Member of the Legislative Assembly for South Belfast since 2005 and 1998. He is a medical doctor and attended University College, Dublin.]

3.30 pm

Dr Alasdair McDonnell (Belfast South) (SDLP)

It is clear from some of those testimonies that there was a side to Baroness Thatcher which those who knew her personally saw and for which they cherished her. I am not here to deny or counter those personal truths, but as a democratic Irish nationalist I must speak with sincerity and honesty about her political contribution and legacy. She always expected and respected candour. Not to register our differences with her politics and approach would be a dereliction of responsibility. Many have said, in earlier contributions that in many ways Baroness Thatcher made a divisive political contribution and has left a divisive legacy in Britain. That, too, is the case in Ireland.

She was a formidable lady and a formidable politician, and only a formidable politician could have made the breakthrough she made — that cannot be denied. Neither can it be denied, however, that she caused great pain, hurt and distress in Northern Ireland. She was ill advised that the very deep political issue, driven by many injustices in Ireland, could be solved by military and security methods alone. Her policy and her approach to hunger strikes hardened and polarised moderate opinion, and demonstrated a lack of knowledge of the island of Ireland and our peoples. Her actions proved counter-productive to her own cause time and time again, handing the IRA political propaganda victory after political propaganda victory. The culture of collusion within the security service, and the licence it had from Government, was also a major problem. The fact that at the time concerns raised by the SDLP were rubbished and dismissed — they have subsequently been vindicated by de Silva and many police ombudsman reports — all served to harden and alienate further constitutional nationalist opinion. That has left many questions, much hurt and a legacy that remains to this day. A large part of that unfinished legacy is how we must deal with the past and help the many victims, not just in Ireland but on this side of the Irish sea as well. The quest for truth will go on.

Our difficulties and political differences did not stop on the shores of these islands. The SDLP not only held a different outlook on Europe, but opposed the resistance to challenging the apartheid regime in South Africa. We disagreed with the attitude towards the African National Congress, and opposed the criminalisation of Nelson Mandela. I note that in the past few days the ANC has displayed great humanity in its response to the death of Baroness Thatcher, and it is with that humanity that I join in solidarity.

We can deal with many difficulties and differences, but history has shown that the signing of the Anglo-Irish agreement, by Margaret Thatcher as Prime Minister and Garret FitzGerald as Taoiseach, was a pivotal and defining moment in our shared history. Indeed, it was a pivotal moment in changing the direction of our relationships in these islands. It was the first significant agreement between Ireland and Britain since the treaty of 1921, and it laid the foundations for the peace process and much of the progress that has taken place in the past 27 years. It changed forever relationships between our two countries and was the foundation of many of the positive changes we have experienced since.

It is poignant that today is the 15th anniversary of the signing of the Belfast agreement — the Good Friday agreement. That effort involved building layers upon layers of understanding, and moving on from that agreement over the past 15 years has involved building more layers of understanding, but we have to agree that the bedrock and the foundation for all that has been achieved was the Anglo–Irish agreement in 1985. The signing of that agreement showed that, as some said earlier, at times Baroness Thatcher did listen to good advice from her advisers. She also listened to her friends — formidable friends such as US President Ronald Reagan; but just as Prime Minister Thatcher might not have recognised the malignant hardening and polarising effect of her policy and attitude towards hunger strikes, she may not have appreciated or recognised the potential benign and long-term softening effect on future relationships of her commitment in that Anglo-Irish agreement.

In placing our problem in these islands in a British–Irish context, the Anglo–Irish agreement challenged the traditional Unionist mindset and equipped political constitutional nationalism to make an even more compelling case against violence to those engaged in violence. Indeed, I believe it laid the foundation for stopping the violence in Ireland. At that stage, the pages were turned to a new history — the beginning of a new history in Northern Ireland, and with it a new history for these islands as a whole. The benefits of the Anglo–Irish and Good Friday agreements are being reaped today by the peoples of Britain and Ireland, who continue to benefit from the positive engagement that started with and continues to flow from Baroness Thatcher's signing of the Anglo–Irish agreement. Baroness Thatcher may not have recognised the full effect of that moment in history, but it is right that I on behalf of Irish nationalism recognise it today, just as the SDLP recognised it at the time of the passing of Dr Garret FitzGerald.

[Conor Burns MP was born 24 September 1972 and after graduating from the University of Southampton worked in communications and financial services. He was elected MP for Bournemouth West at the 2010 General Election.]

3.38 pm

Conor Burns (Bournemouth West) (Con)

Monday was the day we had all been dreading in recent months and years. Much has been written about the state of Lady Thatcher's health in recent years. You will remember, Mr Speaker, only 18 months ago hosting her in your state rooms when she came to support me at an occasion that turned out to be one of her last visits to the Palace of Westminster. May I say, Mr Speaker, that she was grateful for your support and kindness to her on that occasion?

Lady Thatcher came back from so many health scares that we thought she would go on for ever. In the words of the poem:

> If I had thought thou couldst have died,
> I might not weep for thee;
> But I forgot, when by thy side,
> That thou couldst mortal be.

As I watched the television coverage about this remarkable lady, I felt a deep sense of personal loss. Some of us have lost a dear friend, who in my case was not only a friend but a mentor and protectress — someone I loved and cared for very deeply.

I first met Margaret Thatcher back in 1992, when she came to support my hon. Friend and neighbour the Member for Christchurch (Mr Chope) in Southampton, Itchen, his then constituency. Over the years, she was enormously supportive of my efforts to get elected to this place. I remember that in 2001, she came to support me in Eastleigh. We took her to a health club in a visit covered live on Sky News. The chief executive of the entire group had come to welcome her. She announced to him, "These places are a complete waste of time — up and down stairs keeps me fit!"

In 2002, I had what must have been the unique privilege of welcoming Ted Heath and Margaret Thatcher to Eastleigh in the same month. When Ted was coming, I warned the people in my association, "For goodness' sake, don't put out the Thatcher–Tebbit fliers!" Well, they did. Ted reached for one of them, looked at it and said to me, "What on earth are you doing with those two?" I said, "Well, they agreed to come." He then said what I suppose for him was a grudging compliment — "I suppose that is something of a coup." Margaret came down to Eastleigh again in 2005; alas, it was not to be, and Chris Huhne won.

In January 2010, in the run-up to the general election, Lady Thatcher came to what turned out to be the last dinner she ever had outside her home or the Ritz. She came to do an event for me and another candidate which we had given the rather novel title "Women, for men to win". Ann Widdecombe [*former Member of the House of Commons*] was the guest speaker and Margaret was the guest of honour.

In recent years, I spent almost every Sunday evening with Lady Thatcher; on my way to Chester square to see her, I often bumped into you, Mr Speaker, when you were returning from the gym. We had great conversations on those Sundays. They ranged very much depending on how she was on a particular day. If we were in good form, we would go through the papers. I remember last November showing her a poll in *The Sunday Telegraph* that showed the Conservatives 9% behind the Labour party. She asked when the next election was, so I said that there was a little over two years to go. She said, "That's not far enough behind at this stage!" I texted that information to the Prime Minister from the living room of Chester square; I do not know whether it cheered up his Sunday evening at Chequers, but I am sure it reduced my prospects of promotion.

On one occasion, I took a taxi from here to Chester square to see Lady Thatcher on a particularly wet and awful evening. The taxi driver said, "Which end of the square do you want, guv?" I said, "The house with the policeman outside." "Maggie Thatcher's, guv?" "That's right." "What you doin' there, then?" "I'm going to have a drink with her — she's a friend of mine." "What d'you do then?" "I'm a Tory MP." As we pulled up, I went to pay the driver, but he refused to take the fare. I apologise in advance to the Prime Minister for repeating this story, but the driver said, "Your fare tonight, guv, is you go in there and you tell 'er from me that we ain't had a good'un since!" I imparted that message to Margaret, who looked at me and said, "Well, he's quite right." I was then on the receiving end of a lecture about how he probably had a wife and child to support, how I should have paid him and how it was monstrous that I had not.

One of the things we used to talk about was her time in office and some of her remarkable achievements. Quite recently, towards the end of last year, I remember saying to her, "You must have made mistakes." She said, "I suppose I must have done." I said, "Can you think of any specific examples?" She replied, "Well, they usually happened when I didn't get my own way."

Much has been made in the media about the controversial nature of Margaret Thatcher as a politician and of her premiership. We should not shy away from that today, and nor should we on the Conservative Benches be afraid to talk about that. That would be to betray who she was: she was a robust, principled, confrontational character. Yes, she divided; yes, she pursued her policies with vigour and persistence. She believed, as she said to me, that politics at its purest is philosophy in action. She believed in the battle of ideas — something that we would welcome returning to domestic politics today.

If I may say so to the Deputy Prime Minister, Margaret Thatcher was not a Tory at all. In fact, she proudly stated that she was a laissez-faire Gladstonian economic liberal — in the proudest traditions, and I say it as one myself, of the Gladstonian Liberal party. She would have welcomed that.

In some ways, the protests are the greatest compliment that could be paid to Margaret Thatcher. Even in death, the left have to argue against her. She would take great pride in these protests. She would not get angry about them; she would regard them as utterly and completely absurd. All I would say to those engaged in those protests is that they should look at how gracious she always was in what she said whenever her political foes departed the scene — most recently in the statement she issued about Michael Foot.

Her enduring legacy is not just in what she achieved and the fact that the Labour party has not reversed much of it. Her true legacy lies here on these Benches and in those who are coming up behind us. After the 2010 general election, I had the honour of organising a small number of receptions to introduce her to new colleagues. She drew great solace and comfort from the number of those colleagues who told her that they were in Parliament because of her inspiration and because of what she believed and did. Only two years ago Tony Abbott, as the aspirant Prime Minister of Australia, asked to come to see her and told her that his philosophy was informed by watching what she had done when he was at university. While she was divisive to some degree, controversial certainly, she was an inspiration to many people way beyond these shores.

I would like to end by quoting what she said in the closing pages of the second volume of her memoirs — the last authentic book that she published. She reflected on a visit to Warsaw in 1993 and wrote movingly about attending mass at the Church of the Holy Cross:

> Every nook and cranny was packed and the choral singing of unfamiliar Polish hymns was all the more uplifting because I could not understand the verses: it forced me to try to imagine...what the congregation was asking of God.

> Foreign though this experience was, it also gave me a comforting feeling that I was but one soul among many in a fellowship of believers that crossed nations and denominations.

> When the priest rose to give the sermon, however, I had the sense that I had suddenly become the centre of attention. Heads turned and people smiled at me. As the priest began, someone translated his words.

> He recalled that during the dark days of communism they had been aware of voices from the outside world, offering hope of a different and better life. The voices were many, often eloquent, and all were welcome to a people starved so long of truth as well as freedom.

But Poles had come to identify with one voice in particular — my own. Even when that voice had been relayed through the distorting loud-speaker of the Soviet propaganda, they had heard through the distortions the message of truth and hope.

Well, communism had fallen and a new democratic order had replaced it. But they had not fully felt the change nor truly believed in its reality until today when they finally saw me in their own church.

The priest finished his sermon and the service continued. But the kindness of the priest and the parishioners had not been exhausted. At the end of Mass, I was invited to stand in front of the Altar. When I did so, lines of children presented me with little bouquets while their mothers and fathers applauded.

The final paragraph of Lady Thatcher's memoir reads thus:

Of course no human mind nor any conceivable computer can calculate the sum total of my career in politics in terms of happiness, achievement and virtue, nor indeed their opposites. It follows therefore that the full accounting of how my political work affected the lives of others is something that we will only know on Judgement Day. It is an awesome and unsettling thought. But it comforts me that when I stand up to hear the verdict, I will at least have the people of the Church of the Holy Cross in Warsaw in court as character witnesses.

[Sir Gerald Kaufman was born 21 June 1930 and was educated at Leeds Grammar School and Queen's College, Oxford. After working as a journalist he entered Parliament representing Manchester Alnwick 1970–1983 and Manchester Gorton since then. He served Labour Party Leader Neil Kinnock as Shadow Home Secretary and Shadow Foreign Secretary. He famously described his Party's 1983 election manifesto as "the longest suicide note in history".]

3.50 pm

Sir Gerald Kaufman (Manchester, Gorton) (Lab)

I join in paying tribute to my old adversary, Margaret Thatcher. For many, of course, Margaret Thatcher was synonymous with "milk-snatcher" [*as Secretary of State for Education 1970–1974 she withdrew 'free' school milk for children who all used to get 1/3 pint a day*] and it would be idle to pretend that to us in the Labour party, and to millions of our supporters, many of her policies were other than anathema. But Margaret was much more complex than that, both as a politician and as a person, and her international significance was emphasised quite recently when, almost 24 years after she had stopped being Prime Minister, an actress in Hollywood [*Meryl Streep*] could win the "best actress" Oscar for portraying her almost as well as she used to portray herself.

I served in the shadow Cabinet for 10 years when Margaret Thatcher was Prime Minister. I saw her in action, and I often opposed her in action. After she left office — or rather, was ousted from office by some of her colleagues — I had contact with her from time to time.

Of course, as a Labour Member of Parliament, I deplored many of the drastic changes that she made in society. I was Labour's Front-Bench spokesman during the coal strike, which she provoked, prepared for and won, although she was greatly helped by the stupid approach of Arthur Scargill, who destroyed the once almost revered National Union of Mineworkers by refusing to hold a strike ballot — a victory for her — just as Michael Foot, who has been mentioned this afternoon, contributed very significantly indeed to her greatest election victory in 1983.

It was my job to oppose her right-to-buy legislation, whose impact on the availability of social housing persists to this day, which is quite a charge sheet, not to mention the blunders that finished her off: the poll tax and "no, no, no" to Europe. But after all, she was a Tory Prime Minister and was not elected to implement policies that I or my constituents favoured. Unlike Winston Churchill, Harold Macmillan or Ted Heath, she broke the post-war consensus; that was her objective, and that was her achievement.

In personal relationships, and in some policy areas, Margaret Thatcher could be more than civilized — indeed, punctilious and cordial. I was a junior Housing Minister when she was shadow Environment Secretary, and I recall an occasion when one of her Front-Bench spokesmen violated the kind of across-the-Floor Front-Bench deal on which the functioning of this House depends. It was Margaret who sought me out to apologise and to say that she knew nothing about it, and would have stopped it had she known.

After she became Prime Minister, she baulked at railway privatisation. It was imposed by John Major, and its messy consequences we suffer to this day. Although she won her second and third elections with enormous majorities, she was always accessible. She announced that any Member of Parliament with employment problems in his or her constituency could come and see her at No. 10, and I availed myself of that offer when a computer multilayer board factory in my constituency was at hazard. We met in the Prime Minister's study in 10 Downing street and I explained the problem. "But how are we to save it?" she asked. I suggested that it could be taken over by the National Enterprise Board, which had been created by Labour. Kenneth Baker, the junior Minister responsible for this policy area, was present, so she turned to him and asked plaintively, "Kenneth, what did I do with the National Enterprise Board?" I am sorry to say that the factory is now a blood transfusion centre, but, still, she meant well.

Margaret Thatcher was brave. In the parliamentary week following the Brighton bombing, in which terrorists tried to kill her and her entire Cabinet — and British democracy, by seeking to do so — she came here; she was present, bright and perky in the House of Commons, for the Government statement, to which I responded. She was also absolutely right on a considerable number of foreign policy issues. Against timorous nerve-trembling on both sides of the House and attempted international interference, she was utterly determined that the people of the Falkland Islands, who wanted to be British and who still want to be British today, should not be the victims of a fascist dictator. How some

Labour Members of Parliament could actually want to water down a response to an aggressive fascist dictator, I could not understand then and I still do not understand today.

When Saddam Hussein seized Kuwait, she was actively part of the preparations to oust him by force. I was shadow Foreign Secretary at this time and had to seek to carry with me our Back Benchers, some of whom were spineless — *[Interruption]*. I am here to try to obtain a consensus. In the debate, I therefore told the House that Labour policy was based not on supporting the United Kingdom Government, but on implementing United Nations Security Council resolutions. She knew what I was up to, and she dug the Foreign Secretary in the ribs with her elbow and smiled a wry smile. She was also much more far-sighted than most United Kingdom Prime Ministers about rightward trends in Israel and in the middle east. When, as shadow Foreign Secretary, I visited Morocco, I was told by the United Kingdom ambassador there that she had given him a direct instruction to approach the leaders of the then substantial Moroccan Jewish community and urge them to exhort the sizeable number of Moroccan Jewish immigrants in Israel to vote Labour — Shimon Peres — in a forthcoming election.

Until her final debacle, she generally found ways of getting her own way. There had been a Lionel Bart musical called "Maggie May" and the saying went, "Others may not, but Maggie may", and that was very much her watchword. I saw her from time to time after she had left office. On one occasion I attended a social event and when I came in she bustled over to me. I had recently had published in a newspaper an article about protecting children from pornography on TV and videos. She told me how much she admired the article and said, "I carry it with me everywhere in my handbag." To be part of the contents of Margaret's handbag — what greater apotheosis could one possibly hope for, Mr Speaker?

[Sir Gerald Howarth MP was born 12 September 1947 and was educated at the University of Southampton. He held Cannock and Burntwood from 1983 to 1992 and since 1997 the seat of Aldershot. He served David Cameron as Minister for International Security Strategy 2010–2012. In 1970 he demonstrated against exchange controls outside the Bank of England — such controls were suspended by Chancellor Geoffrey Howe in 1979. He also sued the BBC for slander in October 1986, winning costs, damages, and the head of its Director General who resigned.]

3.59 pm

Sir Gerald Howarth (Aldershot) (Con)

This is a sad day for those of us who were privileged to serve as either officers or, in my case, foot soldiers in Margaret Thatcher's great army, but as the Leader of the Opposition said, in what I thought was a very generous speech, it is also an opportunity for the nation to pause, reflect and recall the extraordinary achievements she secured in just 11 years.

Many of my colleagues are too young to remember what Britain was like when Margaret Thatcher won the 1979 election, but we older ones can remember the rubbish piled up in the streets, corpses being left unburied and industry being held to ransom by the likes of Red Robbo. Britain was basically a basket-case. The then Chancellor of the Exchequer was recalled from an aeroplane at Heathrow to come and answer to the International Monetary Fund.

Margaret Thatcher arrived as a new breed; not just a woman, but, as the Prime Minister said, a conviction politician who was driven by a belief that Britain, and the British people themselves, deserved better. She did not need a focus group to decide what she believed in. She was driven by a set of clear Conservative principles, underpinned by a fundamental belief that it was free enterprise that would deliver the prosperity she so craved for our people in the aftermath of the second world war and the malaise to which the Prime Minister referred.

When I became a shadow Minister in 2002, I received a hand-written note congratulating me and advising me, "Know your facts." In that spirit, I wish to remind the House of a couple of facts. Margaret Thatcher believed in sound money, as the Prime Minister said, and in her time public sector borrowing fell from 4.1% to 1% of GDP. The national debt was cut from 43.6% to 26.7% of GDP. She took on the trade union barons and restored the trade unions to their members. It is interesting to look at the figures: in 1979, 29.8 million days were lost to industrial action, or strikes, but that figure was cut to 2 million by the time she left office, and last year it was fewer than 250,000. Such has been the change that this divisive woman wrought to industrial relations in our country.

She also abolished (*suspended and later abolished*) exchange controls. In about 1972 (*1970*) I went on a demonstration outside the Bank of England — I was running the Society for Individual Freedom at the time — and I held a placard that read, "End Exchange Controls". I did not really understand what it was all about, because I had not yet embarked on my banking career, but I had a vague notion that it was some sort of ghastly second world war regulation. The first thing Geoffrey Howe did after becoming Chancellor of the Exchequer was abolish (*suspend*) exchange controls. For those of our young people who do not understand what I am talking about, as I did not then, let me explain. In those days, when we went abroad we were allowed to take 30 quid (*a quid is a pound sterling, and the limit was 50, not 30*) out of the country, and our passports had to be stamped to show that we were entitled to do so. It is important that we take this opportunity to remind people of the changes that have been wrought. I was working in a bank at the time. I took all the regulations relating to exchange controls off the shelves and have them at home to remind myself, and anybody else who might need to, of the iniquity of exchange controls.

She also ended the party line. I do not mean the line that we are so privileged to receive from central office every morning. Again, I remind those who are a little younger that the party line, which we had at home, meant that a telephone, which was graciously provided by something called the General Post Office, could not be used if a neighbour who shared the line was already using it. I remember in the late 1990s all the smart, Armani-suited new Labour types clutching their mobile phones. Those friends and comrades should not forget that had it not been for us privatising the telecommunications industry, they would not have had their mobile phones. *[Interruption.]* The shadow Chancellor can try to phone a friend, but the trouble is that he has not got one. I am sorry — that was a bit divisive.

We have heard of her other domestic achievements, but of course she did not do everything. I, my right hon. Friends the Members for Hitchin and Harpenden (Mr Lilley) and for Wokingham (Mr Redwood) and many others in the No Turning Back group urged her to go further and faster — we were called the "Don't Turn Your Back" group for some obscure reason. I remember that we proposed to her a system in education whereby the money followed the pupil. At an NTB ('No Turning Back' group as in no turning away from Thatcherite principles) dinner, she told us, "Grow up, boys, and be your age. We can't possibly do anything like that." We were all crestfallen and went home very disappointed that the Prime Minister had not listened. Come the general election in 1987, we were out canvassing all day long and would turn on the telly at night to see what was going on at the centre. There was the press conference, with the Prime Minister in the middle and Ken Baker to her side. She said, "We've got this new idea about education. The money follows the pupil." That was what we had proposed to her and she had told us to grow up and that we could not possibly do anything like that. That was the art of Margaret Thatcher's political argument, of which the Prime Minister spoke: she challenged people and made sure that they got their facts right. She challenged that proposal and found that it was a policy worth pursuing.

Abroad, of course, she forged that close relationship with Ronald Reagan and the United States. I heard the story that my right hon. and learned Friend the Member for Kensington (Sir Malcolm Rifkind) mentioned about Ronald Reagan from Bob Tuttle, the former American ambassador. It is absolutely right that they really did admire her. She was no poodle of the United States, however. She challenged them and that is what they admired about her.

She ended the cold war and it is terribly important to understand that at that time we all felt a sense of potential nuclear holocaust. Together with Ronald Reagan and Mikhail Gorbachev, she made the world a better place and liberated millions of Eastern Europeans who had been subjected to tyranny. This divisive lady was responsible for introducing harmony across the iron curtain.

Her will to recover the Falkland Islands is now legendary and I wear my Falkland Islands tie with pride today as a symbol of Margaret Thatcher's determination.

That extraordinary engendering of a new respect across the world for the United Kingdom had commercial advantage. One of the biggest deals we have ever done was the al-Yamamah defence deal with the Kingdom of Saudi Arabia, which today is worth tens of billions of pounds, sustaining high-tech jobs across the United Kingdom. She played a huge part in that. When she went there, she observed all the courtesies of the Arab world — a long dress, long sleeves and a scarf — but I am quite sure that when she flashed her eyes at King Fahd it was all a done deal.

We have heard about the liberation of Kuwait and the winning of the EU rebate. In the latter case, again, she had a simple message for the country. That was one of her secrets. Members might remember Robin Day (*an aggressive TV man*) interviewed her and gave a great spiel about how her belligerence and her determination to get the rebate would put off our European partners. She paused and said, "But Robin, it's our money. We want it back." To date, we have had £75 billion back, so let no one deny her the pomp and circumstance of next week's funeral. (*The funeral supposedly cost 10 million pounds*).

Of course, she did fall out over Europe, and she did sign the Single European Act, as the right hon. Member for Belfast North (Mr Dodds) mentioned. I did not sign it — I was not a Minister — but I did vote against it on Third Reading. When I became her Parliamentary Private Secretary, I said to her, "A lot of people in the House are saying, Margaret, that your belligerence on Europe is hardly justified when you signed the Single European Act." She said to me, "Yes, I did sign it, but I understood it to apply solely to the single market in goods and services. I was assured that it would not be extended to working time and other areas. The fact that I was betrayed is why I feel so passionately about it."

She was a fervent patriot. She profoundly believed in this country; she loved this country and she did not wish to sign up to a united states of Europe — neither do I, nor do my right hon. and hon. Friends on this side of the House. Of course, we were not alone in that. I remember a conservation in the Lobby that was not seen by any of the media involving me, Mrs Thatcher, as she then was, Tony Benn and the hon. Member for Bolsover (Mr Skinner). It was absolutely marvellous to hear the entire expression of unity about how evil, as it were, the common market was in the way it was trying to drive a united states of Europe.

Margaret Thatcher lost office and I was her Parliamentary Private Secretary after that. She was angry; people around the world could not understand it and it is important to remember that she was never beaten by the British people. She was never even beaten by the Conservative party — 54% of us voted for her, but that was four votes short of the majority required. I think that the Conservative party, and the country, suffered as a consequence of that, and I congratulate my right hon. Friend the Prime Minister on doing all he can to try to revive those Thatcherite principles that did so much to revive our country in the 1980s.

I will tell one wonderful story, and then I will wind up my remarks. I went to see Margaret Thatcher after I lost my seat in Staffordshire in 1992 and asked her, "What are you doing this weekend, Margaret?" She said, "Well, I'm going to Paris. I am going to have dinner with President Mitterrand." I asked, "What are you going to say?", and she said, "I am going to tell him that if France signs the Maastricht treaty, *France est mort*." I said, "I think actually that it's 'La France'". She said, "Yes. *La France est mort*." I said, "Well, because it's 'La France', you have to say 'morte'". She went round the room saying, "*La France est morte. La France est morte*", and that weekend she went off to dinner with President Mitterrand. In my view it is no coincidence that on Monday morning, President Mitterrand announced that France would hold a referendum on the Maastricht treaty. The eyes of Caligula and the mouth of Marilyn Monroe, perhaps.

After losing my seat in 1992 in Cannock and Burntwood, I was told that if I did not distance myself from Margaret Thatcher, I would never get a seat again. However, I had a wonderful letter from Enoch Powell who said, "My Dear Gerald, Hard luck but be of good cheer. Fidelity to persons or to principles is seldom unrewarded." Thank you to the people of Aldershot who rewarded me by offering me the first seat that came up after the 1992 general election, which I think rather worried No. 10 at the time. I have not changed my principles; I have been a supporter of Margaret Thatcher from the very first time she put her name forward to be leader of our party and I do not regret that. I think she has been the salvation of the nation, and that she restored our position in the world.

None of us can forget Margaret Thatcher's extraordinary elegance. I remember coming to the Chamber at about 4 o'clock in the morning during an all-night sitting — none of you lot know what an all-night sitting is about, but we used to have them regularly. It was 4 o'clock in the morning, people had had a bit to drink and, for us chaps, there was a bit of stubble and it was really pretty unpleasant. I was sitting on the Front Bench wondering when this purgatory was going end, and then there was a frisson at the back of the Chair. All of a sudden, in walked the Prime Minister, not a hair out of place, hand bag there, smiling. We sort of slid up the Bench and looked at the Prime Minister, saying, "Here I am." She was an inspiration to us all and she inspired huge loyalty. When I asked Bob Kingston, her personal protection officer, what it was like working for her, he said, "I would catch bullets between my teeth to save that woman."

The soldiers whom Margaret Thatcher so admired reciprocated and admired her. I was at the Painted Hall for the 25th anniversary of the Falklands campaign. A lot of people who had been injured, either mentally or physically, were there. When Margaret Thatcher got up to leave, there was the most astonishing roar from men who had been maimed, cheering their warrior leader who had instructed them to go into battle, and they wanted to pay tribute to her.

As people have said, Margaret Thatcher showed immense kindness. In my case, when Neil Hamilton (*a former Member of the Commons*) and I faced extinction after we were defamed by the BBC "Panorama" programme, it took a bit of time to see the chairman of the party — who happened to be Norman Tebbit — but only a couple of days to see the Prime Minister. She listened for 25 minutes and at the end she turned to the Chief Whip, John Wakeham, and said, "These are members of our party in good standing. Please ensure that they get the necessary support." We got that support. We won our libel action and the director general of the BBC was fired, and as a result of Margaret Thatcher's kindness, we were able to resume our political careers.

I will close by quoting Enoch Powell, who, at the time of the Falklands campaign, made an interesting observation. Before the campaign, he had said that the Iron Lady would be tested, but on 17 June 1982, he said this to the Prime Minister:

> Is the right hon. Lady aware that the report has now been received from the public analyst on a certain substance recently subjected to analysis and that I have obtained a copy of the report? It shows that the substance under test consisted of ferrous matter of the highest quality, that it is of excep-

tional tensile strength, is highly resistant to wear and tear and to stress, and may be used with advantage for all national purposes?" [*Official Report*, 17 June 1982; Vol. 25, c. 1082.]

What advantage the nation had in the leadership of Margaret Thatcher, the greatest peacetime Prime Minister this nation has ever seen. Next week, we will have our opportunity to give her the send-off she so fully deserves for her selfless sacrifice to the nation.

[The Rt Hon Michael Meacher MP was born 4 November 1939 and educated at the London School of Economics and New College, Oxford. A university lecturer and researcher he was MP for Oldham West 1970 to 1987 and Royton since then. He served Tony Blair as Minister of State for the Environment 1997-2003.]

4.15 pm

Mr Michael Meacher (Oldham West and Royton) (Lab)

Almost everyone agrees that, in 1979, Britain was set on a course that could not go on. It demanded radical change. At times of deep crisis, the whole country rallies behind a unifying leader, whether it is Churchill in wartime or Attlee in peacetime — the latter constructed a peace that broke with the despair of the 1930s. Mrs Thatcher was a very different kind of leader. She was someone who took the fight to her opponents, and who deployed a scorched earth policy to destroy them. That polarised the country, which is why, even today, she is lionised in the south, as we have heard repeatedly this afternoon, but remembered with a very different memorial in the north.

The task in 1979 certainly required a dominant personality to shake this country out of its somnolent conservatism — all hon. Members agree on that. Whatever else Mrs Thatcher was, she was certainly a dominant figure. She dominated, or came to dominate, her Cabinet, and she dominated her party and the country. Her influence was felt across much of the world.

In that context, I recall a story I recently heard while sharing a platform with my very good friend John Gummer, who is now Lord Deben. When he was Secretary of State for the Environment in the 1980s, he complained that he could not get his Department to take climate change seriously. He rang Mrs Thatcher to ensure that he had the necessary support. When he explained the situation, she said to him, "John, you really shouldn't worry. There are two persons in the Cabinet who are committed over climate change — you and me, so we are in a majority."

Dominance, however, should always have a counterpart in concern for the victims of radical change. One should never destroy without then building up again. Too many industries and too many working class communities across the north were laid waste during those years without an alternative and better future being constructed to replace what was lost. Many of those communities are still desolated today.

In Oldham, the textile industry was wiped out, and a swathe of the country's finest engineering companies were simply swept away. Yes, Labour Members agree that change, and even painful change, is often necessary, but we also believe that it should not be bought at the price of tripling unemployment, tripling child poverty and an unacceptable increase in inequality, which is still with us today.

My office in Oldham has received dozens of phone calls and e-mails on this matter from my constituents, as I am sure have the offices of many other Members. I will quote the exact words of one e-mail:

"Despite what her supporters think, a lot of today's problems result from her policies...the destruction of our manufacturing base, lack of investment in social housing following the sale of council homes, deregulating the banking industry, privatised industries profiteering at our expense. We are still living with the consequences."

My constituent went on: "I'm sure a large percentage of the population who lived through her years in power will feel the same....I hope that my views will be represented in Parliament."

Lady Thatcher will undoubtedly be remembered as a leader of great conviction. However, in my view, greatness has to be tempered with generosity and magnanimity if one is to earn a permanent place in the heart of this nation. I conclude by saying simply that the unwavering conviction that Lady Thatcher possessed so magnificently sets an example for every generation in confronting the problems that challenge them. This generation is confronted by very different problems: the straitjacket of prolonged austerity, the lack of accountability in corporate power, the over-dominance of finance, a grossly unjust system of remuneration and the destruction of the public realm. I say genuinely and forcefully that it is to Lady Thatcher's credit that she has shown that we should not be daunted by problems of that scale and magnitude, but should tackle them head-on and overcome them with the same flame of conviction and resolution that remains her greatest memorial.

[Rt Hon Cheryl Gillan MP was born 21 April 1952 and attended Cheltenham Ladies College and the College of Law. After a career in marketing she became MP for Chesham and Amersham 9 April 1992 and served David Cameron as Secretary of State for Wales (where she was born) from 2010 to 2012.]

4.22 pm

Mrs Cheryl Gillan (Chesham and Amersham) (Con)

The legion of tributes today, the international response and even the distasteful celebrations of her sad death mark out Margaret Thatcher from all other politicians in this country. The remarkable fact that she was only the second woman on the Conservative Benches to serve at Cabinet level makes her achievements even more impressive. (*The first was Florence Hosbrugh 1951–1954 who also served as Education Secretary for Churchill. Only Margaret Bondfield and Ellen Wilkin-*

son preceded her and along with Margaret Thatcher all four were Secretary of State for Education.)

Margaret Thatcher was a woman of great contrasts. It may be said that she bestrode the world stage like a colossus, but she was also capable of great empathy and compassion. She was not only a politician, but proud of her role as daughter, wife, mother and grandmother.

I came into this House just as Margaret Thatcher left, so it is a great sadness that I never got to serve on these green Benches alongside her. For me, she was a cross between my mother and my headmistress. She was a woman to be loved and admired, but also to be feared. She was a woman to hold up as an example for others, but who would expect people to follow her.

For someone with a reputation of wanting to be the only woman in the Cabinet room, I found Margaret Thatcher both inspiring and personally encouraging to other women, particularly those who wanted to enter politics. As a direct result of her comments to me back in 1979, when I sat next to her at a dinner, I believed that I, too, could serve my country as an MP. From some of the speeches that we have heard today and from some that will follow, we will know that she had that effect on many people and empowered them to achieve their potential.

It was Margaret Thatcher's clearly defined philosophy and stubborn adherence to her own beliefs that fashioned the opinions both of her admirers and her detractors. My predecessor in Chesham and Amersham was one such detractor — he entitled his book on the Thatcher years "Dancing with Dogma" (*Sir Ian Gilmour*), to reflect her often intractable views and approach — but even he praised her attention to detail and her mastery of the brief, while perhaps not admiring her footwork on the political dance floor.

Although, almost unbelievably, she had moments of self-doubt, she reserved those for the private arena, mostly to be shared with her devoted and doted-on Denis. On public platforms she always appeared sure-footed, and brave with it.

Politics takes no prisoner, man or woman, and being Prime Minister is no sinecure. I think that, as an individual, she was braver than many men. She took on the vested interests, the dictators and the misogynists, and triumphed. She engineered the end of a cold war, and, against all odds, won a distant one; she curtailed the powers of the unelected unions, and restored it to elected representatives; she removed the dead hand of the state from enterprise, and helped people to improve their lot and their lives through hard work and home ownership; and she established the United Kingdom's ground, quite clearly and uniquely, in a Europe that had its own grandiose ambitions to usurp our British sovereignty. Any one of those feats would have been enough to mark out an individual, but they, and many more, reflect a politician of substance whose like we may not see again in our lifetimes.

[Diane Abbott was born 27 September 1953 to Jamaican immigrants. She was educated at Newnham College, Cambridge, and pursued a career in government and later the media. She became MP for Hackney North and Stoke Newington in 1987 being the first black woman elected to the British Parliament. She is a regular commentator on radio and TV.]

4.26 pm

Ms Diane Abbott (Hackney North and Stoke Newington) (Lab)

I entered Parliament in 1987, when Mrs Thatcher was still Prime Minister in all her pomp and glory, and it is fair to say that she was a remarkable parliamentary phenomenon. She believed in Parliament as the cockpit of political debate, in a way that is perhaps not fashionable today, and she was often the leading lady — whether we agreed with her or not — in some of Parliament's most momentous occasions.

The House will not be surprised to hear that I did not agree with many of the things for which she stood. However, I rose this afternoon not to challenge her beliefs, but to remind the House very gently that, even after all the years that have passed since she stood down as leader of her party, there are still millions of people who felt themselves to be on the wrong side of the titanic battles that she fought. Whether they are people who felt that the poll tax had been imposed on them wrongly, whether they are young people who were caught up in the difficult relationships between police and communities in our inner cities, whether they are people who were dismayed by her unwillingness to impose economic sanctions on South Africa and by her insistence on calling the African National Congress a terrorist organisation, or whether they are people — and I mean communities — who were caught up in the miners' strike, there are still people living today who felt themselves to be on the wrong side of those titanic struggles, and the House should not make it appear that their voice cannot be heard.

Many Members from mining communities are present today, and they will have their say, but let me quote from another Conservative leader, Harold Macmillan. In his first speech in the House of Lords as Lord Stockton, he said:

> Although...I cannot interfere...it breaks my heart to see what is happening in our country today. A terrible strike is being carried on by the best men in the world. They beat the Kaiser's army and they beat Hitler's army. They never gave in. — [*Official Report, House of Lords*, 13 November 1984; Vol. 457, c. 240.]

Whatever the rights and wrongs of the titanic political struggles that she fought — Conservative Members have spoken about them at length — let us remember that in their hearts some of those communities never gave in and deserve to have a voice in the House this afternoon. I am happy to pay tribute to her historic significance and her historic role, and I know that history is written by victors, but those of us who came of age in the Thatcher era know that there was another side to the glories that Government Members have spoken about.

[Sir Tony Baldry was born 10 July 1950 and attended the University of Sussex to read law. While there he successfully sued the local student union for paying for free school milk for local schoolchildren a program axed by then Education Secretary Margaret Thatcher. These payments were declared *ultra vires*.

He has served as MP for Banbury since 1983 and was briefly a Minister of State 1995-1997.]

4.30 pm

Sir Tony Baldry (Banbury) (Con)

I first met Margaret Thatcher when she was Secretary of State for Education and I was a student at Sussex university who was active in student politics. From that, I became Margaret Thatcher's personal aide and research assistant in the October 1974 general election. The Conservative party was in opposition and Margaret was a member of the shadow Cabinet as shadow housing and planning Minister. In those days, Members of Parliament did not have numbers of research assistants — they had just a single House of Commons secretary — so the core campaign team in Finchley was small: Mrs Thatcher's secretary, Alison Ward, now Lady Wakeham, her agent and me. What struck me first about working for Margaret Thatcher was her prodigious work ethic, her indefatigable determination to analyse and understand any brief that she was given and the considerable attention she paid to the last detail. I think that that was helped by the combination of her training both as a research chemist and, for a while, an extremely able junior at the tax Bar. (*Attorney*)

Working for Margaret and producing research briefings for her, I knew that I had to be ready and able to deal with any of the supplementary questions that she might ask — or, at the very least, know who could provide those detailed answers. The simple fact was that at any meeting — I suspect that this was the case throughout her time as leader of the party and as Prime Minister — Margaret was always the best-prepared person in the room, because invariably she had taken the time and effort to ensure that she was the best briefed.

When writing speeches for Margaret in the October 1974 general election, we used two books for primary source material. The first, which has already been mentioned, was F. A. Hayek's *The Constitution of Liberty*, and the other was a book written and published in the 1930s called *A Time for Greatness*. To my shame, I cannot now remember the author's name (*by Herbert Agar*), but I well recall that Margaret's reflection of these two books was along these lines: if the state takes all in taxation and spends all, we all become slaves of the state.

Margaret Thatcher was also incredibly kind, particularly to those who worked for her. Of course, she revelled in the Iron Lady sobriquet given to her by the Russians (*in 1976*) and others — it was a badge of respect for her steadfastness and determination — but there was also a much softer and more caring side to her. Perhaps I can give one example with which I think every Member could empathise. One of my intake, Patrick Nicholls, was a very effective junior Minister, but had had to resign from office following a road traffic offence. Not surprisingly, he was cross with himself and very frustrated, and thought he had let people down.

One evening, Patrick had a telephone call from his Whip, telling him to be in the Division Lobby at five to 10, shortly before the 10 o'clock vote. Patrick asked why and was told simply to be there. Patrick arrived, as instructed, at five to 10, and shortly afterwards Margaret Thatcher walked in, put her arm through his and said, "How are things going, Patrick? How are you?" As the Division bell rang and as the Lobby filled with parliamentary colleagues, the Prime Minister slowly walked through the Lobby, arm in arm with Patrick, chatting to him all the way — a kind and clear gesture of support for someone who had been a hard-working junior Minister and who continued to be an extremely hard-working and loyal Back Bencher.

Margaret also had a great sense of humour. In the 1983 general election, another of our intake, Jeremy Hanley, won Richmond with a majority of just 74 votes. The day after the general election, Margaret, the Prime Minister, telephoned Jeremy to congratulate him on winning Richmond. The Conservative vote in the constituency had been about 21,000. The conversation went like this. Jeremy: "Thank you very much, Prime Minister, for getting me the 74 votes that I needed." Prime Minister: "Jeremy, I got you the 21,000 votes — you just got the 74." Indeed, I often think there were two Margaret Thatchers: the real Margaret Thatcher for those who knew and worked with her and the caricature Margaret Thatcher of some press commentators, satirists and political opponents.

During the winter of 1974–75, I gave some help to Airey Neave in the Conservative leadership campaign. When Margaret became leader of the Conservative party, I joined her private office for a while as the personal link between her and the Britain in Europe campaign that was going on as a consequence of the EU referendum. I therefore had a good opportunity to see how Margaret worked, in the early part of her leadership, with parliamentary colleagues and advisers. Yes, Margaret Thatcher was certainly a person of robust views. She liked a good discussion — robust argument, even — but she was always willing to listen and heed the views of others. There were, I suspect, countless occasions when having heard the arguments — having heard the advice of Willie Whitelaw, or, on more personal matters, heeded the good counsel of Denis — Margaret would accept other people's contributions and advice, perhaps saying something like, "All right, we'll do it your way, but you had better get it right."

It is also a caricature to portray Margaret Thatcher as simply anti-European. I have in my desk at home the originals of a number of speeches that she gave in her constituency and elsewhere during the 1975 EU referendum campaign — speeches clearly amended and corrected in her own very distinctive cursive handwriting. Margaret campaigned wholeheartedly for a "yes to Europe" result in the referendum. As those speeches demonstrate, she clearly believed in a strong Europe being a counterweight to the then Soviet Union and a strong partner to the United States. She clearly undoubtedly believed in a Europe of nation states. She strongly believed in ensuring the speediest possible creation of the European single market and was always extremely frustrated by other member states that sought to frustrate the further creation of a single market for their own particular nationalist interests.

Ironically, I think that this where her frustration may have started with some of the workings of the European Union. Prior to the Single European Act in the mid-1980s, every EU member state had, in effect, a veto on any issue of any importance. This meant that the EU Commission or the President of the Council of Ministers, when wishing to get business through had, importantly, to negotiate with and square any member states that they thought would veto a particular proposal. That meant that any single member state could veto advances in the single market. It was therefore decided, in the Single European Act, to move to a system of weighted qualified majority voting. This, overnight, fundamentally changed the way in which the Council of Ministers and the Commission worked, because now all they needed to do was to secure the support of sufficient member states to get a majority vote. They would therefore start with the member states they considered the most supportive of a proposal and work on them until they got a qualified majority, and if, at the end, there were some member states on the other side of the argument, they were not necessarily particularly concerned. This change meant that while Margaret had succeeded in making the single market work much better, she was no longer able as easily to threaten to exercise a UK veto, and I think in time she found that very frustrating.

I felt enormously privileged to have been appointed even a junior Minister in a Government led by Margaret Thatcher. I was sent to the Department of Energy to help support John Wakeham with electricity privatisation. With the clarity and grip that she had had way back when I first worked for her in 1974, she explained clearly and succinctly exactly what she expected the Department to achieve in respect of not just electricity privatisation, but the future of the coal industry and nuclear power.

Now, there are those who say that Margaret was divisive. To them I would simply observe that Margaret Thatcher was a democrat, and a democrat who won three general elections in a row with increased majorities. (*43, 144, and finally 102*). I was elected in 1983 when Margaret secured a majority of 144 in the Commons. I do not think any of us who were elected in June 1983 were in any doubt that we owed our election to Margaret Thatcher and the affection in which she was held by huge numbers of voters. This, for me, is best recalled in a single soundbite in Banbury market. One of the television stations had come to do some vox pop on the election in Banbury. They went up to a chap who ran the fruit and veg stall. "What do you think about the general election?" they asked. "I don't know much about politics," said the guy, "but this I do know: No. 10 — Maggie's den."

It was very cruel that Margaret Thatcher should have been so unwell for the last years of her life. I first realised that something was not quite right a number of years ago when Margaret was speaking at a fundraising dinner for Somerville college. Lady Thatcher, as she then was, was making a bravura speech, clearly setting out the thoughts and principles that had guided her throughout public life, but she was finding it difficult to bring the speech to a conclusion. I suspect that those of us there who knew her must have suspected that all was not well, and so it sadly proved to be. In passing, it is important to recall how proud Margaret was of having been made an honorary fellow of Somerville, the college which had set her on the path to becoming the UK's first woman Prime Minister, and also how sad she was that was never awarded an honorary degree by Oxford.

It is all ancient history and in many ways water under the bridge, but as an Oxfordshire MP, I always thought it reflected badly on the image and reputation of Oxford university that it had not felt able to recognise Margaret's unquestionable and outstanding achievements in politics and public life. Somerville established a number of fellowships in law and chemistry in honour of Margaret Thatcher, and I suspect that if anyone wanted to make a bequest in Margaret's memory, Somerville is one of the institutions that she would want to see flourish.

Margaret is now at peace and, I am confident, reunited with Denis who, notwithstanding the *Private Eye* (*a satirical magazine published every two weeks*) caricature was a man of good counsel and sound judgment, and a towering column of support and strength for Margaret, a thoroughly decent man. If I were allowed just one image or one memory of Margaret, it would be standing in the winter gardens in Blackpool in the 1980 Conservative party conference, listening to her conference speech, when she said electrically,

"I have only one thing to say. You turn if you want to. The lady's not for turning."

[David Winnick was born 26 June 1933 and was educated at the London School of Economics. He worked in advertising and the union movement before becoming MP for Croydon South 1966-1970 and later Walsall North 1979 to date. While on the left he is considered to be a maverick and he gave Prime Minister Tony Blair his first defeat on a whipped vote in nine years when his amendment to a government bill on detention of terror suspects replaced a 90 day maximum with 28 days.]

4.43 pm

Mr David Winnick (Walsall North) (Lab)

I do not doubt for one moment that Lady Thatcher was kind and considerate in her dealings with those who worked for her. Indeed, I would be surprised if that were not the position. No doubt some of her Cabinet colleagues would have appreciated, at least in the later stages, the same consideration. However, it would be wrong and hypocritical if the views that we expressed at the time — strong views about the policies pursued by Mrs Thatcher's Government from 1979 to when she left office — were not mentioned today.

It is right and understandable that those who support her have spoken and will, I am sure, continue to speak in this debate, but the House is a place where opinion should be expressed freely, even if it is controversial, and those of us who so strongly disagreed with the policies pursued by Lady Thatcher should make our views clear today. It is more political than personal. Of course I regret, like everyone else, the passing of Lady Thatcher. I recognise that by becoming the first female Prime Minister in Britain, she made history, and that cannot be disputed. However, we have to remember what was done during the 11 years — or, to be exact, as she always was, the 11 and a half years — of her premiership in No. 10 Downing street and the way in which those policies were carried out. It was my view, and that of those on the Opposition Benches at the time, that those policies were highly damaging and that they caused immense pain and suffering to ordinary people.

I therefore believe that it is right that, while tributes are being paid to the life of Lady Thatcher, we should not forget what happened at that time. Those of us who were here in the House of Commons used every opportunity to protest on behalf of our constituents who were the victims of those policies, and we were not wrong to do so. This is not so much about Lady Thatcher herself as about the way in which, once the election had been won in 1979, it was decided to pursue policies that almost immediately — certainly within a year or two — caused the outcomes that I have mentioned.

In April to June 1979, the rate of unemployment was just over 5%. In March to May 1984, it was just under 12% and well over 3 million. Those are the percentages, but what did they mean in human terms for the men and women who were made redundant? As we said at the time, many of those people had worked all their lives since leaving school. When they were made redundant in their 50s, they discovered how unlikely it was that they would ever work again. We have to understand the human cost of the policies that have been praised today.

In 1979, 14% of children lived in relative poverty — that was bad enough; the fact that any children were living in poverty was to be deplored — but by 1991, 31% lived in such poverty. Are we really saying that those policies that Conservative Members have been praising today were unrelated to those children living in such poverty and deprivation? The fact that they were living in those conditions should certainly be deplored by Opposition Members.

I have heard it argued many times, not least today, that the policies undertaken by the Thatcher Government were almost inevitable, and that whoever had formed the Government of the day would have had to pursue policies of deindustrialisation involving the closing of factories, foundries and coal mines. But even if we accept that some of that was inevitable, the unfortunate thing was what I can only describe as the indifference to and, at times, brutal contempt for, those who had lost their jobs.

It almost seemed that, instead of offering support and understanding what that meant to the many people involved, the Government of the day blamed those people who were made redundant. It was as though it was their fault, and it was suggested that if only they had got on their bikes, as Lord Tebbit said his dad had done, they would have found work. That is what I mean by indifference and brutal contempt for people who, through no fault of their own, found themselves in circumstances that none of us would want. Does the hon. Gentleman still wish to intervene on me?

[David Morris was born 3 January 1966 and is a former pop singer, hairdresser, and entrepreneur building a chain of salons. He won Morecambe and Lunesdale in 2010 and is a friend of actor David Hasselhoff.]

David Morris (Morecambe and Lunesdale) (Con)

I note that the hon. Gentleman would not give way to me a moment ago. I was made redundant at the time he was describing. I set up my own business due to Thatcherism, I made a success of it and here I am now, preaching it forward.

Mr Winnick: Does that not prove the point? So many people were not in a position to do what the hon. Gentleman did. What he said very much expresses Thatcherism. He says, "I was made redundant. I found another job. Here I am today." What about all the others who were not in a position to do that? What about all the others I have mentioned—those in their 50s, who were never able to work again because, as they grew older, employers said that they were too near retirement age? My point could not be better illustrated, and I thank the hon. Gentleman doing it.

In the black country and the west midlands, we were devastated by the two major recessions that occurred during the 1980s. My hon. Friend the Member for Hackney North and Stoke Newington (Ms Abbott) referred to the terrible hardship suffered by mining communities. Many of us believe that the miners were treated with utter contempt. However much it could be said that Arthur Scargill played into Lady Thatcher's hands, the manner in which the miners were treated is not likely to be forgotten by the communities involved. It is right and proper that that is said today, when tributes are being paid to the former Prime Minister.

Let me also just say this: mention was made, by the Prime Minister and others, that Lady Thatcher had a commitment to parliamentary democracy. I do not doubt that for one moment. She was long a Member of this House — 32 years — and then went to the House of Lords, where she played an active role. It could be said that a certain Mr Gorbachev had a role to play in what happened in Eastern Europe by the manner in which he made it perfectly clear, particularly to the East Germans, that the Russians would no longer, in any circumstances, bolster regimes that were totally discredited.

I do not want to dispute in any way the extent to which Lady Thatcher made a contribution in relation to Eastern Europe. However, it is unfortunate, is it not, that she was so totally unsympathetic to the fight against apartheid in South Africa? To describe the African National Congress as a terrorist organisation and Nelson Mandela as a terrorist cannot be justified under any circumstances. I remember when Nelson Mandela came to Westminster Hall as a very distinguished visitor—as President of South Africa. We paid tribute to him and listened keenly to what he said. I could not but notice that in the front row listening to him was Lady Thatcher. I hope that by then she had realised that she had taken the wrong line on apartheid. We should not just be concerned about freedom in Europe, but in South Africa and Latin America. I was never a fan of Pinochet, a professional mass murderer.

Lady Thatcher was a divisive figure, and she would not for one moment have argued otherwise. One thing on which we can agree in this House is that "consensus" was not her favourite word. The Prime Minister mentioned former Prime Ministers. Of the two Prime Ministers who have made the greatest impression since 1945, in my view, and in the view of the Opposition Benches, Clement Attlee's tremendous changes — the national health service, national insurance and the like — made Britain a far more civilised country. The other figure, to whom we are paying tribute today, is Lady Thatcher. She believed that much of what occurred post-1945 was wrong and should be undermined. My view remains that what the Attlee Government set out to do was absolutely right, and that what Lady Thatcher set out to do — undermine many of the changes brought about immediately after the second world war — was wrong. I know which side I am on.

[John Whittingdale was born 16 October 1959 and educated at University College, London. He worked in politics and finance serving as Margaret Thatcher's Political Secretary 1988 to his 1992 election to Parliament representing Maldon. As Chair of the Media Select Committee he took the very rare step of compelling Rupert Murdoch and his son James to attend and give evidence about phone hacking by their journalists.]

4.54 pm

Mr John Whittingdale (Maldon) (Con)

Today, the House of Commons rightly pays tribute to a great Prime Minister and a great parliamentarian. We who sit as Conservative Members of Parliament salute one of the most successful and influential leaders of our party. Those of us who were privileged enough to know her and to work for her remember an inspiring figure, but also a warm and compassionate person who inspired tremendous loyalty among her staff.

I was 15 when Margaret Thatcher became leader of my party and like so many of my generation and those that followed, I was influenced in my politically formative years by her exposition of ideas and beliefs developed with Keith Joseph and the Centre for Policy Studies. That clear articulation of an ideological philosophy attracted me to become involved in Conservative politics. Three years later, I was lucky enough to meet her for the first time when I began to work for the Conservative party. I was in her office on the day Airey Neave was killed, and some years later I was working for her in Downing street on the day that Ian Gow was assassinated — two terrible blows to her personally.

Margaret Thatcher was a controversial and sometimes divisive figure. It was inevitable given the scale of the challenges she and her Government faced. She had to make difficult and unpopular decisions, but her conviction and strength of purpose enabled her to achieve what she did, often in the face of enormous opposition. She confronted opposition right from the start of her career. The Leader of the Opposition referred to her time at Oxford. She became active in the Oxford University Conservative Association—indeed, its president—because women were not allowed to participate in the Oxford Union. (*A debating society. Women could watch but not participate until the mid 1960s.*) Once she became leader of our party, she confronted huge opposition within our own ranks. Many people resented her background, from a middle-class family in Grantham; they resented her sex and they also resented her ideological certainty. All those things were novel for the Conservative party at that time.

Lady Thatcher's strength of purpose allowed her to confront our country's enemies. We have referred to General Galtieri and the invasion of the Falkland Islands. She played a role in persuading George Bush that she must confront Saddam Hussein when he invaded and occupied Kuwait, and, with Ronald Reagan and Gorbachev, in bringing about the end of communism. She was also a pragmatist and a realist. She was responsible for the Lancaster House agreement, which ended white rule in Rhodesia and ushered in black majority government. She negotiated the hand-back of Hong Kong to the Chinese, and as we have heard, she signed the Anglo-Irish agreement.

I first worked for Margaret Thatcher directly during the two general election campaigns of 1983 and 1987 when I accompanied her on her tour of the country. It was my first experience of her punishing work load, her extraordinary attention to detail and her occasionally somewhat unreasonable demands. I also saw at first hand her instinctive feel for the aspirations and beliefs of the people of Britain. It was her identity with those people that allowed her to articulate so clearly what they wanted and that delivered successive general election majorities for the Conservative party of 144 and 102 — some of us might think that those were the days.

In 1988, Margaret Thatcher asked me to become her political secretary in Downing street. I saw then her huge respect for Parliament itself. She occupied the position of Prime Minister, but she never forgot that she was also the Member of Parliament for Finchley and she believed that it was her duty to come here not just to speak but to vote — to go through the Division Lobby on behalf of her constituents. I used to help her with preparation for Prime Minister's questions, which in those days lasted for just 15 minutes and took place twice a week. She used to spend six or seven hours preparing for that 15-minute session. We used to go through briefs from every Department across Whitehall, which set out the exposition of the Government's policy and the line to take. Sometimes, she did not think it was very good and I would be sent to ring the Minister's private secretary to tell him that the Prime Minister did not like a particular line. Occasionally, she strode across the study, took the phone from my hand and told the private secretary that not only did she not like the line to take, but that she did not actually like the policy, either. Every now and again, she had a remarkable ability to distance herself somehow from the policies of the Government of which she was also leader.

I would like to set right one or two misconceptions. I listened carefully to the hon. Member for Walsall North (Mr Winnick). Although Margaret Thatcher opposed economic sanctions against South Africa, she fiercely opposed apartheid. She argued with the South African Government that they should release Nelson Mandela from prison; that was recognised by Nelson Mandela, if not by the hon. Gentleman.

I would also say to the leader of the Liberal Democrats, who I am sorry to say is no longer here, that, yes, Margaret Thatcher did say that there was no such thing as society, but she went on to say that there are families and communities. She set out the fact that if individuals see people less well off or in need, they bear a personal and moral responsibility not just to let society — some amorphous body — take responsibility, but to act themselves. People claiming now that she said that there was no such thing as society [are giving] an appalling twisting of her message.

I also saw at first hand her immense personal kindness and compassion. As has been said, those were often shown to the most junior members of her staff. On the famous occasion when the waitress spilt the soup on Geoffrey Howe, it was not Geoffrey Howe whom Margaret Thatcher worried about, but the waitress. She always insisted that she could never be late — particularly to funerals, to which, sadly, I used to accompany her occasionally. We used to sit in lay-bys for 15 or 20 minutes; we would have set off early in case there was heavy traffic because she could not allow herself to be late.

I know that both Government and Opposition Members received personal handwritten letters from Margaret Thatcher when they experienced a tragedy in their private lives or with their families. She had enormous compassion. If ever she found out that somebody was alone at Christmas, she would always say that they should come and spend it at Chequers with her. Ronnie Millar, the playwright, told me that he would spend many months trying to think of excuses why he would be busy, because being with Margaret Thatcher at Christmas might not be the most relaxing way to spend it.

After Margaret stood down as Prime Minister, she came on several occasions to support me in Essex. Essex has always been Thatcher country. When she came to my constituency of Maldon at the election in which I first stood as candidate, after she had stood down as Prime Minister, the pavements had crowds four or five deep of people who had turned out to see her. Not all were supporters of hers or of mine, but they wanted to be there because they recognised that she played such a hugely important role in their lives and the life of their country.

Even today, when I occasionally meet parliamentarians, and sometimes even leaders, from different countries, if I say to them that I served as Margaret Thatcher's political secretary, that lights their interest; in many ways, it is what I am most proud of. It was a privilege to know her and an even greater privilege to have worked for someone who was one of the greatest Prime Ministers this country has ever had.

[Glenda Jackson was born 9 May 1936 and won two Oscars for Best Actress in 1970 *Women in Love* and 1973 *A Touch of Class*. She entered Parliament in 1992 for Hampstead and Highgate which became Hampstead and Kilburn following boundary changes before the 2010 General Election.]

5.3 pm

Glenda Jackson (Hampstead and Kilburn) (Lab)

It is hardly a surprise that Baroness Thatcher was careless over the soup being poured over Lord Howe, given that she was perfectly prepared to send him out to the wicket with a broken bat. (*A cricketing reference to Geoffrey Howe's post resignation speech in which he claimed that working for Margaret was like being sent out to home plate with a broken bat.*)

When I made my maiden speech in this Chamber, a little over two decades ago, Margaret Thatcher had been elevated to the other place but Thatcherism was still wreaking, and had wrought for the previous decade, the most heinous social, economic and spiritual damage upon this country, upon my constituency and upon my constituents. Our local hospitals were running on empty. Patients were staying on trolleys in corridors. I tremble to think what the death rate among pensioners would have been this winter if that version of Thatcherism had been fully up and running this year. Our schools, parents, teachers, governors, even pupils, seemed to spend an inordinate amount of time fundraising in order to be able to provide basic materials such as paper and pencils. The plaster on our classroom walls was kept in place by pupils' art work and miles and miles of sellotape. Our school libraries were dominated by empty shelves and very few books; the books that were there were held together by the ubiquitous sellotape and off-cuts from teachers' wallpaper were used to bind those volumes so that they could at least hang together.

By far the most dramatic and heinous demonstration of Thatcherism was certainly seen not only in London, but across the whole country in metropolitan areas where every single night, every single shop doorway became the bedroom, the living room and the bathroom for the homeless. They grew in their thousands, and many of those homeless people had been thrown out on to the streets as a result of the closure of the long-term mental hospitals. We were told it was going to be called — it was called — "care in the community", but what it was in effect was no care in the community at all.

I was interested to hear about Baroness Thatcher's willingness to invite those who had nowhere to go for Christmas; it is a pity that she did not start building more and more social housing, after she entered into the right to buy, so that there might have been fewer homeless people than there were. As a friend of mine said, during her era, London became a city that Hogarth would have recognised — and, indeed, he would.

In coming to the basis of Thatcherism, I come to the spiritual part of what I regard as the desperately wrong track down which Thatcherism took this country. We were told that everything I had been taught to regard as a vice — and I still regard them as vices — was, in fact, under Thatcherism, a virtue: greed, selfishness, no care for the weaker, sharp elbows, sharp knees, all these were the way forward. We have heard much, and will continue to hear over next week, about the barriers that were broken down by Thatcherism, the establishment that was destroyed.

What we have heard, with the words circling around like stars, is that Thatcher created an aspirational society. It aspired for things. One former Prime Minister who had himself been elevated to the House of Lords, spoke about selling off the family silver and people knowing in those years the price of everything and the value of nothing. What concerns me is that I am beginning to see what might be the re-emergence of that total traducing of what I regard as the spiritual basis of this country where we do care about society, where we do believe in communities, where we do not leave people and walk by on the other side. That is not happening now, but if we go back to the heyday of that era, I fear that we will see replicated yet again the extraordinary human damage from which we as a nation have suffered and the talent that has been totally wasted because of the inability genuinely to see the individual value of every single human being.

My hon. Friend the Member for Hackney North and Stoke Newington (Ms Abbott) referred to the fact that although she had differed from Lady Thatcher in her policies, she felt duty bound to come here to pay tribute to the first woman Prime Minister this country had produced. I am of a generation that was raised by women, as the men had all gone to war to defend our freedoms. They did not just run a Government; they ran a country. The women whom I knew, who raised me and millions of people like me, who ran our factories and our businesses, and who put out the fires when the bombs dropped, would not have recognised their definition of womanliness as incorporating an iconic model of Margaret Thatcher. To pay tribute to the first Prime Minister denoted by female gender, okay; but a woman? Not on my terms.

[Graham Brady was born 20 May 1967 and educated at the University of Durham. He worked in public affairs before becoming MP for Altrincham and Sale West in 1997. In May 2010 he became Chairman of the 1922 Committee, an organization that represents the views of Conservative MPs who are not ministers.]

5.11 pm

Mr Graham Brady (Altrincham and Sale West) (Con)

As chairman of the 1922 committee, I want to pay tribute on behalf of Conservative Back Benchers present and past, although I note from the number of colleagues who are standing to make their own contributions that they may well speak for themselves in due course. Like many others, I want to pay a personal tribute. I also want to pay tribute especially as a northern Conservative MP, who now represents the constituency in which I grew up in the 1980s, perhaps answering and responding to the points that were made by the right hon. Member for Oldham West and Royton (Mr Meacher).

On behalf of the 1922 committee, I pay tribute to a leader and Prime Minister who achieved so much — three stunning election victories; turning around a moribund economy; ending decades of decline. She restored our national pride — from being the sick man of Europe, only good at making jokes about ourselves, which I remember as a boy,

I pay tribute to Margaret Thatcher for the inspirational leadership that she gave to the Conservative party; for inspiring Conservative supporters around the country; and most of all, for inspiring millions of people who had never before realised that they were Conservatives. Lady Thatcher's strength, conviction, patriotism and clarity won her the respect of friends and fair-minded critics alike. Perhaps most remarkable was her popularity not only in this country but overseas, and the lasting legacy of freedom, democracy and prosperity, which we have heard about from many colleagues, that she leaves as a leader who helped to win the cold war and who inspired the people of Eastern Europe to fight for their own freedom. Her legacy in this country and beyond will always be remembered with pride by our party.

As with so many hon. Members of my age, my tribute is also intensely personal. Growing up under Margaret Thatcher's governance, it was impossible to be agnostic about politics. Her message was one of opportunity. Whatever your background, you could progress by merit and hard work. Had I not taken that message to heart, I, like so many other Conservative Members — and perhaps, from a different perspective, like quite a few Opposition Members — would not be here in Parliament today.

The last part of my brief tribute to Lady Thatcher is that of a northern Member of Parliament, and it is to address a myth that is in danger of taking hold. My hon. Friend the Member for Maldon (Mr Whittingdale) addressed some other myths that have been spread recently. It is true that the restructuring of our economy in the early 1980s hit parts of the north hard, because a concentration of heavy industry and mining had become uncompetitive and uneconomic, but many metropolitan journalists fall into peddling an easy fallacy, suggesting that the north was uniformly hostile to the message of Lady Thatcher — we were not. Many Labour Members will recall that the seats they now represent returned Conservative Members who supported Margaret Thatcher's strong defence, modernisation of the economy, determination to extend opportunity, and spreading of wealth and home ownership to their constituents. Many of those seats across the north returned Labour Members only after Tony Blair embraced the free market, low-tax message of Margaret Thatcher.

[Rt Hon Frank Field was born 16 July 1942 and educated at the University of Hull. He has represented Birkenhead since 1979. Prior to that he was Director of the Child Poverty Action Group and the Low Pay Unit. He served as Tony Blair's Minister for Welfare Reform 1997-1998. Although a member of the Labour Party he has been ranked as a top 100 conservative thinker by a national newspaper.]

5.16 pm

Mr Frank Field (Birkenhead) (Lab)

David Sheppard (*a former professional cricket player of international standard*) was a left-wing Bishop of Liverpool, who was much admired and also loved. In one volume of his autobiography, he recalls his meetings with Mrs Thatcher — or, rather, the lead-up to those meetings. He recalls the state he would be in — the feeling of illness as the dreaded hour approached. On one occasion, I asked her, a year before she would appoint a new archbishop, whether she would appoint David Sheppard if his name was one of the two on the list that came to her from the royal commission. Her reply was immediate: "Yes, of course." I was slightly staggered by that response, so I asked why. She said, "He always tells me to my face what he thinks and we always have a good argument." It therefore seems proper that in the tributes we pay to this extraordinary person we should follow her example and not be frightened of argument or even of division — we mock her if we are frightened of that.

The Prime Minister and the Leader of the Opposition made powerful speeches about the way in which Mrs Thatcher has shaped the world in which all of us live, and I would just extend that in two ways. The world in which all of us and all of our constituents live has been shaped by Clement Attlee and Margaret Thatcher. The danger for both those people, who brought an ideology into politics and saw it operated, was that some of their supporters might think that just preaching the ideology was enough, rather than also responding to what the real world was teaching them. The right hon. Member for Wokingham (Mr Redwood) talked about the sale of council houses — all of us in this debate sometimes give a slant to history. There were people in the Labour party who also wanted to sell council houses, and the record shows that both the Wilson and Callaghan Governments looked at the idea — the problem was that the civil servants told them that it was not doable. So one of the lessons about Mrs Thatcher is that one should not necessarily take the advice of the civil service if one actually wants to see radical politics.

However, Mrs Thatcher was not uncritical of her own record. On one occasion I asked her, "Mrs T, what was your greatest disappointment in government?" Again as though she had thought long and hard beforehand about it, she said, "I cut taxes and I thought we would get a giving society, and we haven't." She thought we would, by low taxation, see that extraordinary culture in America whereby people make fortunes and want, perhaps publicly, to declare what they are doing with them. That had not taken root here. I think we should look critically at her record. Of course, it is wrong of us to assume what Mrs T would be saying if she were listening to this debate, but I think she would want us to get on to what the differences were and how we take the debate forward.

I want to mention three areas where we are still grappling with her legacy, and with which Members on both Front Benches have not managed to come to terms. First, there is the great question of riches. She was not satisfied with the results of her Government, so should we? Secondly, despite all the gains that the market economy has given this country, there are clearly some areas — part of my constituency is one of them — that its powers cannot reach. We have not come up with policies that can move those areas back to full employment. How do we raise demand in those areas specifically, and how do we ensure that the supply side, to which most of us are now committed, can also take effect through our schools?

The third big area is a problem in our country that she thought she had solved but that now appears in a different guise. We have mentioned, even quite properly on the Opposition Benches, that one of her great struggles was to bring the trade unions within the law decided by this House — not the law that they thought they would abide by. I have been perplexed by some of the recent newspaper coverage of her stewardship, much of which has stated that the country was previously ungovernable. It was governable all right, but not from here and not by the Government elected by the people.

What would Mrs Thatcher say about a global economy, part of which she was so responsible for creating, in which great world companies can choose whether or not they pay taxes and whether giving a donation to the Treasury might be an adequate performance of their duties instead? I would be very surprised if she did not see that as a challenge to our authority, and one with which we need to grapple. All three areas are part of the current agenda for our politics, and that is part of her legacy. I wonder whether she, if still in power, would not be tackling that in a more resolute way than we are currently.

I would like to end with two comments about Mrs Thatcher. We have talked about the power and force of her personality, but she was also brilliant on detail, and that was part of her power in Whitehall. I once had to see her to discuss a defence order for Cammell Laird. Indeed, my relationship with her began after the second meeting I had as MP for Birkenhead, when the shop stewards said, "Cut out all this old stuff. We want a cross-party group and we want you to lead it. Our discussion took place the day she returned from a meeting with President Bush to decide on the first Gulf war. She had every reason to cancel it, but the meeting took place in her study. I had never seen her in such a state. She was marching around the study saying, "You've no idea what a struggle it is putting backbone into him." I said, "Prime Minister, come and sit next to me because I have some things I would like to discuss with you." She kept talking about putting backbone into the American President in order to fight this great war. Finally, she took pity on me and asked, "What do you want?" I made the plea for the defence order and she said, "Fine. Anything else?" When I said no, she immediately got up and continued, "You've no idea the victory I've had today over this." I was really rather excited to be this very small footnote in history.

Of course, courtesy dictated that whichever of the Wirral MPs had lobbied her would tell the others, but in my excitement I forgot to do so. About 36 hours later I saw David Hunt walking down the corridor and I remembered, so I began apologising. He said, "There's no need to apologise, Frank. The relevant Secretaries of State have received a prime ministerial minute and it has been copied to their permanent secretaries." There was a Prime Minister who was making history, for right or wrong — for right, I think — and who was extraordinarily wound up by the events that she had managed to bring about, and she had no staff with her, but before she went to bed that night she wrote that minute to implement what she had agreed. She was wonderful to lobby, because I knew within seconds whether she would do something or whether she thought it was a barmy idea, in which case there was no point discussing it further.

Let me make one last point. Towards the end of her time as Prime Minister, Mrs Thatcher was captured by a court on the Government Benches whose members made it difficult not only for many Government Back Benchers but particularly for someone such as me to see her. I wrote to the court and said that if they continued to block my chance of talking to her and lobbying her, I would kidnap her and tell her what they were doing — and would also lobby her. I got a note back late in the debate saying that the Prime Minister would see me at 10 o'clock. This is a good lesson for the Prime Minister and the Leader of the Opposition. She had a hugely impressive voting record. In my experience, she was one of the last out of the Lobby, and she was there for people to talk to — rather than going in, out and away to do what was thought to be more important business.

As she passed by, I said to her, "Prime Minister, should I follow you?" She said, "People do." As there was no mirror in front of her, I have never worked out whether she was smiling. I hope she was. Following her is a challenge to us.

Do we see her record as though it had been brought down from Mount Sinai on tablets of stone, or would she have recognised, as I have hinted in the few conversations I have had on this specific point, that there is now a new agenda and that whatever principles one has must be applied to it?

The Leader of the Opposition and the Prime Minister were right: to her, what mattered were ideas and whether one could defend one's corner. I mourn her passing.

[Eleanor Laing was born 1 February 1958 and educated at the University of Edinburgh. A former attorney she has represented Epping Forest since 1997.]

5.26 pm

Mrs Eleanor Laing (Epping Forest) (Con)

Margaret Thatcher changed the world for women — for women across the world, for women in Britain and for women in politics and in Parliament. I cannot stand by and watch commentators say that Margaret Thatcher did nothing for women when I know, as many of my hon. Friends in the House and those around the country know, just how much of a difference her very being has made to women.

In the first place, Margaret Thatcher's great belief in freedom and the individual and the fact that her Governments brought freedom and choice to people who had never had it before made a huge difference to millions of women throughout Britain during her years as Prime Minister. We have heard different examples today of what happened to people's individual lives in the 1980s, but overall there is no doubt whatsoever that bringing freedom, choice and opportunity — those were her watchwords — to young women of the 1980s transformed them into the women of the '90s and of this century who are willing to take on the world.

As for women in politics and Parliament, Margaret Thatcher gave us encouragement and advice. I am fed up of hearing the media channels say that she did not want women around and that there was only one woman in her Cabinet while she was Prime Minister. That was not her fault: there were not enough women on these Benches with the experience and seniority to go into her Cabinet. She encouraged women, so that by the end of her premiership and when John Major became Prime Minister, there were plenty of women to go into the Cabinet. They would not have been there had they not had the encouragement and backing of Margaret Thatcher when she was Prime Minister.

Those of us on the Conservative Benches also know what she has done in latter years. Just over a year ago, when she had supposedly withdrawn from public life but while, as many of us know, she was still extremely active in supporting what we were doing, she came to not one, but two or three events that I can think of. Those events involved not just raising money to help women enter Parliament, but her very presence in a room of aspiring people. After a mere handshake from Margaret Thatcher, a young woman would leave an event saying, "I can do this", whereas previously she had thought that she could not. Such was the power and personality of this great lady.

I can forgive female colleagues on the Opposition Benches for thinking that Margaret Thatcher did not encourage women because, of course, it goes without saying that she preferred to see Conservatives elected rather than Labour, or Liberal, female Members of Parliament. In her encouragement and advice, however, on a personal level she was much more like a mother than a Prime Minister. She would hold one's hand and say, "Well my dear, what are you doing about this? What is going to happen about that?" She gave people true encouragement and confidence. Actually, I am wrong to stand here and say that she did that for women — she did it for everyone who had the slightest bit of Conservative blood in their body. She would make the very best of that and help them to realise just how much they could achieve. I do not mean just in politics; she did that for people throughout the country.

People thought that they did not have aspiration and opportunity because before Margaret Thatcher became Prime Minister they did not have opportunities and were told that they should not, and could not, aspire. She gave everybody the confidence to make the very best of themselves — she certainly did that for my generation of women in the Conservative party, and she gave me personal advice that I have always valued and tried to live up to, not necessarily with the greatest results for which she might have hoped. She understood the difficulty that women experience in public life because they are trying to balance their duties to their families, their constituency, Parliament and their general duties. She understood that and made allowances for it. Again, the way she dealt with such matters was to give encouragement. It never occurred to her, of course, that women might need special pleading. Of course she did not want women-only shortlists; it simply never occurred to her that her female status was any hindrance at all, and indeed, that is because it was not.

The other great thing about Margaret Thatcher that no one has mentioned is that in everything she did in public life, and the many hours spent at the Dispatch Box, in Downing street and representing our country around the world, she was always, on every occasion, immaculate and elegant. Here was a lady who was tougher than any man, but she never lost her femininity.

As a result of Margaret Thatcher's brilliance, resolve, determination, courage and example, no woman can ever be told that she cannot rise to any challenge. Margaret Thatcher made the world a better place.

[Kevin Barron was born 26 October 1946 and educated at the University of Sheffield and Ruskin College, Oxford. He had on graduating high school worked as an electrician in a coal mine. He has represented Rother Valley since 1983.]

5.34 pm

Mr Kevin Barron (Rother Valley) (Lab)

Lady Thatcher was a radical politician and will remain a controversial figure. She would have expected that her conviction politics would court controversy even at such a time. Many of her domestic policies caused great concern and harm to many people and communities. I entered the House in 1983, nine months before the start of the miners' strike. I come from a mining background and represent a mining constituency. My overriding memory of the 12-month strike was not the violence that we saw on our television screens — I condemned the violence at the time — but the poverty and hardship that miners and their families went through for the best part of 12 months.

We know that the cause of the strike was the proposed pit closure programme and the consequent effect, particularly on male unemployment, which had been traditionally high in coal mining communities. I am not saying that the Government of the day were wholly to blame for the strike and its consequences, but I believe they had a responsibility to bring the dispute to an early end, which they did not meet.

On Saturday, I attended a march commemorating the closure of Maltby colliery — the coal mine I worked at as a young man. It was the sixth and last coal mine to close in the Rother Valley constituency. The bitterness that stems from the '84-'85 strike is there among people even all these years later. Although tribute can and will be paid to Margaret Thatcher, other voices in the country ought to be heard.

[Christopher (Chris) Chope was born 19 May 1947 and educated at St Andrews University. An attorney he represented Southampton Itchen 1983-1992 and Christchurch 1997 to date. As leader of Wandsworth Borough Council in the early Thatcher era he pioneered the sale of public housing units to tenants at below market prices and his efforts to control the budget earned him the nickname of Chopper.]

5.37 pm

Mr Christopher Chope (Christchurch) (Con)

It was on Monday, when I was in Eastern Europe monitoring elections, that I heard the sad news of Margaret's death. In a sense, it was appropriate that I was out in Eastern Europe witnessing democracy in action. In my view, that would not have been possible but for the work Margaret Thatcher did in destroying communism and opening up Eastern Europe to proper democracy.

We have heard brilliant tributes today, led by my right hon. Friend the Prime Minister, who encapsulated, as did the Leader of the Opposition, so many of the values we hold dear when we remember Margaret Thatcher. I was grateful to the right hon. Gentleman for reminding the House of the difference between consensus and conviction. That is the problem that many Government Members have — the coalition muddles consensus and conviction, which those of us who are conviction politicians find incredibly frustrating.

The theme I should like briefly to pursue is compassion, on which my hon. Friend the Member for Maldon (Mr Whittingdale) spoke so eloquently. Margaret Thatcher was a passionate Conservative, but she was also a compassionate Conservative. When I first met her in 1976 — I was then chairman of Putney

Conservatives — she visited an old people's day centre in Putney, where I saw her in action. She spoke to every single person in the day centre sitting room. She, as leader of the Conservative party, knelt down in order to be able to converse meaningfully with those who could not speak to her easily. That, for me, was a demonstration of her humility and compassion.

People have spoken about the way in which Margaret Thatcher would write letters to colleagues who had been bereaved and so on. A few years ago, my wife was in hospital. The flowers from Margaret Thatcher arrived before my own, which was rather embarrassing. That was the extent to which she was on the ball with her generosity and kindness not only to colleagues, but to their wives.

I agreed with Margaret Thatcher on almost everything. The only big issue on which I disagreed with her fundamentally was her decision not to stand in the second ballot in 1990. If she had stood, I think that she would have won and that the course of history would have been different. I am sad that those of us who went into her study that evening to persuade her to change her mind were unsuccessful. It was typical of her that she sent special notes to all of us who had tried to persuade her to stay on. It was a humiliating experience for that fantastic Prime Minister. Having been in that study and seen her condition, I would not wish it on anybody. Somebody who had served her country with such distinction and who had been a global leader in bringing freedom to much of Eastern Europe was humiliated by people whom she thought were her friends and colleagues. I thought and still think that that was intolerable. May that sort of thing never happen again.

In 1997, Margaret came and supported my election campaign in Christchurch, where we were trying to overturn the majority of about 16,000 that the Liberal Democrats had won in the 1993 by-election. That was her first outing in the campaign. She was confronted by the press because one of our colleagues who was standing in Tatton had suddenly hit the headlines. Margaret demonstrated her ability to deal with the press with a phrase or, as in this case, a very short sentence that could not result in any follow-up. When asked about Neil Hamilton, she said, "Nobody is perfect." In those three words, she closed down the conversation, because she was not passing judgment on his case, but saying something that applies to all of us. That is an example of how she was able to deal with the press and choose words that were effective.

Later on the same visit, we went on a private visit to the Priory primary school in Christchurch, where Margaret demonstrated other attributes: the ability to listen and the ability to speak her mind. She said to a nine-year-old, "What do you want to do when you grow up?" He said, "I want to be a musician." She paused and stared with her wonderful eyes at this young man and said, "And what else do you want to be?" That demonstrated that she did nothing for effect. When she asked somebody a question, she was willing to listen to the answer and make a comment. She gave that person the benefit of her views, whether they liked it or not. I hope that that individual is now a successful musician. If he is not, I hope that he has a back-up, which is what she was saying he ought to have.

It is a fantastic privilege to have this opportunity to pay tribute to, in my view, the greatest Prime Minister of all time. Sometimes one sits in the Chamber and it takes a long time to be called, but it has been a privilege to gather together today and listen to every contribution. If the debate goes on until 10 o'clock, as I hope it will, that will be some compensation for the loss of this great lady.

[Gisela Stuart was born 26 November 1957 in Bavaria, Germany and moved to England in 1974 where she was educated at Manchester Polytechnic and the University of London (External Degree) and became a law lecturer. She has represented Birmingham Edgbaston since 1997 and was the only Labour MP to support the re-election of President Bush in 2004.]

5.44 pm

Ms Gisela Stuart (Birmingham, Edgbaston) (Lab)

When Nancy Astor left the House of Commons, she said "I will miss the House, but the House will not miss me." (*Nancy Astor was the first woman to sit in the Commons serving as MP for Plymouth Sutton 1919-1945; she was born in Danville, Virginia.*) I think that this House, and the other House, will probably miss Baroness Thatcher for longer than many another woman who has served in this place.

Let me say something about Margaret Thatcher and the representation of women. I do so as a Member of Parliament whose constituency has been represented by women for longer than any other constituency in the country — since 1953. The first of those women was Dame Edith Pitt. The then Conservative and Unionist party had to nominate her as the candidate because the local association had rebelled against the original nomination on the basis that it had a perfectly good candidate, albeit a woman, and the party caved in. When Dame Jill Knight was nominated in 1966, the Conservative association said "We have already tried a woman, so we will have a man now", and she said "I will accept that argument, but only if it works both ways." Of course, it did not.

As the Prime Minister said, Margaret Thatcher broke through that glass ceiling. She kicked doors open. Indeed, she kicked doors open for Labour women, in a way that they perhaps did not entirely appreciate, because the trade unions had an enormously powerful role in candidate selections. It benefited us when the unions were forced to provide more openings for women, and when "one member one vote" and many similar changes came along, although Margaret Thatcher would not have thought of those developments in that way.

I do not think Margaret Thatcher realised that the problem was more systemic. Notwithstanding what was said by the hon. Member for Epping Forest (Mrs Laing), before the 1997 election there were more men called John than there were women MPs in the House of Commons. In May 1997, 121 women were elected, which meant that there were more women MPs in one intake than there had been in the entire history of Parliament. I do not think we are right to lay the blame for that at the door of Margaret Thatcher, because it was a reflection of the times. I think that if she had not been the way she was, she would not have been in the position that she was in.

I have asked myself why she is still so controversial. A few years ago, *The House Magazine* gave Denis Healey a lifetime achievement award, and it was Geoffrey Howe who presented him with it. Two old adversaries met in friendship at Speaker's House. Denis Healey said "When you get to my age, there are no enemies any more; there are just people who are still alive with you." Somehow, I do not think that Margaret Thatcher would have seen it in that way. She was fighting to the very end, and I think it was a sign of the times that she had to fight to the very end.

Whole generations have forgotten what 1979 was like. I came here from Germany in the 1970s. I know that Margaret Thatcher would not want us not to learn any lessons from the battles that she had fought — some lost, some won, and some which continue. I am thinking in particular of the role of the market. It is interesting that Margaret Thatcher considered that Hayek's book "The Road to Serfdom" should be compulsory reading. Many Government Members, and probably even more of my hon. Friends, will be surprised to learn that I agree that it should be compulsory reading, as a reminder of the role of the market. [Hon. Members: "Come over to this side!"] No, it is not a question of "Come over to this side".

Similar arguments have been advanced about the force of the market. It has been argued that it actually liberates. The market does not need to be made social, because it is already social. It challenges vested interests, and lets outsiders in. In Germany, that was a social democratic argument advanced by Ludwig Erhard, the father of the social market economy. One legacy of the entrenchment of Thatcherism in the '80s that might have to be looked at now and in years to come is the polarisation of the argument with false options. We are boxing ourselves into corners, which will not be terribly beneficial to either side of the House. If we believe that markets are social and important — in everything Margaret Thatcher did, she realised that they could challenge the status quo, vested interests and outsiders, and bring them in — perhaps we should recognise that they are also socialist.

[Sir Paul Beresford was born 6 April 1946 in Levin, New Zealand and after an education at the University of Otago became a dentist. He represented Croydon Central 1992-1997 and following redistricting Mole Valley 1997 to date. As leader of Wandsworth Borough Council 1983-1992 he pioneered the contracting out of local government services to private companies. He was knighted in 1990.]

5.52 pm

Sir Paul Beresford (Mole Valley) (Con)

I shall be succinct, as I am surrounded by people anxious to speak. I congratulate the hon. Member for Birmingham, Edgbaston (Ms Stuart). Her last paragraph or so was exactly right and expresses how I have felt for some considerable time. Since I became a councillor in 1979, (*surely 1978*), Margaret Thatcher has been someone we have looked to — not always looked up to, but certainly looked to.

My hon. Friends the Members for Christchurch (Mr Chope) and for Maldon (Mr Whittingdale) touched on Margaret Thatcher's compassion and understanding for the people at the bottom, the lowly people — an aspect of her character that does not often come out, but which they certainly brought out. I found out about that myself, when I was a lowly London councillor having trouble with English, my second language. I had come from New Zealand, where politicians were at the bottom of the pile and where, if someone wanted to contact the Prime Minister, they looked his phone number up in the Wellington phonebook — according to mythology, it is still there.

Here, to my amazement, a polite request to see the Prime Minister, explained, was generally accepted. In my day as a councillor, many of the meetings I had with the Prime Minister at my request — some were at hers — went through my hon. Friend the Member for Maldon, who, as he has explained, was her political adviser. When it was the other way around, I could picture his face grinning on the phone as he said, "The Prime Minister would like to see you" — pause — "today" — pause — "Well, at least as soon as you possibly can."

I am sure that my hon. Friend will remember that the way to stimulate a conversation with Margaret Thatcher was to disagree. If somebody disagreed, her eyes lit up and she launched into the argument. If somebody had a proposition, or she had a proposition, she turned the discussion into a friendly argument. My hon. Friend used to sit to one side, but between us, like an umpire at Wimbledon, with his head moving from side to side, with a faint grin, and I would peer out of the corner of my eye to see if I was winning. In any discussion with Margaret Thatcher at that time, I had to be very well prepared, and I was never quite sure when starting an argument disagreeing with her whether she was actually disagreeing with me or testing my hypothesis.

Margaret Thatcher's saying, "The Lady's not for turning", has come up several times today. That might have been true at that particular time, but I found in practice that she would listen to an argument, particularly if there was a political aspect to it, and be prepared to change her position, if the argument was suitable and good enough. She must have done so, because she could not have won so many elections in a row had she had mural dyslexia and been inflexible or unable to see the point of an argument. I think that is why she used to spend time talking to all kinds of people, from Presidents through to business people and the little people, such as me. I remember Lord King telling my business partner and me that he was to see Margaret Thatcher and that he was going to tell her this, that and the other thing. We met him two days after the meeting and asked him how it went. "Oh", he said, "Mrs Thatcher told me this, she told me that and she told me the other thing." I felt good.

As many Members have said, Margaret Thatcher was also prepared to help with campaigning, if we felt it would be of benefit, which I found extraordinary and it provided a real insight into her ability to understand. In 1986, we had a small battle in Wandsworth. We went into an election with a majority of one out of a full council of 61. Her standing in the polls, if I remember correctly, was 19% or 20%. Being a great supporter of some of the things we were trying to do and had done, she offered to drop in on the campaign in support. This was politely declined, and equally politely our "Thank you, but no" was accepted. Do remember, however, that shortly afterwards, that 19% or 20% lifted to a win at the election that shortly followed. It also, regretfully, in a way, meant that we won and we went from a majority of one to a majority of 35. As ever, however, Margaret Thatcher, the Prime Minister, had the last say. I received another one of those phone calls from my hon. Friend the Member for Maldon — a summons to Downing street. I then had a session at which she picked my brains over what Wandsworth was doing, the election result and so on, followed by a request for an urgent formal report. My hon. Friend is a past master at quiet whispering in someone's ear so that they do not miss the point, and as I left with him, he said, "Today is Tuesday. Can we have it by Friday?" I said, "Look, I'm awfully sorry John, but I'm going home to pick up my bags, and then I'm flying out for two weeks." Exactly two weeks later I came back, opened the doors and dropped my cases, and as I dropped my cases, the phone rang. "Well", he said, "Have you written it yet? It's been two weeks. We want it. The Prime Minister particularly wants it."

What I particularly enjoyed in discussions with Margaret Thatcher was that at the end of a discussion she generally had made up her mind, and I was told where I stood. That was extremely useful. On one visit, I sought an audience to explain that the then Inner London Education Authority was serving an education disservice on the children of London, including those in my own borough. My proposition was that the authority could and would provide a better education for inner-London children. I had no inkling of her thinking, but she immediately made it clear that I was pushing at an open door. Legislation followed, and even those who had once supported the ILEA recognised that it was a good move.

[Barry Sheerman was born 17 August 1940 and educated at the London School of Economics. A university lecturer he has represented Huddersfield since 1979.]

6 pm

Mr Barry Sheerman (Huddersfield) (Lab/Co-op)

You were not in short trousers, Mr Speaker, but I think — because I checked your birth date — just starting your A-levels in 1979 (*commencing 11th grade*), when I got elected to the House of Commons on the same day as Mrs Thatcher became Prime Minister. You can imagine my astonishment when I came No. 1 in the list for the first Prime Minister's questions, which meant I was going to ask her first question. Unfortunately, my predecessor, Curly Mallalieu, died that week, and I had to withdraw from that first Prime Minister's questions. It took me a long time to get another question to the Prime Minister. Indeed, the next time I got a highly placed question, Willie Whitelaw was standing in for her. Eventually, on 15 April 1980, I said:

"Will the Prime Minister take time today to reflect on the mounting evidence emerging this week — not only from her Chancellor of the Exchequer — that her economic strategy is destroying Britain's industrial base? Will she further consider a reversal of those policies which have led to a soaring inflation rate of 20 per cent., rising unemployment and crippling interest rates that will soon turn this country into a banana republic, both economically and diplomatically?" — [*Official Report*, 15 April 1980; Vol. 982, c. 1007.]

I mention that only because for a number of years I was a Back Bencher, and for a long time a shadow Minister, drilled to hate everything Mrs Thatcher stood for. Over those years, I came to respect Margaret Thatcher because she commanded the Dispatch Box and was a fantastic parliamentarian. However, we cannot pretend that people did not love and loathe her. In fact, the election results show that more people loved her than loathed her.

When I was at the London School of Economics, I studied with Michael Oakeshott and read Hayek, and I was very much influenced by both those gentlemen. Oakeshott took me through a wonderful study of Machiavelli's "The Prince" and "Discourses", which tell us that for a leader — a prince or Prime Minister — to survive, they have to be lucky. Mrs Thatcher was not only talented as a leader, but lucky. I was on the Opposition Benches knowing what a shambles the Opposition were. We spent more time fighting each other within the Labour party than we had time to fight the Government. It is not good for democracy to have such a weak Opposition as we had post 1979. Sometimes we stand up and say that Mrs Thatcher rolled over the mining communities, and she did. She caused great hardship. Terrible things happened to people in the mining communities, and the miners' dispute should have ended much sooner than it did. My heart went out to the wives of miners selling things to raise money and trying to keep families together. I remember it very well. Although my constituency is not a mining constituency, it is very close to mining constituencies. I understand the people who loathed Mrs Thatcher, but I also understand that at that time those people were let down by the Opposition because we could not get our act together to defeat her.

There have been some very good and perceptive speeches. I agreed with one or two Government Members and did not agree with two or three of my colleagues. I have reflected on what Mrs Thatcher contributed, and I think it was this. What happened in 1979 was a colossal sea change in British politics, and we needed it. We needed something radical to happen to the untidy post-war shambles of a consensus, and Mrs Thatcher was it. It was not about Conservatism or Toryism. The people who said that it was Gladstonian, laissez-faire liberalism were absolutely right, as we know, because that blue liberalism was well known and understood in West Yorkshire. That is what she stood for, and it surprised everyone. Labour Members did not know how to handle it, and partly because of that she had three general election victories. We were trounced. We were a divided party and a divided Opposition, and we had a very long and tough time getting through it. Mrs Thatcher transformed the Labour party. We had to reform and change and get our act together, or we would have ceased to have the presence and power of a major party in our country. We must remember what Mrs Thatcher did for parliamentary democracy.

We are again overdue a radical change in how we regard our parliamentary democracy. We need a voice in this Chamber — I do not know which party it will come from — that says that there are some deep inequities in our society. There are serious problems, different from those that Mrs Thatcher faced in 1979 and in the years of her prime ministership, but very deep. My right hon. Friend the Member for Birkenhead (Mr Field) touched on some of them. There is the tragic decline of our great cities, many of them in the north and the midlands. That has happened all over the developed world — in the United States, we should look at what is happening in Detroit and Pittsburgh. (*Presumably the negatives in Detroit and the positives in Pittsburgh.*) There is something deeply wrong with how our societies are developing, and that is to do with a complex change in international capitalism, as Labour Members would call it, and the international structure of economics.

Something fundamental is happening that we have become a bit complacent about in all parts of this House. We will need somebody with the originality of Thatcher to get us to wake up to what is going on. If we are honest — I make this a constant theme in my speeches; I am sorry — most of us will admit that tiny numbers of people in our constituencies are actively involved in politics. We are in a democracy where only 65% voted at the last election and 6 million people did not even register to vote. The state of our parliamentary democracy is deplorable. We will need someone with a vision, perhaps based on a very different political view, who will say, "If we value this democracy we have got to shake it up."

I have spoken today because I got to admire and quite like Mrs Thatcher, who, as some of my colleagues have said, could be very pleasant indeed. She would give someone a real roasting from the Dispatch Box if they made a comment, but out there in the corridor she would be very kind. That is the truth of the woman. She was phenomenal. She did things that I deplored; she did things I thought were wonderful. There is a balance, and over time we will judge how good it was. We are facing a challenge to our democracy, and we need a Thatcher-like — not the same as Thatcher — radical change that will again wake us up to the fact that our country faces challenges to which, at present, we have no answers.

[Michael (Mike) Freer was born 29 May 1960 and educated at St Aidan's College, Carlisle. A banker, he has represented Finchley and Golders Green since 2010.]

6.9 pm

Mike Freer (Finchley and Golders Green) (Con)

If I may, I shall speak briefly about my predecessor, the Member of Parliament for Finchley and Friern Barnet. Many people have talked about her role on the global or national stage. I wish to talk about the woman who represented Finchley for 33 years, the woman whom my party members remember never, ever as Maggie, but simply as Mrs T or, more fondly, "our Margaret".

From the outset Finchley Conservatives knew they had a winner. One of my stalwarts, Derek Phillips, recounts how as a young Conservative he went into that selection meeting saying, "I'm not voting for a woman." He came out having voted for that woman. He changed his mind in short order when she was clearly head and shoulders above the men, and from that day on, she remained head and shoulders above the men around her.

Much is said about Mrs Thatcher's background. She is described, often disparagingly, as the grocer's daughter and the housewife who knew the value of thrift and of living within one's means, as if there was something wrong with that. For me, Mrs Thatcher illustrates clearly and sharply what shapes our views as Members of Parliament, whether is it ideology, background or our casework. It is probably a blend of all three.

Finchley and Friern Barnet was and is a suburban constituency. Mrs Thatcher would have seen at first hand how Government policies affected the lives of local families — families who had worked hard to buy their home or families who struggled to make ends meet, including the many pensioners in the constituency. When commentators describe her as driven by ideology, they fail to understand the woman. They fail to understand that the constituency was her touchstone.

As might be expected, Finchley has a wealth of memorabilia. I came across an election address dating back to 1974. I also searched for a photograph of one young Finchley student called John Bercow (*Speaker of the House of Commons*) who, I am told, approached Mrs Thatcher at one of the hustings and was firmly told to go and join the Young Conservatives. You will be pleased to know, Mr Speaker that no photographic evidence exists. I have searched.

If I may be forgiven for using a prop, I found an election address dating back to 1974. I shall highlight a few excerpts from it. Mrs Thatcher said in her local election address of 1974, 40 years ago:

> "As a nation we must stop living on borrowed money. We must gradually reduce the debt over a period of three or four years."

That sounds familiar. She went on to say:

> "We must keep public spending within the capacity and willingness of our citizens to foot the bills."

The address goes on to talk about helping first-time buyers with their deposits, of helping council tenants to buy their homes and of easing the rates (*local property taxes*) burden. That was 40 years ago and some would say nothing has changed.

The day-to-day issues that faced Mrs Thatcher as a local constituency MP influenced her policies. Finchley was where she came to recharge her batteries. She knew that when she came to Finchley, she would leave the advisers behind and she would hear the unvarnished truth, as seen by her constituents and, equally importantly, by her supporters and her activists. One of her agents tells the story that within minutes of Mrs Thatcher returning to Downing street, the No.10 machine would be on the phone, demanding politely to know what she had been told in Finchley, because she had returned to Downing street full of vigour, demanding to know what was going on with this or that. Finchley brought home to her what needed to be done.

There is one incident that perhaps explains her drive to abolish the rates and introduce the community charge. This is an example of how I believe her constituency work shaped her policies. The rights and wrongs of the community charge are not for today, but the casework that Mrs Thatcher came across drove home the inequality of a household with several wage earners paying the same as a pensioner. She saw at first hand the struggle that many on low and fixed incomes had with the rates. One experience I will relate. I am told that one elderly resident came to see her in a state of distress. The resident had paid her rates in cash in an envelope to the town hall. The cash went astray. Mrs Thatcher knew the hardship that having to find the rates once had caused, let alone having to find them a second time to make up the cash that had gone astray. It is not commonly known that Mrs Thatcher quietly sent a cheque and paid the rates for that resident. She was far from the heartless caricature portrayed in the media and by her opponents.

Mrs Thatcher took enormous interest in her constituents, and her ability to remember their names and their concerns, often months after first meeting them, was truly astounding. In the early 1990s when I was a local councillor in Finchley, Mrs Thatcher came to a summer fete, which was held every year on a small council estate. She arrived bang on time, for she was a stickler for punctuality. She swept in, in the Jaguar. Out she came, as immaculate as ever. She ignored the local dignitaries such as humble councillors, went straight across to the organiser of the fete, whom I will call Mrs Smith, and said, "Now, dear, how did your daughter get on with her GCSEs? (*Exams taken at age 16, at the end of 10th grade.*) She sat them last year, didn't she? Wasn't she sitting seven?" I was completely bowled over by this. I spoke to her agent and asked if he made copious notes while no one was looking so that he could brief her before she arrived. I was firmly told, "No, she simply remembers." That was the measure of the woman as a constituency MP.

Mrs Thatcher had an amazing knack of being able to put anyone at ease, usually because she knew that what was important to them had to be important to her. The dripping tap that the council would not repair was the most important thing to that constituent, and so it became the most important thing to Mrs T. There are countless examples of her warmth and her compassion. The devotion of those who worked with her and stayed with her after she was no longer the Prime Minister is testament to that. Many of her close protection officers chose to stay with her, rather than move up the ranks. One of them recently told me of a Christmas time at Chequers. He came back to the police mess room to find that Mrs Thatcher had been in. She had tidied up and decorated it with Christmas decorations. She had cleaned out the hearth, laid a fire and left a flask of coffee on the table for her police officers. That is the woman few people saw.

It was said by my noble Friend Baron Baker of Dorking that we shall not see the like of Mrs Thatcher again. Well, we probably will see a woman party leader. We probably will see a woman Prime Minister again. But will we see the intellect, the drive, the passion and the core beliefs to shape events, not bend to them?

Will we see the whole package? I do not think so. "Our Margaret", as my members remember her, was an outstanding constituency MP. Finchley is proud to have selected her, and we are grateful to the Thatcher family for lending her to us.

[Paul Flynn was born 9 February 1935 and educated at Cardiff University. He worked as a chemist in the steel industry before becoming a radio broadcaster and policy researcher. He has represented Newport West since 1987.]

6.18 pm

Paul Flynn (Newport West) (Lab)

Unwisely, I once put down a written question to Prime Minister Thatcher, asking her to list the failures of her premiership. The answer was disappointingly brief. Another MP tabled a question asking her to list the successes of her premiership. The answer cost £4,500 and filled 23 columns of *Hansard*. Modesty was never her prime virtue, but she had many virtues and I would rank her as one of the two best politicians of the last century. The other one was Clement Attlee. It is significant that, about an hour ago, Matthew Parris tweeted:

"Just come across a small, downpage *Guardian* piece from Oct 1967: 'quiet funeral for Lord Attlee'."

Prime Ministers are not made by the trappings of power, or by expensive funerals.

Margaret Thatcher was not like most politicians. We all pretend that we act on the basis of evidence, sense and reason, but most of us — apart from her and Clement Attlee — act on the basis of pressure, prejudice and perception. Those are the things that move us and determine what laws are passed in the House. She was a woman who knew about evidence, however. She knew about scientific evidence, and that is the reason that she was one of the first to embrace the green agenda.

I also believe, however, that Mrs Thatcher was very wrong in many of the things that she did, and my main reason for speaking today is to tell the House what happened to my constituents at that time. No one would question the need for greater financial discipline in the 1970s and into the 1980s; industries were in a mess. However, the great tragedy for Mrs Thatcher was one that befalls many leaders who stay long in office: she became surrounded by sycophants who praised her extravagantly — *[Laughter]*. We have heard a great deal of that today, and much of what has been said is entirely true, but there has also been a huge amount of hyperbole. When she was in charge, what followed was hubris, and hubris was followed by nemesis.

The way in which Mrs Thatcher treated heavy industry in this country involved pursing a mission to discipline the industries and to make them profitable, but she did not know when to stop. I am thinking particularly of the industry that was the backbone of my city of Newport, the steel industry, which is now a pale shadow of its former self. I am afraid that she did not fight for heavy industry in the same way that she fought for the farming industry or for the financial industry, and that had terrible results. Many of the people in my constituency who had devoted their lives to the steel industry had special skills. They defined themselves as steelworkers, but suddenly their skills were redundant. Those people were no longer important; they were robbed of that scrap of dignity around which we all need to build our lives. She went too far, and we all know the result.

There is great respect for Margaret Thatcher as a political personality, and history will judge her as a great Prime Minister. Many of her attributes that have been described today will be seen by most people here as great virtues. Her role was to alter the appearance and persona of England — rather than Wales or Scotland — in the world, but there has been a cost to that. The cost of punching above our weight militarily is that we spend beyond our interests and we die beyond our responsibilities.

There are two deaths that we should be talking about today. Of course we should be talking about Mrs Thatcher, but we should also mention Lance Corporal Jamie Webb of 1st Battalion the Mercian Regiment. He was 24, and he died on 25 March. He was repatriated to this country last Thursday. I do not know whether anyone saw any publicity about that, or whether any attention was paid to the event. He was the 441st of our soldiers to die in the Afghan war. I have visited Brize Norton and seen the sensitively conceived arrangements there. I cannot think of any way in which they could bring greater comfort to the bereaved families of those who have fallen in the name of this country, but I am afraid that the way in which the processions now take place has been designed to avoid drawing attention to these tragedies. Today, along with that of Margaret Thatcher, we should remember the names of the 441 who died for their country, one of whom was Jamie Webb. We should remember their sacrifice and reflect on the fact that the spirit that leads us to punch above our weight often has tragic consequences.

[Rt Hon Simon Hughes was born 17 May 1951 and educated at Selwyn College, Cambridge. An attorney he has represented Bermondsey since 1983. He serves as Deputy Leader of the Liberal Democrats.]

6.26 pm

Simon Hughes (Bermondsey and Old Southwark) (LD)

Two themes have emerged today. The first has been a wish to express our condolences and sympathy. The second has been an expression of admiration and respect from across the House, irrespective of party, for someone who was one of the dominant political figures not only in this country but in the democratic politics of the Western world in the last century. She was one of the strongest and most determined leaders that our country has ever known.

Like my late mother, Mrs Thatcher was born in the great and productive county of Lincolnshire. Given that she also had the same birthday as my dad — 13 October — it was not surprising that we followed her career with greater than usual interest once she entered the Heath Cabinet. As has already been mentioned, she set many examples to follow. She set an example to young people by first standing for Parliament at the age of 24, and to people who do not succeed the first time, in that it took three goes before she got here. She then became her party's leader before she was 50. I remember hearing the news of her election as leader, and of Ted Heath's defeat, when I was standing at the railway station in Bruges during my year as a postgraduate student at the College of Europe. It was clear that that was a significant moment in British political history. It also caused a bit of a dispute in our family. My dad was not keen, but my mum was more admiring.

Through her efforts, Margaret Thatcher changed the place of women in British public life and politics. Let us check the figures. Before she was elected, there had been no general election with more than 200 female candidates, or more than 30 elected women MPs. In the general election of 1992, when she stood down, there were 571 female candidates, and 60 women were elected to this place. The numbers have risen significantly since then. She would not have argued that there was a direct cause and effect, but I am sure that there was one, and thank God for that. It was also significant that, through her election, a scientist became a British party leader and Prime Minister. Her forensic skills and scientific interests were evident, and I am sure that her interest in and worries about climate change stemmed from that.

Margaret Thatcher winning the 1979 election was clearly another defining moment in our history. I hope that colleagues on the Opposition Benches will not try to airbrush the fact that, before that, this country had been through a dire few years economically. It had not been a happy time. We had had to go to the international community for financial rescue, the lights had been going out in the early part of the decade, and we had been working only three days a week. So it was not as though the 1970s were halcyon days. She then delivered three election victories, two of which had majorities of more than 100, always with 13 million or more votes, and always with more than 42% of the electorate supporting her. I noticed — I pay tribute to her successor in Finchley, the hon. Member for Finchley and Golders Green (Mike Freer) — that in her last election she received her highest ever vote, which is a testimony to the way she was respected in her north London constituency.

I first came to this House when she was Prime Minister, in a by-election in 1983. I always believed that all Prime Ministers and Governments do many good things, but do not do everything right — some clearly right, some clearly wrong. I came here as a member of the broader Christian church, as she did, and I realised I would have a difficulty from the beginning. Christians and people of other faiths are called to love everybody, but sometimes loving Mrs T was a bit difficult from the Opposition Benches.

She was clearly right in her attitude towards the Falklands — absolutely right to be determined to recapture the Falklands for Britain. She was clearly courageous beyond expectation in her determination not to be blown off course by the despicable IRA bomb in Brighton in 1984, and she was almost unbelievably successful in her work to bring down the iron curtain.

After she died this week, I worked out that I had engaged with her across the House on 19 occasions between 1983 and her final debate in November 1990. I was able to thank her for supporting work on the Rose theatre, which had been excavated — she did have an interest in culture and the arts. On a few occasions, I had to have a strong go at her with regard to London matters. There was a need to reform London government, but abolishing the Greater London council was absolutely not the way to go. There was a need to mobilise the docklands and urban areas for regeneration, but having no democratic participation was not the way to go. Then there were other issues that were good ideas in part, but often left some things worse off than before. Giving people the right to buy their own council homes was popular and in many ways a good idea, but not giving councils the power to decide whether they wanted to use that power was wrong. Not to make the discounts reflect accurately the length of time someone had been in a home was inappropriate. Not guaranteeing that all the moneys went back to councils was extremely unhelpful, and is one cause of the shortage of social and affordable housing today.

Mrs Thatcher was right to take on the trade unions, which had become over-mighty in the 1970s, but she was wrong to do so in a way that decimated much of manufacturing industry, not just in our coal mines but in other places, such as south Wales. She was right to work, as she did successfully, to bring down the inflation rate from 13% in 1979 to 5% or less in five of the next 10 years. However, presiding over unemployment going up from 4% to more than 9% was not a price worth paying and it had serious, adverse consequences. Although pensioners were better off in terms of the amount of money they had in their retirement, many never forgave her for breaking the link with earnings.

In her very last speech I put it to her that, sadly, she had left the gap between the rich and the poor much wider. I have to say that the gap continued under the Labour Government. She accused me of saying that we would rather the poor were poorer provided the rich were less rich. That was never our view. We needed a fairer society and sadly we did not get one.

I referred to Bruges at the beginning of my speech and I want to end with the Bruges speech she made 25 years ago. It bears re-reading, as I am sure the Prime Minister has on more than one occasion. I end with exact quotes from the speech she gave to the college at which I had been privileged to be a student:

> "Our destiny is in Europe, as part of the Community. That is not to say that our future lies only in Europe...The Community is not an end in itself...The European Community is a practical means by which Europe can ensure the future prosperity and security of its people in a world in which there are many other powerful nations and groups of nations...Certainly we want to see Europe more united and with a greater sense of common purpose... I want to see us work more closely...Europe is stronger when we do so, whether it be in trade, in defence or in our relations with the rest of the world...But it must be in a way which preserves the different traditions... for these have been the source of Europe's vitality through the centuries."

We are proud of her patriotism and give thanks for it. She will be respected throughout the whole of the rest of our political lives.

[David Lammy was born 19 July 1972 to Guyanese parents and educated at the School of Oriental and African Studies, London, and Harvard Law School. An attorney, he was elected to represent Tottenham at a 2000 by-election becoming the then youngest member of the Commons.]

6.34 pm

Mr David Lammy (Tottenham) (Lab)

It is an incredibly long way from Broadwater Farm, (*an area of high density public housing*), via the Bar, to being here as a Member of Parliament. I think it is an even longer way to go from a grocer's shop in Grantham, through Oxbridge and the Bar, to leading one's country as a woman. For that single reason alone, it is appropriate that we come together to pay tribute to Margaret Thatcher.

I look at her legacy from the vantage point of being a young person growing up in Tottenham, with a single parent occasionally reliant on the state and on benefits, during a difficult time for our country. It would certainly be the case that for most of my youth Margaret Thatcher was not somebody I admired, and there were occasions when I actually felt quite scared by much of what she said and what her Government seemed to do. Some 25 or 30 years later, I feel slightly different. My political generation, which includes the leaders of our political parties, coincides with a period in politics of 24-hour media, presentation, soundbite, spin and polling. All of us in this House have met politicians who seem to not really to know their own mind. We have met politicians who say one thing one minute and then, when they have met someone else, seem to say the last thing they heard. Some of us have even met party leaders like that. In that context, I have tremendous respect for someone with conviction and courage, someone who is willing to stand their ground and who is clear on their values. At this time in our history, when things are so hard and there is so much deep concern about our political class, we could do with more conviction from all parts of this House.

I said that I was basing my remarks on growing up in Tottenham, but for the second part of my youth I spent seven years in Peterborough. There, I came across a different kind of working class attitude to Margaret Thatcher. These were people who had left London and gone to a new town. They were making their way and wanted to forge ahead. They were enjoying holidays and owning their homes for the first time. I would go around to their small houses and on their coffee tables they would have the "Tell Sid" brochure, (*an advert for buying shares in a company about to be privatized*) so keen were they to take part in the experiment of buying shares in British Gas. I have to say that my mum got one of those brochures for her coffee table, but that was just to appear as though she was able to buy shares in British Gas.

There were two quiet revolutions of the 20th century that have given us the country and world we have today. The social liberal revolution of the 1960s is perhaps best personified by the quest for freedom and human rights that we associate with another great elder statesman, Nelson Mandela.

The second liberal revolution must most definitely be the economic liberal revolution of the 1980s. Margaret Thatcher was obviously at its epicentre, and for that reason she is a giant figure in our history, and it is right that our country comes together to pay her due respect. However — *[Interruption.]* I am afraid there is a big however, because we also live with the consequences of a hyper-individualised society — consequences that we see in materialism, consumerism, over-corporatism and a sense that unemployment is fine and that those on benefits can fend for themselves. I remind the House that for people in Handsworth, Brixton, Tottenham, St Pauls in Bristol, Moss Side in Manchester and Chapeltown in Leeds, it was a desperate time, with tremendous suffering, and we stand in solidarity with colleagues in the north, particularly in our mining towns and former steelworks, who bear the scars today of that period of social adjustment.

No one has mentioned the Commonwealth, which is an important institution. Despite the advice of Rajiv Gandhi, Oliver Tambo and others who urged economic sanctions, Margaret Thatcher said, "No, I will go it alone." That is a great scar on the history of the Commonwealth.

The history will be chequered for many years. It is right that we pay tribute, but it is also right that we reflect on young people growing up at that time, particularly in our tower blocks and estates, and the suffering they are still going through — not a feral underclass, but workless poor. It began in that period and today it still continues for successive generations.

[Charles Walker was born 11 September 1967 and was educated at the American School in London and the University of Oregon. Before entering the Commons as MP for Broxbourne in 2005 he was in marketing, communications, and the recruiting agency business. Since 2010 he has been a Vice Chairman of the influential 1922 Committee (see above).]

6.42 pm

Mr Charles Walker (Broxbourne) (Con)

I shall try to be brief, Mr Speaker.

I did not know Lady Thatcher. I met her on a few occasions, but I admired her from afar. I rise to pay my respects and to pass on the respects of many tens of thousands of my constituents who would want me to be here today. She was a great woman, a great Prime Minister and she had love of this country emblazoned on her heart.

[David Anderson was born 2 December 1953 and was educated at Durham University. He worked as a coal miner and later as a care worker and has represented Blaydon since 2005.]

6.43 pm

Mr David Anderson (Blaydon) (Lab)

As a former coal miner who became a care worker in the 1980s, looking after frail elderly people — particularly frail elderly women suffering from dementia, incontinence and the inability to bathe and dress themselves — I have nothing but empathy for the family of Margaret Thatcher. They will feel an immense sense of loss that will almost certainly be tinged with a sense of relief. They will feel guilty about that relief, but they should not; it is a normal, healthy attitude when a loved one has been brought low by the reality of our mortality.

As a former miner and trade union leader and as the Member for a constituency whose history was built on the hard work of ordinary men and women, it would be remiss of me not to record the reality of life for people in such constituencies because of policies promoted by Margaret Thatcher. She came to power promising to bring harmony where there was discord. I can safely say that in mining communities up and down the country she brought the opposite. Most mining areas were stable, secure and safe communities where we worked hard and played hard. We did not complain about the difficult conditions in which we worked. All we asked for was the chance to carry on doing that work.

We had built communities over decades, in some cases over centuries, and they had stood the test of time. We built sports centres, swimming pools and cricket and football clubs. We built libraries and developed brass bands, and we ran art classes that gained international fame. That was part and parcel of our culture, but none of it seemed to matter to Margaret Thatcher. She believed that we were no longer any use to the nation because we were deemed "uneconomic".

On what basis was that case made? I believe that the main reason why the United Kingdom coal industry was classed as uneconomic was that we insisted on running safe coal mines, unlike those in the rest of the world. Our history was longer than that of other coal industries. It was littered with numerous examples of avoidable deaths, and we as a country agreed to invest in the best quality equipment in the world and in training people to produce coal as safely as possible. One of the great disgraces in this country is that we import more than 50 million tonnes of coal a year from countries where men are killed in their thousands, yet we closed down an industry that was the safest and most technically advanced in the world. There is still blood on the coal that is burned in British power stations, but it is American blood, Russian blood, Chinese blood or Colombian blood, so that is okay. Well, it should not be okay. As a country, we have millions of tons of coal beneath our feet.

The other area where the so-called economic justification falls down was in the failure of Margaret Thatcher and her Governments to take into account the social cost in communities such as mine, where there was no alternative employment for people who were losing their jobs, and particularly for their children. The village where I lived had seen coal mining for almost two centuries. In a matter of months after closure, we were gripped by a wave of petty crime — burglary and car crime — mostly related to drugs. We have never recovered from it. When someone wakes in the middle of the night and goes downstairs because their home is being burgled, and finds out the next day that it was the son of one of their best friends, it puts into perspective a community that was built on reliance and taking care of each other. That takes a lot of recovering from.

The situation was compounded by the crass decision in 1988 to sell off houses owned by the National Coal Board to private landlords. They brought in people from outside the area who had no respect for the community or for the houses they were given. Twenty years later, houses that were sold to private landlords for £4,000 were bought back by the council for £60,000 of public money, only for them to be pulled down because of the failure of the policy agreed as part and parcel of the decision to ruin the coal industry in this country.

Over the last 48 hours, a lot has been said about the harsh nature of some of the responses to the news of Mrs Thatcher's death, but the House needs to understand the reason. Before, during and ever since the attack on the coal indus-try and the people in it, Governments of both colours were warned of the impact of the policy. We have seen the reaction of people whose frustration is heartfelt. They have lost their sense of place in society. They are being made to feel worth-less. They are being cast aside like a pair of worn-out pit boots. They have seen their community fall apart and their children's opportunities disappear. They are not being listened to, and sadly some of that has boiled over this week.

After today's debate those people may never be listened to again, and Mrs Thatcher's lack of empathy, her intransigence, her failure to see the other side and her refusal to even look at the other side has left them bitter and resentful. They are hitting out in a way that is uncharacteristic of miners and their com-munities. Her accusation that the enemy within was in the mining areas of this country still rankles. I was not an enemy within. My hon. Friends the Mem-bers for Midlothian (Mr Hamilton), for Wansbeck (Ian Lavery), for Blyth Val-ley (Mr Campbell), and for Lanark and Hamilton East (Mr Hood) were not the enemy within. Nor were people like Joe Green, who died on the picket line at Ferry Bridge in Yorkshire, David Jones who was killed at Ollerton colliery, Terry Leaves and Jimmy Jones who were killed in south Wales, or three young boys — Darren Holmes, aged 15, Paul Holmes, aged 14, and Paul Womersley, aged 14 — who died scavenging for coal to try to keep their families warm.

It is understandable that people feel bitter that we are here today to remem-ber the legacy of Mrs Thatcher. All we wanted was the right to work, not just for ourselves but for our kids. It was taken away. The funeral next week will take place 20 years to the day since Easington colliery was closed. Please do not blame the people in my part of the world if they choose that day to pay a tribute very different from that being paid in the House today.

[Andrew Tyrie was born 15 January 1957 and was educated at Trinity Col-lege, Oxford, the College of Europe, Bruges, and Wolfson College, Cambridge. He worked as a bank economist before entering the Commons in 1997 represent-ing Chichester. He is currently Chairperson of the Treasury Select Committee.]

6.49 pm

Mr Andrew Tyrie (Chichester) (Con)

We can see, from the speeches of the hon. Member for Blaydon (Mr Anderson) and others, the deep emotions that Margaret Thatcher still inspires.

So many of us from the Government side are still here for this debate simply because Mrs Thatcher was the inspiration for our going into politics in the first place. There was her sense of public service and duty and her conviction that even the toughest task, including Britain's ungovernability, could be tackled. There was her conviction that the state had lost sight of its essential role of protecting our freedoms, that it was encroaching on them and that it had to be rolled back. Above all, there was her patriotism — she wanted to restore pride in our country and others' respect for it. As far as the last century is concerned, she will come to be seen as the greatest standard bearer for freedom that the House has produced.

My first meaningful encounter with Margaret Thatcher took place at 7.15 am in a windowless back room in Conservative central office just before a press conference during the 1984 European elections. Having been at central office for only a few months, I was unnerved to find myself placed opposite her. She had, it seemed, read all the extensive briefing that we had prepared for her. She fixed me with a stare. Her first question identified an apparent contradiction in the briefing. Before I had time to admit that I did not know the answer, Geoffrey Howe, who was sitting next to me and did, saved me by replying.

Margaret Thatcher was kind enough to add me to a lunch party at Chequers after those elections. No doubt identifying me as the junior man, she told me to sit next to her for lunch. Within minutes, she announced to the table that I was far too thin and insisted on overseeing my consumption of two puddings.

I met Mrs Thatcher sporadically over the following few years. I was at the Treasury, with a ringside seat for the Thatcher–Lawson row, the rights and wrongs of which — and there were both — are for another day. More generally, I had a chance to observe several of her well-known traits. At the heart of her approach was her instinctive understanding that the restoration of prosperity depended on supply-side reform: breaking down the entrenched privileges — of the professions as much as of the trade unions; simplifying and reducing taxes; cutting back the tangle of regulation; and enhancing individual opportunity and aspiration. She wanted to break with the consensus of an over-mighty state and a dependent people.

Some have been arguing recently that Mrs Thatcher's reforms are responsible for the failings of the banks today. I doubt that. Whatever the merits of the prudential regulation that came with the big bang in the '80s, those rules were no longer in place when the crisis broke five years ago; they had been replaced by another set of rules put there in the 1990s in both the US and the UK. In any case, the notion that Mrs Thatcher, who cared most of all about the consumer and the taxpayer, would be an apologist for the banks, is implausible. She would have found the abuse of market power by some bank leaderships for their own gain at the expense of the rest of us every bit as deplorable as the behaviour of trade union leaders.

Most of Mrs Thatcher's legacy on the supply side survives, although her supply-side reforms were, to some degree, reversed by the last Government. Perhaps I should take this opportunity to say that, in my view, the importance of the supply side is still not yet fully recognised by this Administration.

It has been said today that Mrs Thatcher's judgment faltered at the end, and there was perhaps a touch of that hubris that always lurks in No.10's bunker after a long stay. The pain of her reforms still lingers. Over the longer view, none of that, I think, will detract from her legacy. What will linger in the memory is the single most extraordinary achievement of any leader in the post-war era — that of turning a failing country and a basket-case economy into a country that had recovered its self-respect and had a future.

[Geraint Davies was born 3 May 1960 and educated at Jesus College, Oxford. He was MP for Croydon Central 1997-2005 and Swansea West since 2010, following a career in marketing.]

6.54 pm

Geraint Davies (Swansea West) (Lab/Co-op)

I speak as one who was a 14-year-old schoolboy in south Wales when Margaret Thatcher became party leader and as a representative of the Swansea West constituency. Mrs Thatcher was obviously a person of steely determination and focus who cared not about the ebb and flow of opinion or focus groups, but about her strategic vision to deliver change, and that is good. However, she should be judged on her own terms — on whether she did deliver harmony where there was discord and hope where there was despair. Certainly in south Wales, she failed on those two counts. On whether she delivered a better Britain, she did for some and did not for others.

Her leadership was born in the economic and political trauma of the 1970s. Inflation peaked at 25% (*virtually 30%*) thanks to oil price increases, the miners' strike got rid of Ted Heath and then the Labour Government were held together by a Lib-Lab pact that tried to bring down inflation through pay relationships with the trade unions; it had some success approaching 1978.

According to my predecessor Alan Williams, a former Father of the House, (*longest serving MP*) Callaghan said, "I think we can have another round of pay restraint — the unions won't want Margaret Thatcher as the new Prime Minister." How wrong he was. We had the coldest winter for 16 years, strikes lasted until February 1979 and an election was called after a vote of no confidence. Saatchi's then brought forward "Labour isn't working" and delivered Margaret Thatcher. That was a cruel irony, because unemployment went up from 1.5 million to 3.2 million between 1979 and 1983. That was the human cost of bringing inflation down by 4%. That certainly did not deliver harmony at all.

Mrs Thatcher was deeply unpopular then. The Labour left was split and the SDP broke away in 1981. In 1983, the SDP-Liberal Alliance got 25% of the vote to Labour's 28%. Had it not been for that and the Falklands war, Mrs Thatcher might not have won in 1983. When she did, her first focus was to settle scores with the miners who had brought down Ted Heath. She built the coal stocks up in the winters of '83 and '84 and announced that there would be closures and that the National Coal Board would be privatised and sold off. Scargill, of course, fell into the bear trap. He did not hold a vote, there was a 12-month strike — a third of the pits were still working — and a great mining industry was destroyed. As has already been described, we are currently consuming 50 million tonnes of coal a year. but there is no coal industry. Near my constituency, there is the Tower colliery, a co-operative through which the miners bought their own mine, and it operated successfully for 10 years. But communities have been left on their own in despair without support. That is the politics not of hope but of fear, as Nye Bevan put it.

Economic Thatcherism is a matter not just of using unemployment to keep down wages and unions, but of mass privatisation. Crucially, the proceeds of that privatisation — the £70 billion, alongside the £80 billion from oil — were not used as they should have been: to renew our industrial infrastructure, our hospitals, our transport and our schools. The legacy was one of squandering instead: we ended up in a situation where money was being used to keep people on the dole and to provide tax breaks. We ended up with an unmanaged oil system where high exchange rates meant that manufacturing was declining much faster than it should have been.

Ultimately, Mrs Thatcher got re-elected through the Lawson bubble that burst. In the final chapter, while the rich were getting richer, she wanted the poor and the rich to pay the same tax for local services: the poll tax. As we saw the grey smoke emerge from the violent protests in London, the grey suits went round Lady Thatcher and wanted to elect a grey leader — John Major, who, of course, managed to get in. Then, naturally, everything broke down and afterwards we got a new Government who reinvested the proceeds of growth in new schools, hospitals and opportunity. I fear that some of Thatcher's legacy will involve going back and claiming that everything she did was right. What she did not do, however, was to deliver what she should have delivered — harmony and unity, a future that works and a future that cares, rather than a divided nation. I very much hope that we will not continue to press along the road of division and austerity, but will build a new future.

[Philip Davies was born 5 January 1972 and educated at the University of Huddersfield. Following a career in gambling and retail be became MP for Shipley in 2005 and is known as a blunt and fearless interrogator of 'establishment' figures.]

7 pm

Philip Davies (Shipley) (Con)

Margaret Thatcher was my political inspiration. I only wish that I had been here in Parliament when she was Prime Minister, as it would have been a rare treat indeed to be on these Benches and able to support a Government with whom I agreed from time to time.

My earliest political memory was of the Falklands war of 1982. I was 10 years old and remember coming home from school to see what was going on over in the Falklands. It was during that crisis that I built up my admiration for Margaret Thatcher. I was born in Doncaster and was brought up in Doncaster North, the constituency of the Leader of the Opposition. As he made clear, it was a strong mining community. My father was involved with the local Conservative party — there are not many Conservatives in Doncaster — and as soon as I was old enough to deliver leaflets and knock on doors, my father had me out delivering leaflets and knocking on doors. I loved elections — we never used to win any, but I still loved them.

People have often said to me that it must have been incredibly difficult going around mining communities in the mid to late-1980s supporting Margaret Thatcher and a Conservative Government. It was not difficult at all. I believed in Margaret Thatcher to my core, and when we believed in somebody in the way I believed in Margaret Thatcher it was not difficult to go knocking on doors to support the great things she did for this country. It was not Margaret Thatcher who ruined those mining communities; it was Arthur Scargill who ruined them — and let no one forget that.

Margaret Thatcher was a conviction politician. She believed that politics was all about trying to persuade people of what she believed in rather than just telling people what she thought they wanted to hear. That is the kind of politics that I believe in. She did not need focus groups or opinion polls to tell her what to believe. She was instinctively in tune with the British public.

I remember from when I was working at Asda that the best retailers were the ones who instinctively knew what the customers wanted without having to go to a focus group to ask. The worst chief executives of retailers were the ones who always had to be told what the focus groups were telling them and what the opinion polls were telling them. For me, it is exactly the same with political leaders. The best political leaders such as Margaret Thatcher instinctively know what the public want and where they are — they do not need opinion polls — and the worst political leaders are those who have to rely on those polls because they know no better themselves.

Too often, politicians in this country try to be popular. My advice would be, "If you want to be popular, don't be a politician" because of the inevitable consequence that they will become unpopular. Popularity in politics will always be a temporary thing. One thing that can last for ever in politics, however, is respect. Even if not popular, a politician can still be respected, and Margaret Thatcher was one of those politicians. She was a Marmite politician (*Marmite is a dark brown, sticky, vegetable-based food spread with a very distinctive taste which consumers either love or hate*): people either loved her or hated her, but she was universally respected, even among her political foes, because she knew what she believed in, she stood up for it and she delivered it to people. Whether people agreed with her or not, they trusted in her as a politician because she was doing what she thought was genuinely the right thing to do. We need more politicians like that.

Margaret Thatcher won three general elections on the trot, and the best way to sum up her achievement is to recognise that more people voted Conservative in her third general election than they had done the first time she won in 1979. That is a remarkable achievement showing how she built support over those eight years. Tony Blair, on the other hand, won three general elections but lost 4 million voters between the last and the first election. That goes to show the difference in calibre between those two politicians who might otherwise be closely compared.

Margaret Thatcher was voted out by her own party. This occasion gives me the opportunity to put on record my utter contempt for those in our party — people who were not fit to lick her boots — who ousted her in 1990. That did an awful lot of damage — but not just to the country, as it did long-term damage to the Conservative party as well.

Anyone wanting to sum up Mrs Thatcher should look at her final performance from the Dispatch Box as Prime Minister. It was one of the finest performances that has ever been seen in Parliament. I am delighted that the right hon. Member for Bermondsey and Old Southwark (Simon Hughes) was in his place to speak today. He will remember, probably quite painfully, how she wiped the floor with him when he intervened — *[Interruption.]* I think it was Michael Carttiss (*Conservative MP for Great Yarmouth 1983-1997*) who said from the Conservative Benches that she could wipe the floor with the lot of them, and that was absolutely true — she could. During that debate, I wonder how many Conservative Members wondered, "Oh, Lord, what have we done?" They got rid of the greatest Prime Minister this country has ever seen. There will never be another like her. It is a privilege to speak in this debate and to hear some of the great stories that help us to find the true Margaret Thatcher — one I will forever admire.

[Wayne David was born 1 July 1957 and was educated at University College, Cardiff. A former teacher he has represented Caerphilly since 2001.]

7.5 pm

Wayne David (Caerphilly) (Lab)

I believe we should all show respect to Mrs Thatcher, this country's first woman Prime Minister. As Prime Minister of this country, she undoubtedly achieved things in which all of us, on both sides of the House, can share a pride. Most notably, she signed the Good Friday agreement, and under her leadership this country liberated the Falklands and encouraged the freedom of the peoples of Eastern Europe. Let it be said, too, that she played a key role in the development of Britain's role in Europe and the single market. The young Margaret Thatcher was a good European. We should acknowledge too, if not to celebrate it on the Labour Benches, that Mrs Thatcher won three consecutive general elections. There were and still are many people who admired her undoubted strength and resolve, which she had in large abundance.

To show respect, of course, does not necessarily mean that we have to be in agreement. It is worth remembering that many people throughout the length and breadth of this country suffered because of Thatcher's ideology and the policies she pursued. It is important for us all to recognise that — and no part of the United Kingdom suffered more than the valleys of south Wales.

I was born and brought up in a largely mining community — Cefn Cribwr, near Bridgend. Both my grandfathers were miners and both knew from first-hand experience how difficult and dangerous coal mining was. Like so many of my generation in south Wales, the miners' strike of 1984-85 left an indelible mark on me. Let me be clear: the tactics of Arthur Scargill were wrong and played into the hands of the Government; but it was wrong, too, that the Government gave the impression of relishing the opportunity to mobilise the state against working people who were trying to defend their jobs, their families and their communities. In our country, no opponents should ever be described as "the enemy within".

During that long year of the miners' strike, there was undoubtedly real hardship. In my own village, we organised a support group and raised hundreds of pounds to help miners' families. The same happened throughout south Wales. If the hardship of the strike was bad, what happened afterwards was truly awful. Within months of the end of the strike, nearly all the remaining collieries in south Wales were closed. Nowhere was worse hit than the Rhymney valley, the greater part of which I now have the privilege to represent. Two of the biggest collieries in south Wales were within the Rhymney valley — Bedwas and Penallta. Each employed more than 600 men. Bedwas was closed literally weeks after the strike and Penallta followed suit a couple of years later.

Those closures were body blows to the valley. Closing the collieries was bad, but what made things worse was the absence of any real attempt to provide alternative employment or even training for those made unemployed. There was, it is true, a much heralded "valleys initiative" but that, like so many other Government initiatives of the time, was all hype and little substance. In the aftermath of the miners' strike, unemployment rocketed, and so did economic inactivity.

Today, many of the scars of the 1980s are still with us. After 1997, we saw more enlightened and interventionist policies pursued, but we are still nevertheless grappling with the country's historic legacy. In large part because of what happened during the 1980s, unemployment and economic inactivity in the south Wales valleys is still above the UK average, and poverty and deprivation is still a scourge.

I do not believe that the huge social facture in the south Wales valleys was the result of any individual's spite or malice; but it was the result of adherence to monetarist economic theory — a theory which elevated individuals above the community, which put short-term profit before long-term prosperity, and which made people subservient to uncontrolled market forces.

Many Conservative Members genuinely believe that Mrs Thatcher achieved many great things. They are entitled to that view. Undoubtedly Mrs Thatcher did some things that we can all take pride in; but for my constituents, and for many ordinary people throughout south Wales, Mrs Thatcher has left a legacy which they will not celebrate and which they will never forget.

[The Hon Bernard Jenkin was born 9 April 1959 and educated at Corpus Christi College, Oxford. He worked in finance before entering the Commons in 1992 today representing Harwich and North Essex. He is the son of Lord (Patrick) Jenkin of Roding and the husband of Anne Jenkin, a legendary organizer and fundraiser for his party. Consequently he is often compared to Denis Thatcher as a man married to a more famous woman.]

7.10 pm

Mr Bernard Jenkin (Harwich and North Essex) (Con)

The House has already heard much about Margaret Thatcher as a huge political figure — the iron lady who dominated British politics and world politics — but my wife and I grew to know her after she retired from the House of Commons. We came to know someone who was far from the arrogant or heartless figure portrayed by her adversaries. She was someone who must have forced herself to be strong, to hide any self-doubt, to deny herself any weakness, in order to live up to an ideal of herself. She was anything but arrogant.

I do not know how many times we saw her reject the adulation that was so often heaped upon her. She felt undeserving of such praise and standing ovations. She would say how she could never have achieved anything on her own; that her Governments were a team effort, in which many played their part. This was genuine humility, not arrogance. And we have read and heard so much about her acts of personal kindness.

It was her passion for the truth that made her such a dangerous adversary in argument — a danger which she harboured long into old age — and she loved a good spat. She met some bright young candidates before the 1992 election — me included — [Interruption.] I beg your pardon. Two now serve as senior Ministers of state. As they tried to justify UK membership of the exchange rate mechanism, she scorned the one who had worked closely in her Government with heavy inflection. "Oh," she said, "I am so disappointed with you." She listened to the other, who argued that the exit from the exchange rate mechanism would involve too much loss of face for the Government. She retorted: "Loss of face? What is loss of face compared to the loss of 350,000 jobs? If you think that, you're a fool. There's the door!" Not an easy introduction for an aspiring candidate.

What we miss from politics today is her certainty, her seriousness, her clarity of principle, her fusion of the practical with her sense of moral purpose. Those who disagreed with her undoubtedly felt that to be arrogance on her part, but she felt she was a guardian of greater truths and principles, which were far more important than her mere self. This, with her formidable intellect, gave her an extraordinary prescience about the world. How right she was about the exchange rate mechanism, and about the Maastricht treaty and monetary union. I would caution those who try to use her name in support of the EU as it has become, as though she would ever have put her name to the Lisbon treaty or anything like it.

Another myth that this debate helpfully dispels is that she had no sense of humour. When she arrived in Essex in the constituency of my hon. Friend the

Member for Maldon (Mr Whittingdale) for the 1992 election campaign, a junior reporter from the *Essex County Standard* breathlessly caught up with her hectic pace and asked, in front of 200 other journalists, "Do you agree that the Conservative campaign is lacking in oomph?" Mrs T retorted, with heavy irony, "That's what I'm here for, dear."

She will always be revered as a woman of principle with iron determination, even by those who disagree with her. Her premiership was about restoring national self-belief, something few can deny she achieved, and that is what we must now do for ourselves. It has become an axiom in the coverage of reaction to Margaret Thatcher's death that she was divisive, ignoring the fact that the UK was already bitterly divided. We need to hear the scars that industrial decline has left in many constituencies represented on the Opposition Benches, but that should not detract from her achievements; nor should she be blamed personally for what was, in many respects, an inevitable transition of economics.

We should regard some of the more unseemly reactions to her death as a backhanded tribute to her, a reminder of the attitudes she had to overcome in order to achieve what she did, but let the argument about her legacy be based on the facts and not the myths which her opponents would prefer to believe. Spending on health, education, pensions and welfare continually increased under her premiership. The number of people in work increased by 1.8 million. Manufacturing output was significantly higher when she left office than when she was first elected. Wider home ownership and share ownership spread wealth more widely than ever before; social mobility was greatly increased. The incomes of every section of society, including the poorest, increased in real terms. Income taxes paid by the richest 1% of the population increased from 11% to 15% of the total tax take.

As she grew older, we regarded Lady T less and less as a former Prime Minister, more and more as a favourite aunt or grandmother. Sometimes it was hard to believe that this small, frail lady had once held the world in the palm of her hand. The whole nation will be forever in her debt.

[Mike Gapes was born 4 September 1952 and educated at Fitzwilliam College, Cambridge and Middlesex University. He has devoted his life to politics and his party entering the Commons as MP for Ilford South in 1992.]

7.16 pm

Mike Gapes (Ilford South) (Lab/Co-op)

Thinking about what to say today, I looked at my bookcase, and I came across three publications from the 1980s: "Thatcher's Britain: A Guide to the Ruins," to which I contributed in 1983, "Breaking the Nation," published in 1985, and the Fabian Society's pamphlet "ABC of Thatcherism," published in 1989. I do not have time, in four minutes, to quote any of them, but they are well worth reading, although they may be out of print.

I was the parliamentary candidate in 1983 in Ilford North. We had huge, enthusiastic meetings for the Labour party during that campaign, but because of the split in our party, the SDP, the divisions, we had a terrible defeat. The lessons for Oppositions to draw from that period are that it is essential to preserve party unity, and essential to recognise that enthusiasm for one's party and hatred for the other side is not necessarily a guarantee of a victory.

In February 1990, the opinion polls in this country put the Labour party at 56%, under Neil Kinnock, and the Conservatives at 23% under Margaret Thatcher. We know what the Conservative party did in its ruthless manner, which has been mentioned by previous contributors to the debate, but there is a lesson there for all of us in opposition: you cannot count your chickens about what the position might be in two years' time.

In the brief time remaining, I want to say a few words about foreign policy. Mrs Thatcher was absolutely right to sign the Single European Act. She was absolutely right to be in favour of enlargement of the European Union. The consequences of those policies have influenced the politics of this country ever since. That is why we have free movement of people in the European Union. That is why we have the current debate about immigration policy. A lot of that is to do with economic decisions taken at that time. It is well worth our thinking through the consequences for the future.

On other foreign policy issues Mrs Thatcher was wrong. We have heard about South Africa and her attitude to Nelson Mandela, and I am very pleased that Nelson Mandela is still with us today, in this world, and I hope he carries on living for a decent period of time, so that he is able to understand more about the changes that have taken place in this country since the days of Margaret Thatcher, because one thing she did was to cut the overseas development budget. It went down to 0.26% of GDP, yet this coalition — I praise them for it — have kept to Labour's pledge of funding at 0.7% of GDP, which shows that what is being done in the world today is very different from what she did in government.

One other thing that Mrs Thatcher got wrong was her attitude to the unification of Germany. She was vehemently against it, but as a result of that unification, and at great cost to the Germans in the west, we have seen the peaceful transformation of Central and Eastern Europe, as well as the enlargement of the European Union and the end of communism in our continent. Those fantastic achievements could not have been achieved without the support of Margaret Thatcher but, above all, the man responsible was Mikhail Gorbachev, whom she recognised as a man she could do business with. As we heard, she should be praised for that, because she convinced Reagan, although she sometimes tried to rein Reagan back when she was wrong to do so, as at the Reykjavik negotiation, where he was ahead of his time and ahead of the world today in aspiring to a world without nuclear weapons.

[Anne McIntosh was born 20 September 1954 and was educated at the University of Edinburgh. An attorney, she was a Member of the European Parliament from 1989-1999; she entered he Commons in 1997 as MP for the Vale of York and since redistricting before the 2010 General Election MP for Thirsk and Malton.]

7.20 pm

Miss Anne McIntosh (Thirsk and Malton) (Con)

I rise to pay a personal tribute to a very great lady. Baroness Thatcher broke the mould in three distinct ways: she showed the way to women coming after her and showed us that we should aim high; by her example, she opened the door to meritocracy, not political aristocracy; and she spread democracy across Europe and the wider world.

I have cause to be personally grateful to Margaret Thatcher, having fought my first general election in 1987. Of course, we were all offered our treasured photograph with Lady Thatcher, and mine still stands on the mantelpiece in the family home. We were then granted a couple of words with the great lady. She put her arm around me and said, "Now my dear, where do you work at the moment?" I had to tell her that I worked in Europe, but I softened the blow by saying that I did work for the Conservatives in the European Parliament.

I lost that election, but in 1989 I was elected as MEP for Essex North East, which included the town of Colchester. Margaret Thatcher started her working life as a chemist in Colchester and I believe that for a while we were both Essex girls, (*In British culture the phrase 'Essex girl' is a pejorative stereotype of the dumb blonde variety. Its use here is very odd*) though perhaps not at the same time. Her sister then also settled in north Essex and I was delighted to make her acquaintance. My abiding memories of my time in the European Parliament are the speech she made while President of the Council of Ministers, which had wild interruptions from Ian Paisley senior, as we have come to know him, and the overtures she made to Mikhail Gorbachev. I was in Berlin, attending a European Parliament Committee on Legal Affairs meeting, on the day the wall fell, and that will be one of my lifelong memories. That presaged the move for cities such as Warsaw, Prague and Budapest to join the European Union. I am delighted that it was her foresight that encouraged many of us politicians and Conservative party agents to go those major cities in Central and Eastern Europe, and the Baltic states, to explain how political parties were formed and how political elections were fought.

Margaret Thatcher opened up the single European market, allowing British companies to compete in areas such as transport, insurance and financial services. It is difficult to believe now that at that time it was impossible to obtain a cheap air ticket without staying over on the Saturday night. By opening up aviation to a new generation of air travellers, particularly the young, political ideas were allowed to flow more freely.

More than anything, I have fond memories of the inspiration and aspiration that Margaret Thatcher gave to so many of us. As many hon. Members have said, she allowed people choice to better themselves. She allowed many to buy their council houses and own property for the first time, and she allowed many to own shares in previously nationalised companies that had just been privatised. In short, people now living in Thirsk, Malton, Filey, Pickering and Easingwold, and elsewhere across North Yorkshire and the rest of Britain, have a better choice and a better life because of her premiership.

Who would have thought that less than 100 years after women gained the vote, the Conservative party would have been the one that returned the first lady

Prime Minister? She gave people such as me and my generation — Thatcher's children — the confidence to seek a career in public life.

[Chinyelv (Chi) Onwurah was born 12 April 1965 and educated at Imperial College, London. Following a career in the computer industry she joined the Commons in 2010 as MP for Newcastle upon Tyne Central.]

7.24 pm

Chi Onwurah (Newcastle upon Tyne Central) (Lab)

Just as Mrs Thatcher was a child of Grantham, I was a child of Newcastle, although this was in a council flat rather than a grocer's. Just as she grew up always knowing that she wanted to be a politician, I grew up always knowing that I wanted to be an engineer. I grew up in a city and a region that valued engineering — making and building things. It was the birthplace of the railways, and it was the powerhouse of the country, with the coal beneath our feet, the steelyards and the great ships being launched from Wallsend and Sunderland.

When I was accepted to study engineering at Imperial college it was the proudest day of my life — until my election of course. So hon. Members can imagine how my heart sank when the Prime Minister of our country said, not long after, that engineering and manufacturing were the past, that the future was services and that the world would be our workshop while we would keep our hands clean. I had no desire to keep my hands clean. I had already seen what that policy was doing to the north -east: the unemployment; the communities devastated; and the lives of men and women robbed of meaning and pride. The statistics speak for themselves: between 1979 and 1987, the level of employment in the north fell by 1.3 million; 97 mines had been closed by 1992; Sunderland, the largest shipbuilding town in the world, no longer built ships; and Consett had lost the industry that had been a part of its fabric and identity for more than 140 years. I ask Conservative Members to contrast the huge bail-out that a Labour Government offered the financial services sector to protect jobs and investment with the brutal, bone-crushing and soul-destroying destruction that Margaret Thatcher's Government offered the shipbuilding, steel and mining industries, losing those very skills which we now need so very much.

There are those who say, "It was all part of the harsh reality of the new global order", but that is not true. Change was necessary, but it is the Government's job to protect communities from the impact of change. That change could have been managed; there could have been a transition and that could have been invested in. There was another way, and Nissan, which has been mentioned, provides an example of that. It is a great private sector success story that has been enabled by the support and investment of central Government, local authorities and the unions. The 2008 intervention by the previous Government through the car scrappage scheme and bringing forward training enabled Nissan to go through a difficult period and showed that intelligent active government is possible.

Mrs Thatcher's most meaningful legacy in the north-east is the unemployment across the region, but I would not like to close my remarks without paying her tribute. We have heard how she fought hard and tenaciously for the people she thought she represented. My tribute to her will be to continue to fight for the people I represent.

[William (Bill) Cash was born on 10 May 1940 and was educated at Lincoln College, Oxford, becoming an attorney. He entered Parliament at the May 1984 Stafford by-election but since 1997 has after local redistricting represented Stone. In 2011 he published a biography of his ancestor John Bright, a great parliamentarian, to coincide with the 200th anniversary of Bright's birth. Cash is also very proud of another ancestor who supported Samuel Smiles as he wrote *Self Help*.]

7.30 pm

Mr William Cash (Stone) (Con)

I spoke in the confidence motion on 22 November 1990, by which time Margaret Thatcher had decided not to stand again, and in circumstances that I do not believe any other Prime Minister, certainly of her stature, ever experienced. The irony of her going is that, unlike other Prime Ministers, who continued in office until a departure of their choosing, she lived out her retirement in the certain knowledge that on the issue that primarily brought about her fall — that of Europe — she had been right. They put her in a dungeon downstairs, underneath this Chamber. I went down there. She was dressed in black. She was traumatised. It was a disgrace. I do not know how it happened, but it was appalling to witness.

The event that precipitated her fall was the personal statement by the former Chancellor of the Exchequer, now the right hon. Lord Howe of Aberavon. I do not doubt his sincerity, but I challenge anybody to go through that speech and agree with a single word of it. There was a complete commitment to the exchange rate mechanism. There was the issue of economic and monetary union. There was this and that, but she was turfed out of office for no other reason than that they disagreed with her on Europe. Others have said that it was because of the poll tax or because they feared losing their seats, but it was not; it was because of that one main issue.

There is much more that I would like to say, but I will not. I will simply say, in conclusion, that in my judgment there will not be a Prime Minister of her stature for decades to come. I pay tribute to my right hon. Friend the Prime Minister for his veto and for his Bloomberg speech (*on 23 January 2013 David Cameron gave a speech at the Bloomberg offices in London in which he pledged a future referendum on UK membership of the EU*) on the five principles, but I also say that Margaret Thatcher, as Prime Minister, was the greatest defender of our freedom. She understood the European issue. She stood up for the freedom of people in this country and in Eastern and Central Europe. She was a great Prime Minister and I pay tribute to her.

[Geoffrey Clifton-Brown was born 23 March 1953 and educated at Eton and the Royal Agricultural College. A surveyor and farmer he represented Cirencester and Tewksbury 1992-1997 and after redistricting The Cotswolds 1997 to date.]

7.33 pm

Geoffrey Clifton-Brown (The Cotswolds) (Con)

Margaret Thatcher was probably this country's greatest peacetime Prime Minister. That is why I and a number of colleagues are here in the House today. We were inspired by Margaret Thatcher. There has been a certain amount of revisionism by one or two Opposition Members today about the malaise of the 1970s, but if they look at what really happened and at the mess this country was in when she took over in 1979, they will see the huge achievement she brought to this country.

She brought a huge achievement not only to this country, but to the world. She overcame what Winston Churchill foresaw when he made his famous speech at Westminster college, Missouri, and talked about the descent of the iron curtain across the continent of Europe. She saw that and went ahead with her great friend and ally, Ronald Reagan, to form a united front against what he called the "evil empire." We saw the breakdown of the iron curtain, and the people of Warsaw, Budapest, Bucharest, Tallinn and many other European capitals have a lasting reason to be incredibly grateful to her. I do an awful lot of work for the Westminster Foundation for Democracy, which works to build democracy around the world, an initiative that Margaret Thatcher started, for which I am extremely grateful.

The second time I encountered her was at the Conservative party conference in 1984. We were woken by an enormous bang just before 3 o'clock in the morning. It was, of course, the Brighton bomb. She came to the conference with fortitude and said that this nation's will would never be broken by terrorism, and that led to the solution in Northern Ireland.

It was the grocer's daughter from Grantham who broke the glass ceiling, as my right hon. Friend the Prime Minister said, and proved that in this country someone can rise right from the bottom to the top, and that if they work hard and do the right thing, they can rise to the maximum of their ability. She found people who had been in unfortunate circumstances but who, through hard work, had formed businesses and got to the top in this country. We saw a property-owning democracy in this country. Many of the formerly nationalised industries were sold off under her watch and put into the private sector, where they are now flourishing as worldwide businesses. That social movement in this country is one of her huge legacies.

She made this country believe in itself after the Falklands war. Many people had said it could not be done, but she took the risk and we recaptured the Falklands, and I am delighted that a few days ago 98% of the Falkland Islanders voted to remain with this country — *[Interruption.]* It was 99%. I think that only three people voted against.

Politicians of Margaret Thatcher's stature come about only once in a generation. She was the greatest peacetime Prime Minister.

[Dr Julian Lewis was born 26 September 1951 and was educated at Balliol
College and St Antony's College, both at Oxford. He was very active in a range of
political matters before entering Parliament in 1997 as MP for New Forest. His
PhD is in Strategic Studies.]

7.36 pm

Dr Julian Lewis (New Forest East) (Con)

It is a shock for those of us who are old enough to have been politically active
in the 1970s and '80s to realise that a 40-year-old MP today was just four years
old when Soviet deployment of deadly SS-20 missiles began in 1977. At the same
time, here at home, Labour MPs, including a sitting Cabinet Minister, were
being deselected in their constituencies by Marxist and militant infiltrators. I am
pleased that the hon. Member for Huddersfield (Mr Sheerman) rightly acknowl-
edged that it was Margaret Thatcher who saved the Labour party by forcing it to
expel the extremists and return to moderation.

To that I will add another short list that others could undoubtedly extend.
Margaret Thatcher gave the unions back to their members by making postal
ballots for trade union elections compulsory. She freed the Falklands and, indi-
rectly, caused the downfall of dictatorship in

Argentina — something that President Kirchner (*President of Argentina*)
would do well to remember. She secured the future of Britain's Trident nuclear
deterrent, as I trust my right hon. Friend the Prime Minister and the Leader of the
Opposition will continue to do, despite the blandishments of the absent Liberal
Democrats. She insisted on the deployment of NATO cruise missiles, without
which the hard-line grip on the Kremlin would undoubtedly have lasted longer.
She worked with Presidents Reagan and Gorbachev to secure the intermediate-
range nuclear forces treaty of 1987, which eliminated cruise missiles, the Persh-
ing missiles and the Soviet SS-20s, paving the way for what happened two years
later.

No one did more than Margaret Thatcher to bury the far left at home and
defeat totalitarian leftist extremism abroad. The history of freedom is in her debt,
as are we all.

[Mark Pritchard was born 22 November 1966 and was educated at London
Guildhall University. He was brought up in an orphanage and later in foster care
in public housing. After a career in marketing he has represented The Wrekin
since 2005 and is married to Sondra from California who was a PanAm flight
attendant.]

7.38 pm

Mark Pritchard (The Wrekin) (Con)

I would like to put on the record my thanks to all her loyal staff over so many years, not least Crawfie and Mark Worthington, her dedicated chief of staff right up to the very end, who is no doubt working on her behalf as we speak.

For me personally, and for millions of people in this country, Margaret Thatcher was an inspiration. She was also an inspiration to people all over the world. At home, she was the personification — the epitome — of aspiration. She rightly reminded us that whatever a person's background — whatever their race, religion, gender or sexuality — if they worked and studied hard they could get on and succeed. No mountain was too high to climb and no dream was too ambitious to fulfil.

She was also right to believe in sound money, as the Prime Minister pointed out earlier, and in strong defence, and to believe that the state should have a strong role, but not a domineering role or a nanny role. She was right to believe in the power of the individual to win, whatever obstacles were put in their way by their background or their circumstances, and to believe that Britain still had a vital role to play in the world.

For millions abroad, she was a torchbearer for liberty, freedom and democracy. She gave hope to the hopeless. She gave courage to the disheartened at home and abroad. For millions in the grip of the Soviet Union, she was the Iron Lady, prepared to stand up against oppression, tyranny and opposition. The same oppression reigns over North Korea and Iran today, and we must show the same resolve.

Margaret Thatcher governed for all and led for all. She was a conviction politician and not, as we have heard from some on the Opposition Benches, a prejudice politician. Perhaps the best tribute we can give Lady Thatcher today is to join in her unending belief that Britain's best days are yet to come. I join my right hon. Friend the Prime Minister in paying tribute to Lady Thatcher and saying that she was a great Prime Minister, a great leader and a great Briton. She was Mrs Aspiration.

[John Baron was born 21 June 1959 and educated at Jesus College, University of Cambridge. An army captain (1984-1987) he later worked in banking. He entered the Commons as MP for Billericay in 2001 later redistricted to form Basildon and Billericay.]

7.41 pm

Mr John Baron (Basildon and Billericay) (Con)

Margaret Thatcher was once asked who wore the trousers in her household. It was at the height of her power, and she retorted quickly, "I do, but I also wash and iron them." It made a good impression and reminded everybody of the fact that she was a very humble person with great humility. Many colleagues on both sides of the House who are more eloquent than I have testified to her many qualities and achievements, her strength of character, her belief in conviction politics and her belief in freedom, democracy and opportunity.

I would like, if I may, to focus on one accusation levelled against her both by Opposition Members in this debate and by the media more generally, which is that she was a divisive figure. If those who levy that charge mean that she intentionally went out to create division, conflict or whatever else, I disagree. If they mean, however, that she, through her policies and convictions, forced people to face the facts and to face what was obvious, I wholeheartedly concur.

I am honoured to take part in this tribute debate — we have heard some great speeches today — but there is a danger that we will forget just how bad the economic situation was in the 1960s and 1970s, as well as what she had to tackle and to deal with to bring this country round. We forget that for the best part of two decades successive Governments had pursued inflationary policies to try to gain full employment or something near to it. The unions had become all-powerful and they could not be tamed, with successive wild-cat strikes. All sorts of economic chaos resulted. We had Chancellors going to the IMF cap in hand, the three-day week, the lights turned off, the rubbish piled high in the streets and the bodies not being buried in cemeteries.

If I can add anything of value to this debate, looking at the age profile of many of my colleagues, it is that having lived through the 1970s I can testify to what it was like. It was absolutely dire — [Hon. Members: "It was horrible."] As my colleagues say, it was horrible. The atmosphere was full of pessimism. There was no hope and no aspiration. We were the sick man of Europe. She, through her policies, her conviction and her belief in aspiration, opportunity, kicking back Government controls and reducing Government spending, brought this country around. If testimony is required to how successful she was, we need only to look at the fact that very few of her major policies — I can hardly think of any — were reversed by the Governments who succeeded hers. Perhaps her greatest legacy is that she converted the Labour party from a party that was doing no good for this country, in the sense that it was pursuing extreme left-wing policies, and dragged it kicking and screaming to the centre of the political landscape.

In conclusion, she once said that it is no use being someone in politics, one has to do something with politics. That will be her lasting legacy and this country will ever be grateful for that approach.

[Nick Gibb was born 3 September 1960 and was educated at the University of Durham. He worked as a handyman, on a kibbutz, and later trained as an accountant. He became MP for Bognor Regis and Littlehampton in 1997.]

7.45 pm

Mr Nick Gibb (Bognor Regis and Littlehampton) (Con)

Many in this House can speak more eloquently about Lady Thatcher as a person than I can, particularly my hon. Friends the Members for Bournemouth West (Conor Burns) and for Maldon (Mr Whittingdale), who made moving speeches. To me, Lady Thatcher was a more distant figure whom I met at party events and as a parliamentary candidate hoping for a photograph with her for the elections. Whenever I met her, I always found her kind, supportive and interested in how I was getting on.

As a student, when I was a member of the national committee of the Federation of Conservative Students, we met Mrs Thatcher in Downing street. I was writing a pamphlet calling for the end to the National Union of Students' closed shop and urged her to include it in her trade union reforms. I remember her looking at me straight in the eyes and saying, "I'm glad to see you're coming round to my way of thinking". I was, of course, as were large parts of our nation and many other nations across the globe. (*As early as 1970-1974 as Education Secretary Margaret had wanted to deal with this issue of the NUS Closed Shop. You had to join the union to get your degree.*)

Others have talked about Lady Thatcher's role in ending the cold war, her part in bringing freedom and prosperity to the former Soviet empire and the positive lasting legacy of her speech to the College of Europe in Bruges, but it is her role in turning around Britain and restoring our economy, which benefited many millions of people in this country, that I believe is so important. Lady Thatcher provided leadership to a cause and to a country. She led the battle of ideas with the idea that an overweening state crowds out the private sector and free enterprise and the innovation that comes with them; the idea that tax rates of 83% and 98% stifle initiative — a battle she won so convincingly that no subsequent Government have dared even to contemplate raising rates to such levels; and the idea that the money supply was key to controlling inflation, which was again a battle that she won so convincingly that it was a Labour Government who established the Monetary Policy Committee. She fought the battle of ideas with courage and, in doing so, inspired a generation.

I was 14 when Mrs Thatcher became the leader of the Conservative party and it was her leadership, her articulation of ideas and her determination to do the right thing that inspired me — and many others — to take an interest in politics. Her economic reforms resulted in GDP per head rising in real terms from £7,700 in 1979 to more than £10,000 by 1990. The wealth that that created did not did not just go to champagne bars in the City. It resulted, for example, in the proportion of houses with central heating rising from just 54% in 1979 to more than 80% by 1991 and in the proportion of owner-occupied housing rising from 55% to 66% by 1990. She truly was a transformational leader — a leader who changed this nation for the good and for good — yet the hostility to her from the left and, indeed, from some on the Conservative side of the House was remorseless. She stood up to that hostility because she believed she was right, and she was right.

As a newly selected parliamentary candidate all set to fight the Labour stronghold of Stoke-on-Trent Central, I was devastated when in November 1990 Conservative Members of Parliament deposed her as the leader of our party. To this day I wish my party had not done so, but as Cecil Parkinson, another great statesman of the 1980s for whom the battle of ideas was always the spur, said:

"Her ideas and vision live on."

He was right, too: her ideas, her vision and her achievements will always live on.

[Andrew Rosindell was born 17 March 1966 and attended Rise Park and later Marshalls Park School. He worked as a journalist, PR consultant, and researcher before being elected as MP for Romford in 2001.]

7.49 pm

Andrew Rosindell (Romford) (Con)

It is an honour to rise today to pay tribute to someone whom I have always believed to be our greatest peacetime Prime Minister, and one of the finest — if not the finest — political leaders of the Conservative party, whom many of us know to have been a compassionate and kind human being. Lady Thatcher had courage, determination and principle, but she had patriotism deep inside her. She loved this country; she was inspired by standing up for Britain and she showed that in and out of office and wore it with pride. She wore the Union flag regularly on her jacket, and showed that when the chips were down and it mattered most, her instincts were always to put the interests of our country first. In no better example was that tested than when Argentina invaded the Falkland Islands in 1982. I wonder whether those islands would be free today had she not been our Prime Minister.

She was a kind person who treated everyone as an equal. She was humble, and good in many ways that the public never got to see. She had a Christian upbringing and throughout her time as Prime Minister, and throughout her life, she upheld those Christian values. She supported the Queen and our constitution. When the Queen and the royal family had a difficult period in the early '90s, she was on the television and in the media making it clear that the country should unite behind Her Majesty. She understood what it was to stand up for Britain and why it was so important to do so.

Margaret Thatcher showed bulldog spirit as well as compassion for the British people and people across the world. She fought for freedom for the people of Eastern Europe, and the people of Latin America were free because she defeated the dictatorship in Argentina. She liked younger people and encouraged the next generation. Many of us here today from the Prime Minister downwards were inspired by Lady Thatcher. It is her legacy that we inherit and that we must protect, uphold and advance still further. We must fight to put the interests of our country first, as Lady Thatcher always did and would have continued to do had she remained in office for longer.

[Daniel Kawczynski was born 24 January 1972 in Warsaw, Poland, and after relocating to the UK was educated at the University of Stirling. He was an account manager in the telecommunications industry before entering the Commons as MP for Shrewsbury and Atcham in 2005.]

7.52 pm

Daniel Kawczynski (Shrewsbury and Atcham) (Con)

When I was first selected as the parliamentary candidate for Shrewsbury in 2002, I was asked by the Conservative Women's Organisation to come to the Conservative social club. There was a huge portrait of Margaret Thatcher and a seating plan of the dinner from when she came to Shrewsbury in 1981. All the ladies — Mrs Elaine Weston and others — spoke to me in glowing terms and with tremendous respect about their enormous pride that Margaret Thatcher had visited Shrewsbury. Although 20 years had passed since that occasion, they could recount almost every single aspect of her trip to Shrewsbury, such was their profound love and admiration for this lady. Others have spoken about conviction politics, but when politicians are generally not seen in a good light, we can all learn a great deal from the tremendous respect that this lady generated among millions of people in our country.

When I was first elected to Parliament in 2005, I remember being invited to have dinner with Margaret Thatcher at the Carlton club. Sitting next to her at dinner, I was absolutely mesmerised. My heart was beating very, very strongly, and it was one of the most fascinating experiences of my life. Afterwards, when photographs of us were taken, I remember towering over her because of my height of 6 feet 9 inches, but thinking how she towered over me in every other respect.

As somebody of Polish origin, I can say that Margaret Thatcher's visit to the shipyards at Gdansk in 1988 was transformational and gave the people of Poland great hope that there was the possibility of defeating communism. Nobody did more to give the people of Eastern Europe that tremendous hope that a better day would come. I remember visiting my beloved grandfather who was a great Polish patriot. Late at night, we listened to the BBC World Service — of course, it was illegal to do so — very quietly and with the curtains drawn so that nobody would hear us. I remember tears swelling in my grandfather's eyes, such was the tremendous hope that she gave through those broadcasts to those imprisoned people living behind the iron curtain.

Finally, I remember being chairman of the university of Stirling Conservative association in 1992. Our local MP was Michael Forsyth and we were told that we would lose all our seats in Scotland in 1992, and that we would lose Stirling. I was desperately upset and spent the election going up lamp posts putting up "Vote Conservative" signs because I was so tall the socialists could not pull them down. I was so disheartened because I felt that Neil Kinnock was so left-wing that if that man got into office he would destroy everything that my heroine had built up for this country.

My first chance to meet Margaret Thatcher was when she came to speak at a nearby rally. She gave me hope, and the next day I went with my best friend to the bookies. (*Main Street legal gambling shops*). I had only £700 left until I started my summer job, and I put £500 on the Tories to win with a majority of more than 20. Thanks to Margaret Thatcher, I made the best investment of my life.

[Lee Scott was born 6 April 1956 and was educated at the London College of Distributive Trades. He worked in sales and fundraising before becoming MP for Ilford North in 2005.]

7.56 pm

Mr Lee Scott (Ilford North) (Con)

I will say a few brief words about my memories of Margaret Thatcher. I met her on four or five occasions, the first of which was in the constituency of my hon. Friend the Member for Romford (Andrew Rosindell). I said to her at the time that I was a bit concerned about my desire to be a Member of Parliament. I left school aged 15 and did not have many qualifications, but I had a desire to work and help people. She said to me, "If you have the desire to do it and want to work and help people, then do it." She inspired me to be here today and, like many Members from across the House, I can honestly say that I would not necessarily be here today if it were not for Margaret Thatcher. She will always have my gratitude for that.

On other occasions, when Margaret Thatcher walked into a room people knew that it was somebody special and that they were in the presence of a figure who would go down in history. If we put the clock forward 100 years, I am sure that people will still remember Winston Churchill, Margaret Thatcher, Mr Attlee, perhaps even Mr Blair, certainly the current Prime Minister — [Hon. Members: " Hear, hear.] — I had to get that in. Without any doubt, however, they will remember Margaret Thatcher as a great Briton and somebody who saved our country. May she rest in peace. God bless her.

[Nigel Adams was born 30 November 1966 and was educated at Selby High School leaving aged 17 to set up a telecommunications company he later sold to a publicly quoted enterprise. He has represented Selby and Ainsty since 2010.]

7.58 pm

Nigel Adams (Selby and Ainsty) (Con)

I recall as a schoolboy at the end of the 1970s the national decline, the endless strikes, the lights going off, and the rubbish not being collected. Ordinary people were simply fed up with how our once proud country had been turned into a basket case. Margaret Thatcher turned our country around and saved it. She wanted to improve ordinary people's lives by giving them more personal freedom and encouraging them to stand on their own two feet. She certainly did that for me. I was a young person from a working-class background, the grandson of coal miners. All of a sudden, there was a national figure and a leader of our country who made it clear that people can achieve success, whatever their background or walk of life. That was a politician I could relate to. She is the reason why I am standing in this Chamber today.

I had the pleasure of meeting Baroness Thatcher on a couple of occasions. Like my hon. Friend the Member for Shrewsbury and Atcham (Daniel Kawczynski), I was petrified to be in her presence. I greatly remember, and will always cherish, her words of encouragement to me when I was a candidate and, after the election, when I told her I had won the Selby and Ainsty seat.

Baroness Thatcher was a conviction politician and a truly great Briton, and we owe her a great debt.

[Harriet Baldwin was born 2 May 1960 and was educated at Lady Margaret Hall, Oxford, and McGill University, Montreal, Canada. She worked in banking for 20 years before winning West Worcestershire in 2010.]

8.1 pm

Harriett Baldwin (West Worcestershire) (Con)

It is a remarkable statistic that only 100 women in the history of this country have become Conservative MPs. Lady Thatcher played a crucial role not only in inspiring us, but in raising money for us. I met her at fundraisers for "Women2Win" or for individual female candidates, including current Members of the House.

Lady Thatcher was always absolutely remarkable in her steadfastness and support for women in the Conservative party, but — this comes better from a Conservative woman MP — she was also always absolutely immaculately dressed. She always looked fantastic. Has it not been wonderful over the past few days watching those old news reels and seeing that, on every occasion she faced as the first female leader in the Western world, she always wore exactly the right thing? Whether she was in a tank in Germany or dancing with a former movie star — Ronald Reagan — she always looked impeccable. That held true even very recently, when my hon. Friend the Member for Bournemouth West (Conor Burns) invited some of the new intake MPs to meet her. She asked, with that piercing curiosity, "What's your majority?"

It is only right that we pay tribute to Lady Thatcher's personal assistant, Cynthia Crawford, who lives in Worcestershire, and who made such a huge contribution to Lady Thatcher's life. Cynthia was such a loyal friend throughout Lady Thatcher's retirement years. She ensured that Lady Thatcher always looked impeccable — they worked together very well on that.

Another secret about Lady Thatcher's later years is that, as a result of that friendship, she came frequently to Worcestershire. She spent quiet retreats and holidays at the cottage in the woods in Malvern, where she found peace and beauty in the country. She grew to love the Malvern hills — she was inspired by Elgar, who was born there. It gives me and the people of West Worcestershire great satisfaction to know that she enjoyed the beauty of the great constituency that I have the privilege to represent. I am so pleased that she found peace there on earth, and I wish her peace in the next life.

[Nadhim Zahawi was born 2 June 1967 and was educated at University College, London where he read Chemical Engineering. After a marketing career he co-founded and became CEO of YouGov. He was returned in 2010 as MP for Stratford-on-Avon.]

8.4 pm

Nadhim Zahawi (Stratford-on-Avon) (Con)

When I was selected as a parliamentary candidate in February 2010, Margaret Thatcher was one of the first to send a handwritten letter of congratulations, with an invitation to join her for drinks. I turned up in London — she had invited a handful of new candidates — and she wanted to know how things were in Stratford-on-Avon. I explained that the people were worried about the state of the country's finances. Her sound advice was this: "We need to win, Nadhim, to ensure that we can fix things again, and make the tough decisions the country needs."

Lady Thatcher's gift to this country was to make it great again. Her gift to the world was to confront aggressive communism and the cold war. Many colleagues have spoken eloquently about what Margaret Thatcher meant to them. I want to end by quoting two short notes I have received that show what she meant to those whom she cared most about: the people of her country.

The first is from a serving soldier in the Household Cavalry, who writes: "She was a real legend who walked her own path, stirred passions on both sides of the fence and made a sick Britain great again."

The second note is from Dr Naeem Ahmed, who works in the NHS. He writes: "My dad is a 1st generation Bangladeshi who arrived here at 13."

Dr Ahmed's dad was upset at Margaret Thatcher's passing, and said: "She was a leader on the side of the small businessman".

The testimonies of those young men prove that the great lady will live on.

Margaret Thatcher made this country understand the importance of living within its means. She knew that only when we achieve that can we be ambitious for, and positive about, our position in the world. Next week, the country she loved will mark her passing. It is right that we do so with the full ceremony of Church and state, because 30 years ago, in a storm-lashed corner of the south Atlantic, she stood up for the inalienable rights of British citizens, despite coming under great pressure to look the other way. In doing so, she showed the world that we are not yet finished, and that Britain's name and Britain's word still matters. She gave us hope that our finest hour lies not in the past, but in our future. For that, the nation owes her its thanks.

[Daniel (Dan) Byles was born 24 June 1974 and educated at the University of Leeds and Nottingham Trent University. By age 27 he was the youngest major in the British Army and is a mountaineer, sailor, ocean rower, and polar adventurer. In 2010 he became the MP for North Warwickshire.]

8.8 pm

Dan Byles (North Warwickshire) (Con)

Margaret Thatcher was a great inspiration to me and my family, and particularly to my mother. When my parents divorced when I was nine years old, my mother became the single mother of two children. She was inspired by Margaret Thatcher's example and words and did not look to others for help when she faced the classic problems that single mothers face. How do they provide for their children? If they cannot afford child care, what do they do during school holidays? What do they do when their children are sick? With no experience whatever of running a business, my mother established a small shop with our home above it, which enabled her to look after my sister and I, and yet be there for us when we were not at school.

Both my parents left school at age 16 and neither went on to university. My sister left school at age 16 and did not go on to university. I will always be incredibly grateful to the Conservative Government that Margaret Thatcher led in the 1980s for the assisted places scheme. I had an assisted place at Warwick school. As a result, I was the first and only member of my family to stay at school beyond 16 and go to university. Ultimately, as a result, I gained a commission in the British Army and eventually became an MP. I therefore feel honoured to be here today.

I will keep my speech very brief, Mr Deputy Speaker, and finish by reading the full quotation for the Deputy Prime Minister:

"There is no such thing as society. There is a living tapestry of men and women and people and the beauty of that tapestry and the quality of our lives will depend upon how much each of us is prepared to take responsibility for ourselves and each of us prepared to turn round and help by our own efforts those who are unfortunate."

[Michael Ellis was born 13 October 1967 and educated at the University of Buckingham becoming an attorney. In 2010 he was elected MP for Northampton North.]

8.10 pm

Michael Ellis (Northampton North) (Con)

Lady Thatcher rose from being a grocer's daughter in a northern English town to become a titan of the 20th century — a true colossus on the political stage. She was a deeply principled leader and was prepared to do unpopular things. In that, she is followed by my right hon. Friend the Prime Minister. What strikes me most is her tangible moral courage and her indefatigable bravery. Her political courage, about which many colleagues have spoken, was rooted in principle and in a determination to do what she thought was right for this country.

One of her best friends was Airey Neave MP, a hero of the second world war who was blown up by an IRA bomb in a cowardly attack here at the Houses of Parliament in 1979. She was defiant about that afterwards. Likewise, she displayed steadfast defiance in the face of the murderous IRA attack at the Grand hotel in Brighton in 1984, which killed five people. She insisted on carrying on and gave her conference speech the following day, apparently despite a serious warning of another bomb. She was indefatigable and courageous in every respect.

Although it is popular for those who did not know her to caricature Lady Thatcher as uncaring, it is quite clear that she was deeply compassionate and considerate, as her staff and those who were bereaved will today testify. She worked harder than anyone else; she was better informed than anyone else; she was magnificent.

As several Presidents of the United States have said, she was one of America's greatest friends. She recognised the tremendous force for good and for international democracy that the United States is in the world and the leadership that it still gives to the oppressed around the world. It should not be forgotten that she was also a true friend to the Jewish people and to Israel.

I pay tribute to those who were devoted to her in her personal life, such as Mark Worthington and my hon. Friend the Member for Bournemouth West (Conor Burns). They have been assiduous in their care and devotion, and clearly loved her dearly.

In conclusion, she was a paragon of duty and service. Despite not knowing her anything like as well as several of my colleagues, may I still say that I will miss her?

[Bob Stewart was born 7 July 1949 and was educated at the Royal Military Academy, Sandhurst. He served in the British Army 1969-1996 rising to the rank of Colonel. He became MP for Beckenham in 2010.]

8.13 pm

Bob Stewart (Beckenham) (Con)

Many hon. Members have paid tribute to Margaret Thatcher's care for the armed forces. Thirty years ago, after my rifle company, A Company the Cheshires, was blown to bits, she flew into Northern Ireland and came with me to Musgrave Park military hospital. Thirty-five of my men had been wounded and six had been killed. She went around the beds and stopped, talked, wept, caressed, sat with and inspired those men. I was incredibly impressed.

A year later, again in Northern Ireland, Margaret Thatcher visited my company at Aughnacloy in south Tyrone. She flew in with the Special Air Service (*the UK's elite army special forces unit*) and I briefed her. I asked her, "Prime Minister, do you have any questions?" She said, "Make sure, Bob, that I meet all the soldiers who were wounded a year ago." She did. My goodness, that lady — that Iron Lady — had the heart of a lion and that lion's heart was made of gold.

[Margot James was born 28 August 1957 and was educated at the London School of Economics. She achieved early fame after being regularly photographed with Margaret Thatcher both at the Conservative Party Annual Conference and on the morning when members of the Federation of Conservative Students presented their leader with 50 red roses to mark her birthday. Following a very successful career building a health oriented PR and clinical trials company in 2010 she became MP for Stourbridge.]

8.15 pm

Margot James (Stourbridge) (Con)

Shortly before he died, my father said to me, "If you get to meet Margaret Thatcher, tell her from me there were only two politicians in my lifetime who made a difference and she was one of them." The other was Churchill.

My father spoke from personal experience. Born in Coventry, he left his council school at the age of 14. He got going in business with a single lorry and delivered coal from the black country around the Birmingham area. By 1963, he had built his business up into a publicly quoted company. By then, one of his interests was a car delivery business. Ten years later, the whole enterprise was teetering on the edge of bankruptcy thanks to the Transport and General Workers Union. "All out" was the familiar refrain and it meant that any money that anybody had any hope of making would disappear in ever more fantastic wage settlements, sustained by wildcat strikes, violent picket lines and the ruthless closed shop system.

There is much talk of Margaret Thatcher being a divisive figure. She certainly became a hate figure for those whose power she challenged and eventually overcame. I sympathise very much with people who lost their jobs in the manufacturing industries that declined in the 1980s. However, a myth has grown up — propounded, I am afraid, in this Chamber this afternoon — that the policies pursued by Margaret Thatcher's Governments were responsible for the decline in manufacturing and the closure of industrial plant and coal pits. That is to deliberately ignore the fact that the decline began soon after the war and accelerated dramatically in the 1960s and 1970s.

The strikes, restrictive working practices and outrageous pay settlements led to a very negative climate for investment. Technological change was either resisted wholesale or was allowed on sufferance and, crucially, on condition that the same manning levels were maintained. Britain therefore lost and lost again in world markets.

By the late 1960s — a full decade before Margaret Thatcher became Prime Minister — it was cheaper to import coils of steel than to buy them from the overmanned British steel works. By the mid-1970s, our old industries were kept going only by ever-increasing Government subsidy and by nationalisation. That was ultimately unaffordable and diverted money from investment in new industries and services that would provide employment in the future. To lay the blame at Margaret Thatcher's door for all that is to shoot the messenger.

I did have the chance to pass on my father's message. I did so in the presence of my late mother who, at the age of almost 90, finally got to meet Margaret Thatcher. All Mrs Thatcher could say to my mother was, "How kind of you to come." She exuded such kindness and humility that I have never forgotten it. It is a shame that the public did not see more of that trait.

To conclude, the convictions, passions and principles that guided Margaret Thatcher came to be known as Thatcherism. Her determination to stand up for Britain in Europe, for the freedoms of those who were oppressed by the Soviet Union, for the working people who wanted a stake in their future and to get on, and, above all, for the pride of Britain, is unequalled in my lifetime. It was a privilege to witness it all and I am deeply grateful to have benefited personally, both politically and in business, from the policies that she pursued with such bravery and determination. May she rest in peace.

[Heather Wheeler was born 14 May 1959. She served in local government and worked in insurance before winning South Derbyshire in 2010.]

8.19 pm

Heather Wheeler (South Derbyshire) (Con)

I represent an old mining area, and, as folk might imagine, some of the e-mails that I have received have been quite lively. However, I have been reminded that unemployment in my area is now 2.8%. The old mines have gone. People remember the difficulties that arose between the Union of Democratic Mineworkers, whose members did not strike, and the National Union of Mineworkers, whose members did, but people now have jobs. People have reinvented themselves.

Some of the e-mails that I have received have been very passionate about the future that Mrs Thatcher gave to our country, and the aspiration that she gave to it. I certainly know that I am in this Chamber because of her. As a 17-year-old, I wrote a paper about why British Leyland should be privatised rather than nationalised, because it was losing £1 million a week. What an outrageous situation it was — although quite why a 17-year-old knew facts like that, I cannot imagine.

The change in our country has been phenomenal, and all the groundwork was laid by Mrs Thatcher. I was so pleased to meet her, and I love the photograph that I have of her with me. When I finally became leader of our council — which had always been a Labour council — the first thing that I did was to put a portrait of Maggie Thatcher in my office. I do not think that there had ever been a picture of her in any of the council offices before, except on a dartboard. That was a major change, and it meant that South Derbyshire was turning around. The future was bright — the future was blue — and we owe her so much.

[David Morris — see above]

8.21 pm

David Morris (Morecambe and Lunesdale) (Con)

To me, Mrs Thatcher was a huge inspiration, not because of her willingness to make difficult decisions but because she made me feel, at a time of bleak prospects, that there was hope for the future. I started my first business as a Manpower allowance recipient, and, indeed, I entered my first job as a "yopper". I do not know whether anyone else remembers the youth opportunities programme. At that time, after the late 1970s, we did not have much of an industry left. I grew up abroad because my father could not afford to live here in the late 1970s, but he came back after Margaret Thatcher became Prime Minister, purely and simply because — as he said — "I can afford to live in my own country again".

Those who are young and of no political persuasion whatsoever may start to understand that this country has a lot of good going for it, but no one seems to say that it has a lot of good going for it. I have lived all over the world, and I have seen unimaginable poverty. I have lived in places where families were begging on the streets. That experience is hard to describe. Then I came back to Britain, where there was a free health service and free education. Here I reach out to the Opposition: all that was begun by the Clement Attlee Government. However, Thatcher actually embellished it.

We are here today to honour a lady whose political legacy — as was said earlier — will outlive us all, and will continue well into the future. Today I was very disappointed to see, in the left-leaning press, reports of the shenanigans of young people celebrating her untimely demise. If those people had been around 35 years ago, as I was, they would understand what things were like in the late 1970s. Young people cannot imagine a time when the bins were not collected, when there were power cuts and a three-day week, when the dead were not being buried, and when — worst of all — our democracy was being held to ransom by the trade union movement. Thanks to Margaret Thatcher, they need not suffer from such appalling problems. She made higher education possible for the masses. Sadly, I did not benefit from it, but now I am here with you lot, which says a great deal.

We should see things in perspective. Eighteen months or two years ago, David Hasselhoff came to the House. Everyone remembers him singing on the Berlin wall when it came down. He turned to his manager and said "Larry, did I tell you I brought the wall down?" His manager said "I think it was that Iron Lady they are making a film about at this moment in time." He said "You're right, Larry. I should audition for the part of Ronald Reagan, shouldn't I?" He is trying to save the wall for the sake of remembrance, but we should remember the legacy that Margaret Thatcher gave. As a child of the Thatcher era, I was privileged to grow up and prosper, and I am privileged to be here on this day as a Member of Parliament to — in a way — celebrate what she left behind.

[Dominic Raab was born 25 February 1974 and was educated at Lady Margaret Hall, Oxford as well as at Cambridge. An attorney, he joined the Foreign Office before becoming in 2010 the MP for Esher and Walton. His book *The Assault on Liberty* was very well received and reviewed.]

8.24 pm

Mr Dominic Raab (Esher and Walton) (Con)

Unlike many who have spoken today, I met Lady Thatcher only once, but I was nevertheless touched by her unique blend of resolve and kindness. She wrote to me after the last election, as she wrote to many of my new colleagues, urging us to "carry the fight to our opponents whenever the time comes".

Her twilight years never dimmed that most tenacious of spirits.

Of course she had her critics and her enemies — did anyone ever get anything done without them? — but this was a woman who won three elections by appealing across tribal political divides and across society. For me, what stands out about her legacy is the fact that she was an underdog fighting for the underdog. Yes, she was renowned for her economic leadership; yes, she reminds us today that we have a choice, and that if we rise to the challenge, our better days lie ahead and not behind us; but she would never have held office for so long had she not carried people with her.

She may have caused division within the Westminster village, but in the country, because of her, 6 million took a stake in British businesses, and 1 million bought their council homes. (*Low ball — more like 2 to 3 million*) For many more — including refugees like my father, who came here with nothing — she nurtured the flicker of aspiration, inspiring people, regardless of their background, to believe that as a result of hard work, their dreams of prosperity and a better quality of life lay within their grasp. That message resonated not just in Britain, but around the world. As cold war historian John Lewis Gaddis has observed, "It was a blow for Marxism, for if capitalism really did exploit the masses, why did so many among them cheer the 'iron lady'?"

She was fired by a moral clarity that drove decisive action against perilous odds. We think of the Iranian embassy siege, and of the Falklands. Her most basic insight on Europe, shortly after she took office, remains prescient. She said:

> "We believe in a free Europe, not a standardised Europe. Diminish that variety within the member states, and you impoverish the whole community."

That neatly sums up the malaise that afflicts the European Union today.

As others have said, Margaret Thatcher made the political weather. She forged a new consensus. That is why, after the 1997 election, the cover of *Time* magazine pronounced her legacy the real winner. That is why Tony Blair wrote in his memoirs:

> Mrs Thatcher was absolutely on the side of history...in recognising that as people became more prosperous, they wanted the freedom to spend their money as they chose; and they didn't want a big state getting in the way of that liberation by suffocating people in uniformity, in the drabness and dullness of the state monopoly... Anything else was to ignore human nature.

When Caesar learnt of Mark Antony's death, he lamented:

> The breaking of so great a thing should make
> A greater crack.

Today, we ensure that the passing of so great a statesman echoes from this Chamber. Margaret Thatcher was the ultimate conviction politician: our greatest peacetime leader.

[Fiona Bruce was born 26 March 1957 and studied law at the University of Manchester and Chester Law College. From 1981 on she worked as an attorney, founding her own law firm before being elected in 2010 MP for Congleton. She is not to be confused with Fiona Bruce, presenter of *Antiques Roadshow* on PBS.]

8.27 pm

Fiona Bruce (Congleton) (Con)

I remember experiencing, as a student in the 1970s, the power cuts and the three-day week. I remember studying by candlelight. I recall literally crying with sadness and shame as I watched rubbish piling up in our streets on television screens and heard of families who were unable to bury their dead. Then came Margaret Thatcher, a Prime Minister who showed remarkable political leadership in standing up to and ending that industrial anarchy. She restored our nation's much-needed dignity, and my profound respect for her, and that of millions of people across our nation, was birthed then and has endured ever since.

Clearly, she blazed a trail as a woman, and as importantly for me, she stood out as a conviction politician. She had clear beliefs, and she lived and led by them, and in doing so inspired me and many others — beliefs such as the importance of personal and social responsibility and accountability; of hard work and enterprise; of the imperative of endeavouring to balance the books, whether with a household budget, a business or when managing public funds; of family and strong communities created and sustained by active citizenship; of a sense of duty, service and a moral code, no doubt influenced by her father, a Methodist lay preacher; and of a strong nation state, but not a state that nationalises society.

For me, having and adhering to those convictions as she did, distinguished Margaret Thatcher from a mere politician and raised her to the status of stateswoman. Just by being there as Prime Minister, she was a standard bearer for women, but she was very much a wife and mother too, and I would like to pay tribute to her and Denis for their enduring commitment to their strong marriage, which I am sure in large part enabled her to fulfil her role as the nation's leader. As a woman, no doubt she was many times deeply hurt within herself by the outrageous slings and arrows that accompanied political leadership, but with Denis's support she weathered them all with dignity and composure in the service of this nation, and for her brave example we owe her our thanks.

She must too have been hurt when her view of society was utterly traduced, after words she used in a magazine interview were quoted totally out of context. Of course she believed in society, and in strong, enduring societies made up of committed relationships of men, women and families, each playing their part. In that same interview, she spoke of our "duty...to look after our neighbours".

It reflects ill on those who misinterpreted her on this issue.

Likewise, to attribute to her the excesses of materialism, selfishness and greed, as some in the media have done, is wrong: an equally gross distortion. Enterprise, as I learnt from her over the years of building a business, is about creating something that contributes to the welfare and well-being not just of the individuals working within it, but of the community and country. It is about having a sense of social responsibility as to what to do with success, if that follows.

Margaret Thatcher epitomised for me the fact that one individual, given hard work and commitment, can make a remarkable difference. I am sure that even she would have agreed that no one gets everything right all of the time, but her example has inspired me to believe that whether at home, at work or in our communities, whether in voluntary groups, public service or further afield, every single individual has the potential to make a real and positive difference and a remarkable contribution, whatever their circumstances, sphere or start in life.

It has been a privilege to pay tribute in this place to Margaret Thatcher, one of the greatest leaders our country has ever known. In closing, may I reflect again on the kindness that she exhibited to so many. May I finish with a tribute from several ladies who serve in the Members' Tea Room? I asked them today whether they knew her, and unprompted they immediately responded, "Oh, she was lovely. A true leader. A wonderful lady. We loved her."

[Robert Buckland was born 22 September 1968 and was educated at the University of Durham. An attorney, he became MP for South Swindon in 2010.]

8.32 pm

Mr Robert Buckland (South Swindon) (Con)

At a time when politicians seemed to loom very large in the lives of us all, Margaret Thatcher loomed the largest. Thinking about it, the role of politicians now looms somewhat less in our lives precisely because of what she achieved. She came to power in an age when far too many of the major decisions affecting day-to-day life in this country were made directly by the state, which possessed far too much control over too many of the levers of power in Britain. Her greatest legacy is that she ceded control over many of those levers and gave power back to the people.

Margaret Thatcher's uncanny knack of understanding the aspirations and concerns of the people of this country was reflected in her deep commitment to wider home ownership and her passionate belief in trusting families and individuals to make the most of the key decisions affecting their lives. She shared the instinctive suspicion of the British people for those who wielded and abused unaccountable power. Her fight to tame militant trade unionism here at home and her fight against Soviet hegemony abroad were testament to that innate understanding. The message for us today, in the House and beyond, is that we should not shy away from facing up to those who abuse power, whether in the form of a poorly regulated banking sector or monopolistic self-interest.

Much has been made of Margaret Thatcher's background as a scientist, and there is no doubt that that was important, but she was also a lawyer. She was a qualified member of my profession, and I firmly believe that that honed her skill not only for debate but for analysing evidence and for testing it in argument before putting it to the people. She developed policy by debate and discussion, but once her mind was made up she was determined and took action. She did not shy away from the maxim that it was deeds, not words, that mattered.

The hon. Member for Huddersfield (Mr Sheerman) described Mrs Thatcher as a Gladstonian Liberal, but she was far more than that. She was driven by ideas but not ideology, which makes her very firmly a Conservative. She understood the value of meaningful tradition, and her beliefs in freedom, the rule of law and the old Tory slogan, "Trust the people", shall and must endure.

[Mark Menzies was born 18 May 1971 and educated at the University of Glasgow. He worked in retailing before becoming the MP for Fylde in 2010.]

8.35 pm

Mark Menzies (Fylde) (Con)

My mother was widowed at an early age and forced to raise me on her own. She was a Labour voter. She worked in a factory and she was a trade union member. She often had to get up at 5 o'clock in the morning to catch the bus, determined that she could give me the best possible chance in life. A good education and stability were important to my mum. Balancing working shifts and doing her own child care was always a huge challenge. One of Margaret Thatcher's key policies provided my mother with a huge lifeline. I refer, of course, to the assisted places scheme, for this policy had a huge benefit in my life. People from my background in Scotland did not go to private school, nor did they go to university, and the scheme gave me and others that opportunity. It not only allowed private boarding school education to become affordable to someone like my mum but succeeded in broadening my horizons at an early age.

While private education is not necessarily the best option for everyone — indeed, Lady Thatcher herself showed what can be achieved through the grammar school system — I know how fortunate I was to receive a place on the scheme. It certainly gave me confidence and a jump-start in life that would never have been possible without Lady Thatcher's hard work and belief in the power of education. I almost certainly would not be in the Chamber today without that push. As I say, my story is not unique. Some 800,000 children were ultimately supported by the assisted places scheme between 1981 and its abolition in 1997, with an average of £10,000 in total spent on their schooling — just a few thousand pounds per year.

Like many in this Chamber, I was privileged to meet Lady Thatcher on a number of occasions, but none sticks out in my memory as much as the first time I met her, when I was a teenager. I was nervous, and she was prime ministerial, but she took time to talk to me, and she made me feel like the only person in the room. One thing I never did was to say thank you for the assisted places scheme, so may I, Mr Deputy Speaker, correct that mistake now? Through the auspices of the Chair and through this tribute debate, I say thank you, Margaret Thatcher, for the assisted places scheme and for giving children such as me an opportunity that we would never otherwise have had.

[Mary Macleod was born 4 January 1969 and educated at the University of Glasgow. She spent 20 years in business consulting before entering the Commons in 2010 as MP for Brentwood and Isleworth.]

8.38 pm

Mary Macleod (Brentford and Isleworth) (Con)

I would like to make three brief personal points about how Baroness Thatcher touched my life and why so many loved her and will miss her. First, Lady Thatcher was the embodiment of aspiration. She studied science when few women were doing so. She was one of only 25 women to be elected in 1959, when only 4% of MPs were women; now, there are 146, or 22%. Lady Thatcher was someone who absolutely believed in aspiring to the highest levels, and she proved that it could be done and that nothing was impossible. My parents always brought up my sisters and me to believe that we should aim high, work hard, try our very best, give any task 100%, and fulfil our potential. Baroness Thatcher was the epitome of this — that it does not matter who you are, where you come from, what your background is or what your gender is. You can absolutely succeed and achieve your goals and dreams, and it is what you deliver and do right now that counts in life.

Secondly, Lady Thatcher was an inspiration to me and to a generation of women in this country, as we heard from my hon. Friend the Member for Epping Forest (Mrs Laing) and also from the hon. Member for Birmingham, Edgbaston (Ms Stuart), who said that Baroness Thatcher kicked the door open even for Labour women in Parliament. I, also, was a child of the Thatcher era and was in school and university when Lady Thatcher was Prime Minister. I did not think it was strange or unusual to have a female Prime Minister. It felt natural. After all, we also had a female monarch. Lady Thatcher made me believe that anything was possible. If a woman could be Prime Minister, surely other women, too, could rise to the highest levels in business and in politics. As President Obama said,

> "As a grocer's daughter who rose to become Britain's first female prime minister, she stands as an example to our daughters that there is no glass ceiling that can't be shattered".

It was Baroness Thatcher who inspired me to become a Member of Parliament, and it was she who kept me going when it took me 13 years to get into Parliament. I was told then that Lady Thatcher went through more than 40 interviews to get selected for Parliament. If it took her that number, then another rejection that I received was always that much more bearable. She came to help me in my election campaign in March 2010 because she really wanted me to win my seat. She came to Chiswick with my hon. Friend the Member for Aldershot (Sir Gerald Howarth) and her presence filled the room. She inspired everyone, from the youngest to the oldest. I believe that generations of women across this country and around the world will always remember her. She led the way, and it is now up to women around the country to follow her example and rise to the challenge too.

Thirdly, Lady Thatcher showed what it was to be a politician of clarity, confidence, conviction and courage. What an incredible role model she was. She knew clearly what she wanted to do and achieve, and she delivered it. She said in 1989:

> I am extraordinarily patient, provided I get my own way in the end.

She had a strength that was second to none. She had the courage to do what was right and not always popular. She had a vision for Britain and transformed this country. She had many tough fights to battle through, but she held to that vision and her conviction. Her courage and strength were seen in so many ways, and in 1982 she said about the Falklands war:

> Defeat? I do not recognise the meaning of the word.

Our country will always need more politicians like her. That is why I will always encourage more women to stand for Parliament, people who have a clarity of purpose and a passion, conviction and courage to deliver real change.

In conclusion, we have lost an incredible leader. We have lost a great reforming former Prime Minister. We have lost a great woman and a great friend. Baroness Thatcher was a wonderful example to all right hon. and hon. Members here today to be politicians of passion, strength, courage and conviction and to fight for Britain's interests every step of the way. As she said herself,

> Where there is despair, may we bring hope.

Her legacy will continue to inspire not only us, but generations to come.

[Mark Pawsey was born 16 January 1957 and educated in estate management at Reading University. A businessman, he became in 2010 the MP for Rugby a seat once held by his father Jim Pawsey.]

8.43 pm

Mark Pawsey (Rugby) (Con)

Just a year after the momentous Conservative victory of 1979, a newly elected MP, having won a Labour seat with a fairly slender majority, thought it would be a good idea to invite the Prime Minister along to his constituency. The newly elected MP was my father and the constituency was the one I represent today. I thought it would be interesting to look at the local paper's report.

The Prime Minister undertook a walk-about in Rugby town centre, much as the current Prime Minister was to do 30 years later. The 4 July 1980 edition of the *Rugby Advertiser* tells us that there were some hecklers in Rugby town centre. As a conviction politician, she attracted opposition. The paper tells us that some of the people were star-struck. There were emotional tears from supporters, and others asked, "Is that really her? Are you sure it isn't Janet Brown?" As some Members will remember, that was the comedienne impressionist of that time.

The paper tells us about Mrs Thatcher's caring side — she signed the plaster cast of a lucky seven-year-old. And finally, it tells us something about her humility. The final sentence in the report is: "As a delighted PM got into her car outside Rugby School — more than an hour late for her next visit to Daventry — she remarked: 'There were even more people here than I expected'."

I have asked my father about his recollections of Lady Thatcher from his time here, and much of what hon. Members have said today rings very true. He told me how supportive she had been when he talked about the concerns of a local manufacturer at Prime Minister's questions. She invited him into her office to discuss what more could be done to support that company. He also told me about the late-night votes that took place at 2 and 3 o'clock in the morning. Members in this intake apparently have it easy, with our votes at 7 and 10 o'clock. He told me how Mrs Thatcher would appear at 2 or 3 o'clock — not a hair out of place, as fresh as paint and full of life — to keep up the spirits of the parliamentary party.

Many Members have spoken about Lady Thatcher's input into their political careers. Her effect on my career related more to the business sector. In 1982, when I was in a secure job as a sales manager for a successful company, I heard her speeches referring to the provision of fair incentives and to rewards for skill and hard work. That kind of environment sounded good to me, and those speeches helped me to decide to risk my future by setting up and running a small business.

I eventually decided to aim for a political career, however, and my finest moment was when I joined one of the small groups referred to by my hon. Friend the Member for Bournemouth West (Conor Burns) and had the opportunity to meet the great lady herself. It has been a great honour for me to pay my tribute to her today.

[Damian Collins was born 4 February 1974 and was educated at St Benet's Hall, Oxford. He worked in advertising, marketing, and communications before 2010 when he became MP for Folkestone and Hythe.]

8.46 pm

Damian Collins (Folkestone and Hythe) (Con)

Mrs Thatcher was an icon of the 20th century, as many Members have said, but her real legacy will be the way in which her policies changed the lives of ordinary people such as my grandparents, who were among the hundreds of thousands who bought their council house, the workers who were given the right to decide whether to strike or whether to join a trade union and the many people who started their own businesses during the Thatcher years and were given opportunities that had been beyond the reach of many people in the past. There are thousands of legacies and thousands of stories across the country to illustrate how people remember her.

The one big thing I want to mention today, as the Member of Parliament for Folkestone and Hythe, is Mrs Thatcher's determination to do big and bold things that other Governments had struggled with in the past because the objections to them had seemed insurmountable. Among those was the decision to press ahead with the channel tunnel. That was controversial at the time, but the economic regeneration of east Kent and the benefits of the high-speed rail network through the area have all stemmed from that decision. I was interested to read the statement made by Jacques Gounon, the president of Eurotunnel, after Lady Thatcher's death. He said:

"Without the vision and drive that were so characteristic of Lady Thatcher throughout her life, the Channel Tunnel, probably the greatest infrastructure achievement of the 20th century, would never have been built."

[Oliver Colvile was born 26 August 1959 and in 2010 became MP for Plymouth, Sutton and Devonport.]

8.48 pm

Oliver Colvile (Plymouth, Sutton and Devonport) (Con)

While I was thinking about what I was going to say today, I spoke to a very good friend of mine, Michael Love, who used to be Mrs Thatcher's agent. He told me a very amusing story — I thought it was amusing, others may not find it so. On the eve of the Conservative party conference, the Prime Minister and party leader used to make sure that she addressed the Conservative agents. My right hon. Friend the Prime Minister continues this great tradition, which, I am told, she started. She said to Mike, "Could you kindly give me some pointers that I might be able to use?" He said, "Yes, one of the things that you should understand" — a secret I might share with the House — "is that agents see all parliamentary candidates as the 'legal necessity'." She duly took notice and included it in her speech, saying, "I do know that some of you think that we, as parliamentary candidates, are nothing more than legal necessities, but I have to tell you that some of us are more important than just legal necessities." I think that went down incredibly well.

During the course of the 1983 general election, I had to organise her visit to Mitcham and Morden. It was a marginal seat and we needed to ensure that we held on to it. We were going to take her to Morfax, which manufactured wheelbarrows used to blow up bombs in Northern Ireland. We suddenly realised that we could not take her there, because it was also responsible for creating bits of the Exocet 2, which were used during the course of the Falklands war. Instead, we took her to Renshaw, which manufactured marzipan. She was told in no uncertain terms that she had to wear a hairnet, and that everybody else, including the press and the media, had to wear a hairnet. She was brilliant and did so superbly. As one can imagine, however, members of the press and the media took no notice whatever of the health and safety regulations and decided not to, and so the whole morning's production had to be thrown in the bin, as the company was concerned about hair in the Christmas cakes.

[Penny Mordaunt was born 4 March 1973 and read philosophy at Reading University. She worked in communications and campaigns including a spell as

Head of Foreign Press for George W Bush in 2000 before in 2010 becoming MP for Portsmouth North.]

8.53 pm

Penny Mordaunt (Portsmouth North) (Con)

Mourning the loss of Ronald Reagan, her great friend and Western co-architect of the demise of the Cold War, Lady Thatcher said:

"We here still move in twilight. But we have one beacon to guide us that Ronald Reagan never had. We have his example."

We have hers: her confidence that a conviction politician could lead her country; her unshakeable belief in the best of human nature; her optimism that this country could be led back to international respect and renown; her focus on making a real, tangible difference to people's lives; her self-confidence, not founded in arrogance but in belief in equal access to opportunity and in meritocracy; her ambition that others should achieve their ambitions; and her courage to do what she believed to be right and to take responsibility for it, to face down terrorism and the foes of freedom.

Margaret Thatcher was a warrior who fought for freedom, of the individual and of nations. She believed in the nation state, but where her opponents could see only the state, she saw the nation. She believed in Britain and the British people, in our history, our destiny and our capacity to play a leading role in the world.

For those who were born after Lady Thatcher's premiership — a vast cohort that now includes many young adults — her legacy may be hard to comprehend, for the simple reason they have only lived in the Britain she forged. Nowadays, talk of freedom when freedom can be taken for granted seems overblown, the nearness of danger in the cold war now intangible, the destructive power of the unions so distant as to seem always doomed, triumph over an invading dictator predestined and Britain's high standing in the world an unshakeable fact. Yet personal freedom, victory in the cold war, proper industrial relations and a dynamic market economy, triumph in the Falklands and respect for Britain's voice in the councils of the world were not inevitable accomplishments. That is why they were accomplishments — her accomplishments.

As we mourn Lady Thatcher, I hope she will inspire us afresh. We should take pride in her life, her achievements and what this country was able to do under her leadership and henceforth as a consequence of it. We should celebrate a remarkable life of service and a remarkable woman.

[Priti Patel was born 29 March 1972 to Ugandan immigrant parents and was educated at Keele University and the University of Essex. She worked in press and public relations before 2010 when she entered the Commons as MP for Witham.]

8.57 pm

Priti Patel (Witham) (Con)

I was proud to grow up during the Thatcher years and to see at first hand the inspirational way in which she introduced powerful changes to improve our country. As a young girl in the 1970s, and the daughter of immigrants, I was fully aware of the disastrous state this country was in. Our economy, society and politics lay crippled after decades of decline. We had become the sick man of Europe and we were seen as weak across the world. Hope, aspiration and entrepreneurship were being suppressed by the instruments of the state — militant trade unions and vested interests that stood opposed to change and reform.

Margaret Thatcher was different. She broke away from politicians who thought the status quo was the norm, and an option, and that we should just go along with the managed decline of our country. As my father always said, she ushered in a new era of hope and optimism, and she was a strength for our country.

Like Margaret's parents, my mother and father were small shopkeepers. Without Margaret Thatcher's economic reforms, which liberated and transformed this country, my parents would not have become the entrepreneurs and self-employed individuals that they went on to become.

There is no doubt that in Margaret Thatcher we had a Prime Minister who not only understood the importance of hard work — she herself had a tremendous work ethic that my family certainly looked up to — but obviously understood sound money, what it meant to be aspirational and, importantly, what it meant to be a wealth creator. She recognised what it meant to the people of this country to be allowed to get on with running their own lives and to have politicians take a back seat.

Margaret Thatcher was determined to smash the obstacles that held people back. She was a champion of opportunity, battling against the forces of privilege and the establishment. In my view, she was the ultimate warrior for the working class and for aspiration. She knew how to unlock Britain's strength to empower individuals and businesses. She laid the foundations for council tenants to buy their homes, lowered and simplified taxes, reduced the deficit, secured the rebate from Europe and brought democracy to the trade union movement. She worked alongside the great Presidents Reagan and Gorbachev to end the cold war and liberated the Falkland Islands.

Advancing the cause of freedom to empower people was always at the forefront of Mrs Thatcher's conviction, her political beliefs and ultimately her actions. We had a Prime Minister who demonstrated that anyone from any background could, through strong beliefs and hard work, rise to the pinnacle of their chosen profession. To me, as a young woman growing up during the Thatcher era and as an MP now, seeing how she led the way has been inspirational. She showed that women could smash through the glass ceiling by reaching the highest political office.

Mrs Thatcher was an inspiration to me and a great source of political advice as I embarked on my political career. I had the privilege of knowing her and of having her political counsel on many occasions. She was, ultimately, a real Conservative. She knew what it meant to be one — to be a patriot and a true leader of our nation.

Like many in the county of Essex, my constituents felt that they could trust and support Margaret Thatcher to safeguard the interests of this country and defend it. There is no doubt that they are saddened by her death, but as we mourn the passing of this tremendous human being — a great Prime Minister and a wonderful person — people in Britain and worldwide can take great comfort from knowing that her legacy will continue through the millions who have benefited from what she brought to this country and through the freedom that she gave millions overseas. We will remember that tremendous legacy for generations to come.

[Alok Sharma was born in India 7 September 1967 and took a degree in Applied Physics with Electronics from Salford University. In 2010 he became MP for Reading West.]

9.2 pm

Alok Sharma (Reading West) (Con)

It is a great honour to speak in this debate paying tribute to Baroness Thatcher. Many colleagues have spoken with great eloquence about their personal experiences of Baroness Thatcher and her kindness. I did not know her personally and that is my personal loss. However, she was an inspiration to my family, my parents and me.

My father often remarked that Margaret Thatcher was not just the first British female Prime Minister, but the first British Asian Prime Minister. He was not joking — he does do jokes, but never about Baroness Thatcher. He always said that she might not look like us, but she absolutely thought like us. What he meant was that she shared and empathised with our values, experiences and ethos. She faced prejudice not because of her race but because of her gender. As the Prime Minister said earlier, in his moving tribute, she understood what it took to break through the glass ceiling. For immigrant families such as mine, she was aspiration personified.

The Prime Minister and the Government are absolutely right to push forward policies to rebuild an aspiration nation. Baroness Thatcher was the original architect of the modern British aspiration nation. She believed in people working hard and being rewarded for it. She believed in education as a great leveller. She believed in helping entrepreneurs, business and the private sector to create the wealth to pay for our public services. She believed in respect for the rule of law. Those are all values espoused by many immigrant communities, such as the one I come from.

My parents started their own business in the late '70s. As anyone who has run a business or tried to run one knows, it is pretty hard work when it first gets started. My parents certainly went through some pretty tricky times, but the one thing of which they are absolutely certain and I am absolutely certain is that if it were not for the economic policies that Margaret Thatcher and her Governments followed, they would not have prospered — and without them, I would certainly not be here today.

Americans often talk about the great American dream, and I can say that Margaret Thatcher inspired the great British dream. What she said to all of us, whether we were from the working class or were immigrants from wherever it might be, was that it was possible for each and every one of us to reach to the stars in Britain. That is something of which I am incredibly proud. Margaret Thatcher is someone to whom my family and I have an enormous debt of gratitude, and there are millions of families like mine up and down this nation who feel exactly the same way.

It was because of Mrs Thatcher that I got involved in the Conservative party. That is why I, like many other colleagues, started delivering leaflets for the Conservative party at the age of 11. I rejoiced in her victory of 1979 and I rejoiced again in her historic victory in 1987, having spent a few weeks being the bag carrier of my right hon. Friend the Member for Wokingham (Mr Redwood) during the general election campaign.

Her leadership was aspirational, inspirational and transformational. She was a global phenomenon — a towering international leader who profoundly touched and affected people across the globe, not just in this country.

[Simon Reevell was born 2 March 1966 and educated at Manchester Polytechnic. He became an attorney and 2010 was elected MP for Dewsbury.]

9.7 pm

Simon Reevell (Dewsbury) (Con)

I have been struck over the last few days by the number of times I have heard the word "divisive" being used on the television — as if every one of Margaret Thatcher's policies created division, especially so in the north of England. That is not right. There are no complaints in Dewsbury about us taking on Argentina and throwing foreign invaders out of the Falklands, or about us helping to throw Iraq out of Kuwait. In Kirkburton, no one moans about us standing alongside the USA and against the USSR in a process that saw democracy come to countries of the former Soviet bloc. In Mirfield, there is no suggestion that IRA prisoners should have had political status, and in Denby Dale they do not say that the trade union legislation should be repealed so that the unions become so powerful that it is possible to turn up for the night shift with a sleeping bag and expect to get paid. Across the whole of my constituency, people nodded their heads as warnings of European federal ambition from over 20 years ago were replayed on Monday night's television.

Of course there are differences of opinion. The gentleman in Thornhill who told me he would always be grateful to Maggie because being able to buy his council house changed his life had a different outlook from that of a man in Emley who was kind enough to tell me I seemed a nice lad, but then explained that as an ex-miner he could not vote Tory. Of course, it is the latter area — industrial policy — where controversy might lie. In the early 1980s, when I had had so many problems with my Austin Metro that they sent a man from Longbridge to look at it, he shrugged his shoulders and said it was a Friday car — built at the end of the week when people were in a hurry to be away. That was not Margaret Thatcher's fault. They did not have Freitag cars at VW, and VW still builds cars. None of the manufacturers in my constituency would be thankful if the clock was turned back to the 1970s.

But what of the coal industry? On Monday, I watched an old clip of a younger Mr Scargill on television. He was telling his then audience that a miner's job was not just that miner's job; it was his son's job and his grandson's job. No it wasn't: my granddad was a Yorkshire miner and he worked in conditions that were said to be cruel for the pit ponies but okay for the men. He was blown up underground twice, each time going back to work as soon as he was healed. He did not do that in the hope that his children and grandchildren would still be doing it for decades to come; he worked like that to try to ensure that his children and grandchildren would not have to work underground, swallowing dust and dirt and facing the threat of explosion and even drowning. And he was as big an NUM man as anyone else in the pit.

I remember the miners' strike because members of my family were caught up in it. For some it was about jobs, but for others it was about power — about who ran the country. The democratically elected Government run the country, and from 1985 everyone understood that. That does not mean that there were not mistakes, but the Britain of 1990 was a far better place than its counterpart of 1979; better in the sense of who we were, of how we saw ourselves, and of how others saw us.

The period from '79 to '90 was overwhelmingly one of positive achievement, and it is nothing short of remarkable that one person was the driving force behind an entire nation rediscovering its pride and re-establishing itself in the world.

That is why I, along with many of my constituents from Dewsbury, in Yorkshire, in the north of England, will pay our respects on Wednesday of next week.

[Dr Thérèse Coffey was born 18 November 1971 and attended Somerville College, Oxford and University College, London where she earned a PhD in chemistry. She worked as a chemist and later retrained as an accountant. In 2010 she became MP for Suffolk Coastal.]

9.11 pm

Dr Thérèse Coffey (Suffolk Coastal) (Con)

There is no question but that Margaret Thatcher defined politics for a decade, if not a generation, if not a lifetime. There are two other people I want to thank today. I want to thank you, Mr Speaker, for allowing the debate to happen. I also want to thank the chaplain for the prayers that were said, which I thought were very special.

Margaret Thatcher was certainly an inspiration to many in this place, and many in the country. Even now, the polls after her death show that more than half the population thought she was a great Prime Minister; any party leader and Prime Minister would hope for such ratings. I expect that every Conservative Member elected in 2010 mentioned Margaret Thatcher as an inspiration in their selection speech. In fact, I expect those people who did not probably did not get selected. Dare I say it, although the great lady of course left office in 1990, her legacy lived on, and there is no doubt that the members of our party loved Margaret Thatcher, and I believe they were right to do so.

Of course Margaret Thatcher broke through the glass ceiling, becoming the first woman Prime Minister. It is said that she found it harder to become a Member of Parliament than she did Prime Minister, but both were herculean tasks, which she achieved, with the help of her male friends, some mentioned already — such as Airey Neave, who was assassinated — and the help and support of others. To her end she would encourage people to enter public and political life, and I think many women in Parliament today are here for that reason.

Of course, Margaret Thatcher was the only science graduate to be Prime Minister. Not for her was history, perhaps, or thinking about the weight of history. In fact, she made history. Her skills as a scientist, in the use of data and rigorous analysis, were an important part of what persuaded her. Her view could be changed if someone had the facts, rather than the emotions of other subjects.

I read chemistry at Oxford and I chose her college, because I had fallen in love with Margaret Thatcher by then. I had done so because I grew up in Liverpool. Hon. Members have talked about communities transformed, and we have heard about the success of entrepreneurs and small business. Opposition Members may think that we look back through rose-tinted spectacles, but people's lives really were changed. People were released; they were allowed to choose, to get on and to be free.

Of course there were impacts on communities, particularly those reliant on one major employer or industry. I lived in Liverpool when the riots happened. They did not affect my neighbourhood but they affected school friends, one of whom was supposed to come to stay with us to get away from the horrendous things that were happening. I also remember Derek Hatton, who said the most despicable thing yesterday. What I remember of him is that he destroyed my city. Militant Labour was the employer involved, and my parents, both teachers, were among the 30,000 who received their redundancy notices overnight. I have been hearing about how people were cast aside, but militant Labour tossed aside the clerk, the cleaner and the street sweeper, as well as the teacher. That is when I woke up and realised that politics mattered, and the following year I got involved in a by-election. Admittedly, the right hon. Member for Knowsley (Mr Howarth) won that, but I stood up; I saw that Margaret Thatcher was leading the country and making a huge difference to people's lives, and I wanted to be part of it.

The constituency I now represent perhaps benefited from some of the issues arising from the militancy of the dockers' strike in Liverpool. Similar things happened elsewhere. Felixstowe grew as a port during that time. When Mrs Thatcher came to Felixstowe in 1986 to speak at the Conservative central council she referred to the modern industrial relations that the good trade unions had with their employers at the port of Felixstowe. We see the same thing now in much of our manufacturing industry, where some of the unions are working well. However, one thing she did was to ensure that it was the democratically elected Government who ran the country, bringing to an end to the closed shop, the "all out" and the flying pickets that crippled industry at the time.

I do not believe that Margaret Thatcher hated the state. What she hated was the state telling the people what they should want. She wanted the state to serve the people and put their needs first. She trusted people to choose. Her very first speech was about the private Member's Bill in which she opened up council meetings to the press and the public; (*Margaret Thatcher's maiden speech in 1959 was to introduce her own bill and was made from the Dispatch Box on the Front Benches. This happened because she had come 3rd out of 310 backbenchers who had entered the annual draw for time to introduce a Private Members Bill*) she made sure that happened. She also did things such as putting parents on school governing bodies so that they were involved in the direction of the schools. She had backed the police, of course, but she had recognised that there was trouble there and that there was a need to reinstate trust, so in the Police and Criminal Evidence Act 1984 she introduced the tape recording of evidence sessions. She started to bring those kinds of reforms in where they were needed.

Above all, Margaret Thatcher put the "Great" back into Great Britain, at no time more so than during the Falklands war. She believed in ideas and she trusted the people. She put that choice to the electorate three times, and the British public backed her, with an increasing number of votes from 1979 to 1987. She was truly my heroine. Margaret Thatcher, may she rest in peace.

[Alec Shelbrooke was born 10 January 1976 and was educated at Brunel University in mechanical engineering. In 2010 he was elected MP for Elmet and Rothwell.]

9.18 pm

Alec Shelbrooke (Elmet and Rothwell) (Con)

Two people in the political world had the biggest influence on me. The one who made me a centre-right politician was Ronald Reagan — I will talk about that another time — but Margaret Thatcher did three important things to me and formed who I am, as a child of the '80s. First, she did not just abolish the glass ceiling that had been there from time immemorial — she smashed it to smithereens. That is why I, like a great number of my hon. Friends, stand here as a child of a comprehensive school; our parents had very normal jobs and we did not go to a fee-paying school. I ended up with an engineering degree and I am now a Conservative Member of Parliament, and my sister is an orthopaedic surgeon. We went through that comprehensive school system, and Margaret Thatcher said to us, "If you work hard, there is no limit to what you can achieve." We took that on. It was about a work ethic.

There are five comprehensive schools in my constituency, and when I visit them I tell the children, "I went to a comprehensive school, too, and nothing can stop you achieving whatever you want." Margaret Thatcher did for me what the tabloid press have done for children these days, who think that if they go on "The X Factor" they will become a pop star. She made us realise that if we worked hard we would achieve our dreams and that it was not just about fame and fortune.

Conviction was very important. It is about standing up for what we believe in, rather than taking the path of least resistance. Political history around the world is littered with leaders who took the path of least resistance. Conviction politics is vital. I want to give a live example for people out there today: the privatisation of British Telecom, which my hon. Friend the Member for Aldershot (Sir Gerald Howarth) mentioned earlier. It is not just that before privatisation people had to wait six months to get a telephone line, or that they needed permission from British Telecom to put an extension in their house. We look today, after the death of Margaret Thatcher, at how advanced telecommunications have become in our society.

She did not privatise British Telecom in the 1980s because she foresaw that we would all be using Twitter, Facebook, the internet and e-mail and have constant access to news; she did it because she knew that the state could never do for those industries what commerce and people with experience of running businesses could do for them. All those people who have used Twitter and Facebook to make the most vile comments in recent days should remember that they can do so because they have easy access. They should try to imagine what it would be like if they had to wait six months to get a mobile phone before doing so.

My hon. Friend the Member for Christchurch (Mr Chope), in an excellent speech, said that he did not disagree with a single one of Margaret Thatcher's policies, except her decision not to stand in the second round. I agree. I do not think that I disagree with anything she did, but there is a lesson that I think we could learn on something that was not done. I passionately believe that she was absolutely right to tackle the union menace that had crippled this country and made us the laughing stock of Europe. When we look at the growth factors in Western Europe and what was happening in this country, we see that we were doomed. That culminated in the miners' strike. There were rights and wrongs, but that is not a debate for today. However, I will say that it was wrong that more was not done after those communities lost their mines.

I think that a lesson has been learnt. Our current Prime Minister has picked up on the idea of the big society and, by looking at what happened in the 1980s as a whole, what it means to help whole communities. Yes, they were the right decisions to make and the convictions were right, but there are always consequences that must be dealt with. He rightly describes himself as a one-nation Conservative, and I agree. It is about managing for the whole country. However, I believe that Margaret Thatcher's intention was to do that. It cannot be said that she was there only for the rich, because she empowered the poorest people in society and, as has been said, she knew that education is the great leveller.

Conviction is the hardest form of governance. It will never be popular, but it is the only honourable way to govern.

[Robert (Bob) Blackman was born 26 April 1956 and was educated at the University of Liverpool. A long standing local and regional politician he entered the Commons in 2010 as MP for Harrow East.]

9.24 pm

Bob Blackman (Harrow East) (Con)

As we sit in the Chamber on almost the 21st anniversary of Margaret Thatcher's ceasing to be an MP and leaving the House of Commons, it is right and proper that we should honour her legacy and her life, both political and personal.

I remember the early days. Most anecdotes have been from when she dominated the House of Commons, but I well remember that it was a difficult time for her when she was first elected as leader of the Conservative party. As a fresh-faced young student, I attended one of her first speaking events after she had been elected as leader, at the Federation of Conservative Students' conference. At the time, the FCS was dominated by a Heathite element and there was deep suspicion about what Margaret Thatcher would do to the party and the country if she became Prime Minister. She espoused firm principles and a belief in free enterprise, sound money, strong defence, individual responsibility and, above all, personal liberty. As she addressed that conference, one could see the ripples of change among the young people attending the conference, probably for the first time. She transformed many of us so that we became clarion calls for change across our campuses. We fought the battle for four years after she became leader and we got our reward in the 1979 general election. We fought a war of ideas on campuses and in universities and we won, with her support and her firm view.

One anecdote that has not been told concerns the fact that when she was first elected leader and went on that first speaking tour, a brief went out from Conservative central office that she was teetotal and abhorred alcohol. As many Members will know, that was not the case. She attended a meeting at a Conservative club in the north-west and, of course, the briefing had not reached them. She had been around a series of different events, and the chairman of the club said, "Mrs Thatcher, would you like a drink — a whisky, perhaps?" The person from Conservative central office shook, thinking that there would be an explosion, and Mrs Thatcher said, "Thank goodness there is someone in this party who enjoys a drink."

I well remember the 1979 general election, the changes that came and the squeals of horror as the first Budget was unveiled. Next week, we will no doubt continue the rather anodyne debate about whether the top rate of tax should be 45% or 40%. We should remember that in those days it was 98%, and 68% on earned income. She abolished that penal taxation and changed the position of society once and for all. It was decisive — and quite right, too. She embodied everything that modern people aspire to and that is her lasting legacy to us.

We should also remember the terrible times that have been mentioned, with the battle for the recovery of the Falkland Islands and the personal dilemma about sending our troops to war to possibly die in defence of their country and our dominions. That decision was not taken lightly. No doubt she lost many hours of sleep when that was going on.

I well remember leaving the Grand hotel in the late hours in October 1984 and hearing subsequently about the blast that had gone off. At the time when that happened, during the early hours of the morning, none of us knew whether the Prime Minister or the members of the Cabinet were still alive. It was with great relief the following day that we found out that the worst had not happened. It could have been so different. I am sure that that, together with the impact of losing dear friends in this place, impacted on her view of the policies on Ireland.

We should remember the lasting legacy of Margaret Thatcher, whether it is the 2 million people who own their council houses as a result of her policies, the 20 million people who bought shares when she produced a shareholding democracy or the millions of people in Eastern Europe who owe their fundamental freedoms of democracy and liberty to the iron will of the Iron Lady. That is her lasting legacy.

[Mark Reckless was born 6 December 1970 and was educated Oxford, Columbia Business School, and the College of Law. As an economist and attorney he won many plaudits before entering the Commons in 2010 as MP for Rochester and Strood.]

9.29 pm

Mark Reckless (Rochester and Strood) (Con)

I came to the debate before Prayers and found that there was nowhere to sit on the Benches, so I sat just to my right on the floor. Just above me to the right was my hon. Friend the Member for Bournemouth West (Conor Burns). He told me — I was not aware of this — that that was the seat on which Margaret Thatcher sat after she stopped being Prime Minister. I felt that it would be a privilege to sit through the seven and a half hours of debate and tributes, and that I would not seek to speak, but I wish to address one area.

The day before yesterday, the noble Lord Bell said that Margaret Thatcher believed in principles, which perhaps set her apart from virtually any politician of today. I am not sure that that is fair and I believe that my right hon. Friend the Prime Minister, and many who sit behind him, were inspired by Margaret Thatcher, and that much of the politics in which she believed has found its way into our Government. In different ways, I believe that we are taking forward her legacy.

When I was at school, perhaps my oldest friend was Daniel Hannan, who is now an MEP. Together we observed the progress of the Thatcher Government, and we took a greater and greater interest, particularly in Europe. At the time, I was beginning to take an interest in economics and seeking to understand the interface of politics and economics. At the time, Margaret Thatcher and the now noble Lord Lawson were involved in a disagreement about shadowing the Deutschmark, and on that issue I believe that Margaret Thatcher was simply right. Even at the time, it seemed to me that it was just too good; we had had a consumer-led recovery, but as a teenager in my naive way I thought it was getting out of control. Nevertheless, I heard that there could not be a problem because the pound was at the same level against the Deutschmark and we had cut interest rates to keep it below three Deutschmarks. There was a disagreement between the Chancellor and the Prime Minister that I think was resolved terribly unfortunately for our country, but it was the Prime Minister who was right.

Towards the end of Margaret Thatcher's time in office, Europe became the central driving issue. There is too much of a trend to say that in the last days of her premiership she had somehow lost her touch or that the man-management was not there. The issue of Europe did not develop afterwards; it was there in the central disagreement on economic policy in her Government.

I do not believe that Margaret Thatcher's personal split with Geoffrey Howe was about personality. On 25 June 1989, Geoffrey Howe with the noble Lord Lawson said to Margaret Thatcher that unless she set a timetable to join the exchange rate mechanism, they would resign. She believed that Geoffrey Howe was behind that, and a month later she removed him from his post as Foreign Secretary. Eighteen months later she made a statement when she came back from the Rome summit, which we recall for "No. No. No.", and which led to Geoffrey Howe's resignation and his later speech that set in train the events leading to Margaret Thatcher's downfall. Listening to that debate again this morning, what struck me was how she answered Tony Benn when he said to her, "You now say this, but how do we know that this is any more than you seeking partisan short-term advantage by wrapping yourself in the flag? It was you who took us into the ERM without consulting the British people, you who signed the Single European Act, and you who sat in a Cabinet that took us into the Common Market without a referendum."

Margaret Thatcher answered him and said that she would have used different words. In essence, however, she agreed with him. There was a mea culpa. On those issues, he had been right and she regretted the stance that she had taken. She said those things while she was Prime Minister, and I believe that it set in train the process that led to her fall. However, she also inspired a new generation of politicians. There is the question whether we will ultimately be part of an ever-closer union in Europe or again be an independent country. Margaret Thatcher at least kept open that possibility by restoring our national strength, so that it could once again be resolved in favour of independence.

[Thomas Docherty was born 28 January 1975 and entered the Commons in 2010 as MP for Dumfermline and West Fife.]

9.34 pm

Thomas Docherty (Dunfermline and West Fife) (Lab)

It is a privilege to close this debate on behalf of Her Majesty's Opposition.

We have heard excellent contributions from right hon. and hon. Members on the Back Benches of both sides of the House, and from all parts of the UK. Because of time constraints, I cannot mention them all, but I want to single out just four. We heard thoughtful contributions from those who served under her, such as the right hon. and learned Member for Kensington (Sir Malcolm Rifkind) and the right hon. Member for Wokingham (Mr Redwood). We heard from Members who knew her personally. The hon. Member for Bournemouth West (Conor Burns) made a deeply felt contribution. He spoke with eloquence and emotion, particularly about his experiences of her in her later years.

However, while we recognise Baroness Thatcher as an extraordinary figure, we have heard many right hon. and hon. Members speak with great feeling and conviction about her influence on them and their constituencies, including my hon. Friend the Member for Blaydon (Mr Anderson). I represent a former mining community in Scotland, and I believe it is only right that the House has heard from Members who represent similar communities. The debate has shown the wide-ranging views in the House. I am sure that Baroness Thatcher, as a great parliamentarian, would appreciate how the debate has been conducted.

[Andrew Lansley was born 11 December 1956 and educated at the University of Exeter. Following a spell as a civil servant and Conservative Party employee he entered the Commons in 1997 as MP for South Cambridgeshire. He was Secretary of State for Health 2010-2012 and since then has served as Leader of the House of Commons and Lord Privy Seal.]

9.37 pm

The Leader of the House of Commons (Mr Andrew Lansley)

It is a great privilege to bring this debate in tribute Baroness Thatcher of Kesteven to a close.

I am grateful to the Leader of the Opposition and his colleagues for their generous remarks. The Leader of the Opposition was followed not least by the right hon. Member for Manchester, Gorton (Sir Gerald Kaufman), who was characteristically thoughtful and generous. Margaret Thatcher did indeed break the consensus — that was her purpose and her achievement. It is perfectly possible, as he and other Opposition Members have said, to disagree with her policies but recognise the character of that achievement. The hon. Member for Newport West (Paul Flynn) said that history will judge her as a great Prime Minister, and indeed it will.

Other Opposition Members who opposed her policies did not necessarily engage in quite the same generosity of view. Margaret Thatcher would not have been surprised. She always expected her convictions and determination to achieve change to lead to opposition and argument. As my hon. Friends have said, she always relished that argument. In fact, when I was listening to the hon. Members for Walsall North (Mr Winnick), for Hampstead and Kilburn (Glenda Jackson) and for Blaydon (Mr Anderson), I could practically hear her at the Dispatch Box enjoying herself — she would have wanted to be here participating in that argument. She knew that the principles for which she always stood firm had to be fought for not just by her generation, but by every generation. That is the tribute that she would most want. It has been demonstrated in many speeches today that those values are recognised, are being upheld and will be pursued with the same conviction in the future.

Many Members have given great testimony of her public character. Not least, we have heard about her courage in the face of terrorism, whether it was the IRA and the Brighton bomb or the murders of Airey Neave and Ian Gow. We have heard about her courage in facing up to the invasion of the Falklands and taking the decisions that were never easy, but were entirely necessary to see off a dictatorship.

Margaret Thatcher was a radical and a reformer. Her achievements were the result of turning her conviction into a determination to achieve change.

This debate is remarkable not least for capturing a sense of her personal kindnesses and support. Of course, she was the first women Prime Minister and leader of a party. That is at the heart of how she inspired so many in the House, particularly women Members of Parliament, and women in politics across the world. She not only inspired women in politics, but supported them. I am grateful to my hon. Friend the Member for Epping Forest (Mrs Laing), the hon. Member for Birmingham, Edgbaston (Ms Stuart), my right hon. Friend the Member for Chesham and Amersham (Mrs Gillan) and many other Members who said how they had been helped and supported by her. I note that Margaret Thatcher's support and kindness extended to many Members of the 2010 intake. They might not have served in this House with her, but they were inspired by her and even personally supported by her. That is remarkable.

We have heard good examples of Margaret Thatcher's humour. Margaret Thatcher inspired loyalty, a point which my hon. Friend the Member for Maldon (Mr Whittingdale) captured. He worked for her loyally, as did so many in this Chamber and beyond. She inspired loyalty among her staff and extended her loyalty to others, including by recognising people's service and sacrifice. The House is grateful to my hon. Friend the Member for Beckenham (Bob Stewart) for describing how she supported the wounded in the military hospital in Northern Ireland.

Many people in this House were inspired by Margaret Thatcher and worked with her. I had that opportunity myself. In 1979, I heard her speak in support of John Hannam in Exeter. She set out her objectives of breaking the power of the trade unions, restoring sound money and making Britain great again. She did those things. It is a remarkable thing in politics to be able to say "I am setting out with certain objectives" and then to do those things. However, she did so much more, and we have heard about so many of those things during today's debate.

Years later, when I was director of the Conservative Research Department and my right hon. Friend the Prime Minister and I were at the receiving end of demands for briefing and policy work, I witnessed that ability. Margaret Thatcher had a compass to steer by. A meeting with her was not a meeting at which people offered a range of views and she tried to assess where the balance lay; it was a meeting at which she adduced all the evidence and arguments, and applied her principles and convictions to them. She might express her support for free enterprise, for instance. My hon. Friend the Member for Chichester described her support for freedom and liberty against an over-mighty state. She might express her support for personal liberty, as distinct from the idea that all responsibilities could be handed over to some society without a sense of the responsibility of individuals, families and communities to step up and do what needed to be done. My hon. Friend the Member for North Warwickshire (Dan Byles) illustrated that by means of a full quotation.

I saw all that for myself, just in that last year before Margaret Thatcher ceased to be Prime Minister, and I found it remarkable, but what I also found remarkable were her private warmth and kindnesses. When I was private secretary to Norman Tebbit at the time of the Brighton bomb and immediately after it, she extended to Norman and Margaret Tebbit innumerable kindnesses. They included looking after Norman Tebbit at Chequers (*the British equivalent of Camp David*) while Margaret Tebbit was at Stoke Mandeville (*a specialist hospital for spinal injuries*) just down the road.

It has been made clear by so many contributions from the Government Benches today that we understand how Margaret Thatcher steered this country out of decline and hopelessness. She enabled what had been the sick man of Europe to gain international respect and subsequently admiration, and even to be seen as a country to be emulated. She transformed this country, and, as the hon. Member for Huddersfield (Mr Sheerman) pointed out, she even transformed the Labour party. The tribute that we can best offer her is not just to remember that, but never to go back and always to build on her achievements: to be a country that is strong, free, respected and enterprising, and to be a people who are responsible, knowing, as my colleagues said more than once today, that the best for this country is ahead of us rather than behind us. That was her conviction. She was convinced that, given the principles that sustained her, that could be true.

Margaret Thatcher served in the House for 33 years, and she served this country every day of her life. Today, in recognition of her service and her achievements, we in the House have paid our tributes. Next Wednesday, as a country, we will have a chance to offer our thanks and to say our farewells.

I commend the motion to the House.

Question put and agreed to.

Resolved,
That this House has considered the matter of tributes to the Rt Hon Baroness Thatcher of Kesteven LG OM.

9.48pm
House adjourned.

House of Lords

Death of a Member: Baroness Thatcher
Tributes

[Lord (Jonathan) Hill of Oareford (Conservative) was born 24 July 1960 and attended Trinity College, Cambridge. After a career in politics and PR he was made a member of the Lords on 27 May 2010 and became Leader of the House of Lords and Chancellor of the Duchy of Lancaster on 7 January 2013.]

2.37 pm

The Chancellor of the Duchy of Lancaster (Lord Hill of Oareford)

Whatever our views and whatever our backgrounds, I think that we would all agree that she made a huge difference to the country that she loved, that she helped to pick Britain up off its knees, that she changed our place in the world and that she transformed the very shape of our political debate. I think that we would also agree that she was a staunch defender of our parliamentary system and the part that it should play in our national life.

The personal journey that she made, particularly at that time, from the grocer's shop in Grantham to the highest office in our land, was a truly remarkable one. The outlines of that journey are well known. Margaret Hilda Roberts was born in Grantham in 1925. Head girl of her grammar school, she went to Oxford during the war, graduating with a degree in chemistry. In 1951, she met and married Denis, the rock of her life for more than 50 years. In 1953, she gave birth to twins, Carol and Mark, to whom we extend our deepest condolences, along with the rest of her family and her many friends.

135

Having entered Parliament in 1959, she was in the Cabinet by 1970. Even today, 11 years from first election to the Cabinet would seem swift, but 50 years ago, for one of just a handful of female MPs, it was extraordinary. Even more remarkably, by 1975 this non-establishment figure had become leader of the establishment party, confounding the predictions of many. Those same people then foretold a quick exit. They foretold her never reaching the steps of No. 10. In fact, she herself said that she believed she would never see a woman Prime Minister in her lifetime. How she proved them and, indeed, herself wrong.

These bare bones of fact do not, of course, explain the reason for her success. They do not capture the strength of her personality, the beam of the spotlight and the force of her will that I remember vibrating through the government departments where I worked in the 1980s. Nor, I think, can we measure the extent of her achievements without first understanding the grim inheritance of the 1970s. Successive Governments had tried and failed to tackle our economic and political woes. We had become the sick man of Europe. People asked, not fancifully, whether Britain was indeed possible to govern. We were a divided country, and at times our very future seemed to hang in the balance. That is the background against which the sifting process of history will make its judgments. That is the background which helps to explain her approach and makes her achievements stand out so clearly. She did not take the easy way. She certainly did not take the consensual way. She led because of belief, she was guided by conviction and she was harnessed to the purpose of making Britain great again.

Tough economic policies were needed to turn the country around. She knew that the status quo was unsustainable and that some things had to change. Her programme of deregulation and denationalisation, and of reducing the power of trade unions, was painful, particularly in some parts of our country, but it made Britain a global competitor once again. The recapture of the Falkland Islands, her resistance to the IRA despite the high price paid by many of those closest to her, her friendship with President Reagan and her shared vision for a world free of the Cold War made Britain once again a world leader. The threat of nuclear war that seemed to hang over us in the early 1980s was lifted. It was indeed an iron lady who helped draw back the iron curtain from Eastern Europe, extending freedom to millions. In those countries, too, she will always be remembered. These are mighty achievements. She was an extraordinary leader of her party, of this country and of the world during what were extraordinary times.

It is true that great leaders are not always easy people. I think that it is fair to say that patience was not a virtue that Mrs Thatcher had in abundance, and that she did not always instantly get the point. The great Ronnie Millar (*a playright of note*), who helped with her speeches for many years, told me the lovely story of an occasion when he was trying to reassure a rather nervous Margaret Thatcher with some soothing words just before she was due to speak at her first party conference as Prime Minister. "Piece of cake, Prime Minister". "No, not now, thank you, dear". Those who knew her best all testify to the warm side of her character: the countless personal kindnesses, the loyalty and the small, thoughtful acts.

For someone who so defined a decade, it was perhaps not such a surprise that a new decade ushered in change and that after eleven and a half years the longest serving 20th century Prime Minister resigned and, a little over 18 months later, joined your Lordships' House. It was perhaps typical of Mrs T-now Lady T -that she began with a maiden speech on Europe-on Maastricht, in fact. Perhaps it was typical also that she began by reminding her new home of one or two home truths. She began:

> Mine is a somewhat delicate position. I calculate that I was responsible as Prime Minister for proposing the elevation to this House of 214 of its present Members. That must surely be considerably more than most of my predecessors-and my father did not know Lloyd George! (*A reference to the well-known stories that titles such as peerages were effectively sold while David Lloyd George was Prime Minister*). [*Official Report*, 2/7/92; col. 897.]

Sadly, that was to be one of few speeches to which we would be treated in the subsequent decades. The light that had burned so brightly began to dim as she suffered the loss of Denis, and ill health. However, although we may not have been blessed with her words, her presence was keenly felt and was sustained by her many friends here.

Perhaps Margaret Thatcher's greatest strength as Prime Minister was her refusal to accept Britain's decline. In taking that stance, the obstacles she faced were monumental, but her belief in the ability of the British people to better themselves, and of our country to better itself, was paramount. She was a once-in-a-lifetime Prime Minister and one of the most remarkable leaders this country has seen.

[Baroness (Janet) Royall of Blaisdon (Labour) was born 20 August 1955 and educated Westfield College, London. She is the current Leader of the Opposition in the House of Lords.]

2.45 pm

Baroness Royall of Blaisdon

As the tributes to her which have flowed since the news of her death was announced have shown, there is no doubt that Margaret Thatcher was, and will remain, a polarising figure. For some, including many on the Benches opposite, Lady Thatcher inspired then, and inspires now, a devotion to a politician who they believe not only, as the Prime Minister said on Monday, "saved" this country but was the political ideal to which they aspired and, indeed, is the political model that they believe that they still need now. From that viewpoint, not only was she the dominant politician of her generation but was one of the most influential Prime Ministers this country has ever seen-someone who has claim, as David Cameron said in his tribute to her, to be Britain's greatest ever peacetime Prime Minister. Not all those on the Benches opposite share that view. Some, like the noble and learned Lord, Lord Howe of Aberavon, and the noble Lords, Lord Lawson of Blaby and Lord Heseltine, and many other noble Lords, are part of her story but in very different ways. Not all of them were always and at all times in full agreement with her. For some, including on my Benches and in my part of the political spectrum, Mrs Thatcher, as she was then, was a divisive figure and someone to whom they were, and remain, fundamentally opposed; someone whose very name, even now, almost 30 years since she became Britain's Prime Minister in 1979, can raise heights of emotion, of passion, of anger, of despair and more; and someone who they believe can never be forgiven for what she did to individuals, to communities, to industries and to the country. That is a legitimate position of disagreement to hold, but to hold parties to celebrate the death of someone is wrong, in bad taste and something that I deplore.

However, as the tributes have shown, disagreements with Mrs Thatcher, her vision, her ideals, her politics and her policies have not prevented even her political opponents from being able to assess fully the enormity of her impact as the United Kingdom's longest-serving Prime Minister of the 20th century and as this country's first, and so far only, woman Prime Minister.

I pay particular tribute to Baroness Thatcher in that role. She was unquestionably a truly remarkable woman, and although I did not agree with many of her policies, I recognise that it was extraordinary for a woman — a grocer's daughter, wife and mother — to be a successful research chemist before becoming a barrister and then going on to become an MP, a Minister and to lead the Conservative Party and become the first female Prime Minister, especially at the time when she did it. Baroness Thatcher was a model for many women, including many women in politics. She burst through the glass ceiling and proved that it could be done, but she did not hold out a helping hand for others to follow. I admire strong women — and she was certainly strong and wielded immense power over colleagues as well as the country. However, as with my late noble friend Lady Castle, for whom I worked in the first six years of Baroness Thatcher's premiership, she also knew how to use her womanly wiles. Barbara said that her power over male colleagues derived from the fact that she had "a brain as good as most of theirs plus ... the arts of femininity".

However, in relation to the issue of women, personally I wish that Baroness Thatcher had used her strength in different ways. I know that she showed many kindnesses to female colleagues, both MPs and her staff. However, despite the many talented Conservative women in Parliament, they were never — apart from another former Member of your Lordships' House, Lady Young — promoted to the Cabinet. Since 1929, when Margaret Bondfield joined the Cabinet, there have still only been 33 women Cabinet members. As the first ever female Prime Minister, Lady Thatcher could have done so much for female politicians, and for working mothers and women struggling to hold their families and communities together, but she chose not to do so.

However, there is some in what which Baroness Thatcher was and did that I admire: her personal strength and courage, shown so bravely in her response to being bombed at the Grand Hotel in Brighton in 1984, and her early support for Mikhail Gorbachev, with whom I had the good fortune to celebrate his 80th birthday here in this House two years ago, and for glasnost and perestroika in the former Soviet Union. All this was important in changing the dynamics of our continent and helping to bring the Cold War to an end, as was the part that she played in driving forward the single market.

Lady Thatcher's determination and belief were the principal drivers in Britain regaining the Falklands, but they led also to misjudgments such as Section 28, now rightly repudiated by today's Conservative Party, or gauging the ANC wrong in South Africa. Her legacy and impact in and about Europe is still absolutely with us today.

I know too, from my own personal experience, just how formidable a political opponent she was. In the 1980s I was proudly working for my noble friend, now the noble Lord, Lord Kinnock, then the leader of the Labour Party, and I saw first hand, to the cost of our own campaigns, just how effective a politician she was and how much parts of the country supported her at that time.

Lady Thatcher had a real appreciation of middle England's hunger for aspiration, giving people a greater chance to own their own home. She recognised that our economy needed to change, but the painful changes that were made were not carried by the broadest shoulders and have left an unbalanced economy with which we are still grappling. History will form a judgment on the legacy of Baroness Thatcher as a political figure in Britain, and in the world. Agree or disagree with her, she was unquestionably a towering figure in this country and beyond our shores. I leave those judgments to others better qualified than me to make them.

I will conclude my remarks by saying something about Lady Thatcher as a member of your Lordships' House. She entered this House in 1992, more than 20 years ago, and was automatically and, rightly, immediately a senior figure in this place. When I first came to your Lordships' House I was mesmerised by this frail but still powerful woman who through sheer determination had transformed our society, dividing opinion and dividing the country. Not for her the consensual notion of one nation that I passionately espouse. As increasingly frail as she became, as a result of that enormous impact, her appearances in the House at key moments and on key Divisions were electrifying.

In more recent years, of course, Lady Thatcher's appearances were less frequent. I pay tribute to those who were of particular assistance to her, and especially mark the support-the real, caring support-given to her by the noble Lord, Lord Forsyth of Drumlean, in her later years.

[Lord (Tom) McNally was born 20 February 1943 and was educated at University College, London. He is the leader of the Liberal Democrats in the House of Lords having served as a Labour MP who defected to the Social Democrats which later merged with the Liberal Party to from the Liberal Democrats. He serves as Minister of State in the Ministry of Justice in the Coalition Government.]

2.52 pm

The Minister of State, Ministry of Justice (Lord McNally)

Due to some serendipity, for about five years at the State Opening of Parliament I found myself sitting on the Bench opposite next to Mrs Thatcher and spending time with her as we awaited the Queen's arrival. The one thing I want to share with the House took place in the year her husband died, when she had already had a number of minor strokes and did not speak a great deal. She suddenly turned to me and said, "My husband died earlier this year". I said, "Yes, Baroness Thatcher, I know". She paused again and then said, "I miss him very much". That tremendous partnership between Baroness Thatcher and her husband, which was so much a factor in her own political life, is remembered today.

There are times when, for all the grandeur of the surroundings of this House, we have to play second fiddle to activities down the Corridor. Today, however, although the tributes in the other place will no doubt be eloquent and apposite, it is in this Chamber, as the Leader of the House has reminded us, that we will hear the memories and judgments of those who experienced first hand the Thatcher phenomenon. If one considers the number of people whom she sacked, promoted, defeated or berated, they must make up a goodly number of those present in the House today. In short, the importance of the next couple of hours is that not only does this House know where the bodies are buried but some of the bodies are present here.

In January 1965, when paying tribute to the life of Sir Winston Churchill, Harold Wilson referred to "the sullen feet of marching men in Tonypandy" — a reminder that Churchill, in a long life, had sometimes been at the heart of bitter social conflict, as well as showing great leadership in the times of national crisis. So it was with Margaret Thatcher, and that reality was reflected in the remarks of the noble Baroness, Lady Royall. I quote again from Harold Wilson's tribute to Churchill. He said that "the tempestuous years are over; the years of appraisal are yet to come" [*Official Report*, Commons, 25/1/65; col. 672].

I shall not attempt such an appraisal today. Instead, I shall rely on two perspectives given not at the time of her death but some years ago.

Seven years ago, the *New Statesman* invited its readers to nominate their "heroes of our time". Somewhat to the surprise and embarrassment of the *New Statesman*, Baroness Thatcher was the highest-rated British politician. The paper explained this result as being due to the fact that no one was in any doubt about what Mrs Thatcher stood for and what she believed in, and it was those qualities of steadfastness and clarity of purpose which had been recognised by the *New Statesman* readers.

My second assessment comes from another surprising source. As a Member of the other place in 1982, I was present for two exchanges that took place between Enoch Powell and Mrs Thatcher. To appreciate fully the quotations that I am about to give, your Lordships will have to imagine that slightly nasal, Black Country twang in which Mr Powell spoke, but which I shall not try to imitate. The first is Enoch Powell addressing Mrs Thatcher after the Falkland Islands had been invaded. Speaking on 3 April in the House of Commons, he said:

> "The Prime Minister, shortly after she came into office (*as Leader of the Opposition, not as Prime Minister*), received a soubriquet as the 'Iron Lady'. It arose in the context of remarks which she made about defence against the Soviet Union and its allies; but there was no reason to suppose that the right hon. Lady did not welcome and, indeed, take pride in that description. In the next week or two this House, the nation and the right hon. Lady

herself will learn of what metal she is made". — [*Official Report*, Commons, 3/4/82; col. 644.]

My second quotation is from some 10 weeks later — 17 June 1982 — after the British victory in the Falklands war. Enoch Powell said:

"Is the right hon. Lady aware that the report has now been received from the public analyst on a certain substance recently subjected to analysis and that I have obtained a copy of the report? It shows that the substance under test consisted of ferrous matter of the highest quality, that it is of exceptional tensile strength, is highly resistant to wear and tear and to stress, and may be used with advantage for all national purposes." — [*Official Report*, Commons, 17/6/82; col. 1082.]

That was the only time in my experience that Enoch Powell made a joke. (*These two quotes were framed by Ian Gow MP, given to Margaret Thatcher for Christmas 1982, and hung in her office for many years.*)

There is no need to airbrush out of history or to ignore the fact that most of us on these Benches spent a good deal of our political lives fiercely opposing many aspects of what became known as "Thatcherism". However, that does not prevent us recognising the qualities that were highlighted both by the *New Statesman* and by Enoch Powell-qualities that have quite rightly brought us together today to pay due respect and proper tribute to Margaret Thatcher as a figure of enduring importance in our national life.

[The Lord Bishop of Oxford (John Lawrence Pritchard) was born in 1948 and educated at St Peter's College, Oxford, entering the Church of England in 1972.]

2.59 pm

The Lord Bishop of Oxford

My Lords, I rise to pay tribute to Baroness Thatcher, sharing with noble Lords a string of strong memories of a remarkable woman, the first woman to occupy the office of Prime Minister.

As others have said, the change that she made to the face of Britain was complete. It opened up new avenues of possibility in all directions: share ownership, home ownership, liberalisation of the markets, entrepreneurial innovation, and so on. She strengthened Britain's role in the world immeasurably with clear policies on defence, the Falklands, Northern Ireland, communism, Europe, South Africa and more. No one was in any doubt that there was a force in the land.

I spent the last years of the 1980s in County Durham, so I know some of the deep divisions that Lady Thatcher's policies caused. "Billy Elliot" country was not an all-singing, all-dancing landscape. (*Billy Elliot is a reference to a 2000 movie about an 11 year old boy who wants to be a dancer growing up in northern England during the coalminers' strike of 1984-1985*). It is almost impossible to find moderate opinion for or against on her style of leadership, but the one thing that we can all acknowledge is that she was a leader of absolute integrity in terms of her own beliefs. She was an iconic conviction politician.

The Church of England had its moments with Lady Thatcher, of course. The suggestion that the date for the enthronement of the Archbishop of Canterbury be moved so that it avoided a clash with the Budget of 1980 was one early instance. Happily, on that occasion, the lady was for turning. In the end, it was the Budget that was rescheduled.

As we know, the church traditionally has a role of critical solidarity with Governments of all persuasions, so the production of the influential report *Faith in the City* and the Archbishop of Canterbury's Falklands sermon, in which he remembered the bereaved on both sides of the conflict, both caused momentary mayhem in the press. That was to be expected when issues of principle were at stake. It did not dent her respect for the church, or our regard for her steely qualities. It was entirely fitting that the place where she particularly enjoyed the chance to walk securely and privately in her latter years was the grounds of Lambeth Palace, which successive archbishops placed at her disposal.

We should remember, too, her roots in Methodism and the influence that the Christian faith played in informing her beliefs about personal responsibility and the importance of religion in public life. Methodism was born in the pursuit of justice and hope among working people. It had, and still has, a radical edge, and it is from that edge that Margaret Thatcher drew much of her strength. You do not have to agree with every decision that she took to acknowledge the strength of her character and her determination and passion in all she did.

As we have said, history will continue to debate the legacy of Baroness Thatcher for years to come, but she clearly defined politics not just for her generation but for many generations. Some of us perhaps wish that, on a few more occasions, the lady had been for turning — for turning has a good pedigree in Christian theology — but we can still applaud her many achievements while regretting some of the excesses. We will most certainly not forget her. May she rest in peace.

[Lord (Herbert) Laming was born 16 July 1936 and studied at Durham University. He became Convenor of theCrossbench Peers 5 September 2011 having risen to the Lords in 1998 after a career as a senior social work administrator.]

3.03 pm

Lord Laming

It is perhaps understandable that on an occasion such as this we draw on personal experiences, although I must say that I have nothing like the depth of experience of some of my colleagues who worked with Mrs Thatcher day by day. I first met Mrs Thatcher in the mid-1970s, when she was the after-dinner speaker at the annual conference of the directors of social services. The House will not be surprised to learn that she made a characteristically challenging speech, leaving the audience in no doubt that, given the opportunity, she had real ambition to change local government and, in particular, social care services.

At the end of the event, the president of the association told her that he had arranged for a good malt to be delivered to his room, and hoped that she and a few others would join him for a brief nightcap. I have no doubt that part of his motivation was, as it were, to put her right on a few things that she had said. However, he did not expect, in the early hours of the morning when they were all flagging, Mrs Thatcher to be driving on in full flow setting out the important issues that she intended to tackle. I feel sure that he-as it was a he-was not the first to regret even the hint of an attempt to patronise her; nor was he the last to experience her phenomenal energy, drive and conviction, or her steely determination.

Almost a decade later, as Prime Minister, Mrs Thatcher commissioned Sir Roy Griffiths, the then deputy chairman and managing director of Sainsbury's, to conduct a major review of the social care services for vulnerable adults. The noble Baroness, Lady Pitkeathley, and I greatly enjoyed working with Sir Roy and we were given the opportunity to be called his advisers. I was with Sir Roy on the day he met the Prime Minister to go through the main thrust of his report. He was a wise man and had learnt the importance of careful preparation in the face of what was likely to be a forensic scrutiny.

Sir Roy told me that all had gone well, primarily because he concentrated on the main thrust of his report. In a nutshell, this was simply that when a vulnerable person is dependent on a relative stranger to meet their personal needs, their primary concern is about the quality and sensitivity of the service delivered and not about the nature of the organisation that delivers it. I feel sure that this way of thinking hugely pleased Mrs Thatcher, not least because at that time local authorities operated an almost total monopoly of home care services, day centre services and residential homes for all people, whatever their disabilities or special needs. In addition, they also regulated the few independent providers operating in that area. That was the beginning of a fundamental transformation of those services, which are of such importance to the well-being of our fellow citizens.

I hardly need to remind the House that for very good reason we have very often had cause to praise the Children Act 1989. That bedrock legislation changed childcare practices in this country. Almost 25 years on, it has stood the test of time.

In short, during the years when Mrs Thatcher was Prime Minister, the foundations were laid for huge changes in every aspect of the social care services in this country. Inevitably, many of these changes were and are contested but one thing that was never in doubt was the determination of the Prime Minister to see them through. The record of Baroness Thatcher as a woman in a male-dominated environment, as a tenacious politician and as a formidable Prime Minister is for all to see and certainly will endure. May she rest in peace.

[Lord (Michael) Jopling was born 10 December 1930 and was educated at Durham University. He served as a Conservative MP and Cabinet Member rising to the Lords in 1997.]

3.08 pm

Lord Jopling

My Lords, I speak as one of the dwindling band of those who appeared in the 1979 photograph of the Cabinet. I speak also as one of an even smaller band of members of her shadow Cabinet in prior years.

Much has been said over the past few days about Margaret Thatcher. Indeed, much of it has been said several times, but let me add two or three of my memories. I remember Margaret Thatcher above all as a particularly kind woman. I give one example. At the first Christmas for which she was Prime Minister, in 1979, she said to me, "Do you know of any of our people in the House of Commons who are going to be alone — through death, divorce or whatever — over this Christmas period? If you do, I would like to ask them to Chequers to come and stay over Christmas". That, I thought at the time, was one of the most generous things from somebody with all the pressures on them of being Prime Minister.

There are some who say that she was a very bad listener. I would argue strongly with that. Maybe she was not a very good listener when some of her colleagues were embarking on what I call waffle. However, often I was at a meeting of Ministers when a Secretary of State had to come and propose a new policy. She would begin the discussion in her typically strident way, saying, "Well, Secretary of State, I am not very attracted to what you want to do, but let us hear it, if you must". He would then explain what he wanted to do. Others would come in. Having listened, she would say, "Well, Secretary of State, if that is what you want to do, you'd better go on and do it. But if it all goes pear-shaped, don't come back to me to bail you out".

Of course, Margaret Thatcher loved, probably above all, an informed political debate. I have a memory of a very small lunch in Downing Street, when Pierre Trudeau come over from Canada to complain because we were not expediting as much as he would have liked the legislation to release British control over the Canadian constitution. At lunch, we quickly got that out of the way. Then Margaret Thatcher and Pierre Trudeau, who clearly disliked each other, embarked on a gloves-off confrontation of political philosophies. Francis Pym and I were the only outsiders present. It was a memorable experience to be a fly on the wall and listen to those two going hammer and tongs together.

The one word, I suppose, that many will think of with regard to Margaret Thatcher is "leadership". Many people today who look back on Margaret Thatcher's period with enmity were not alive when she was Prime Minister. A myth has grown which has led to the contentious attitude of some people today. They forget that, in 1979, Britain was on its knees. What needed doing had needed doing for decades. She set out to do those things. She changed Britain. She changed much of what went on in the world. She played a major part in bringing down what Ronald Reagan described as the "evil empire" of the Soviet Union.

Finally, I find the hostility that one hears from some people today hardly surprising. I do not believe that she would feel at all surprised by that hostility, bearing in mind what she had to do and the fundamental changes that she needed to bring about.

[Lord (Robert) Armstrong of Ilminster was born 30 March 1927 and was educated at Eton College and Christ Church, Oxford. His long career in the Civil Service peaked as Secretary of the Cabinet 1979-1987 and he rose to the Lords in 1988.]

3.14 pm

Lord Armstrong of Ilminster

Perhaps something should be said from the perspective of one who, as a civil servant and Secretary to the Cabinet, worked closely for and with her for eight of the 11 and a half years for which she was Prime Minister. Statistically speaking, the turnover of Prime Ministers has been higher than that of Cabinet Secretaries. Most Cabinet Secretaries have served more than one Prime Minister and sometimes three, such as my noble friend Lord Butler of Brockwell, or even four, as my predecessor Lord Hunt of Tanworth did. I am a relatively rare bird in that I served only one Prime Minister.

I was summoned one morning in July 1979 to a meeting with the Prime Minister at No. 10, which I hoped-but did not know-would result in an appointment as Secretary to the Cabinet. I was taken upstairs to her room and shown in at the door of the study. As I went through the door, she looked up at me and said, "Robert, you're looking very tired". It was not the most promising opening to an interview in which I was hoping to be offered one of the most onerous jobs in the public service, so I stammered out something about having been up rather late the previous night. Then she said, "Robert, I have asked you to come in order that I can tell you that I want to appoint you as Cabinet Secretary to succeed John Hunt in October". Of course, I was delighted and accepted the offer. I went downstairs and told the private secretary that the Prime Minister had offered me the job and that I had accepted it. But I said, "It was a little bit odd that she started by saying, 'Robert, you look very tired'". That private secretary said, "Oh, don't worry about that — she's saying that to everybody this morning".

The noble Baroness, Lady Royall, spoke about Lady Thatcher's lack of aspiration to be a feminist, if I may sum it up in that way. That may have been fair but she was nothing if not feminine and many of her colleagues, and many of those who were her civil servants, will recognise that. My recollection goes back to the first visit that we had from President Mitterrand of France to Downing Street, in 1981. We were all dreading it because he had no English, or claimed not to, so that everything had to be interpreted — and, of course, he was French.

Noble Lords: Oh!

Lord Armstrong of Ilminster: Lady Thatcher had greatly disliked his predecessor and Mitterrand was said to be a socialist, but the meetings went rather well. Despite the interpretation, they went smoothly and there were good speeches by both parties at a dinner. When the President finally came to leave the next afternoon, I went with the Prime Minister to see him off at the front door of No. 10 Downing Street. As we walked back, I said to the Prime Minister in what I suppose was a tone of some surprise, "That visit went rather well, didn't it, Prime Minister?" She said, "Yes, I suppose it did". Then there was a pause and she said, "Of course, he likes women, you know".

Noble Lords: Oh!

Lord Armstrong of Ilminster: Looking back, I recognised that the President had been — how shall I put it? — flattering her femininity throughout the meeting, and that she had recognised that and enjoyed every minute of it.

More than once during the time that I was with her, she told me that her role as Prime Minister was to be the guardian of the strategy. She had a clear vision of what that strategy should be and of the policies required to carry it out. She displayed great courage and determination in pursuing this strategy and in introducing and sustaining the policies which it required, and she could exercise great firmness and all the strength of her personality in making sure of the active support of her colleagues and her civil servants in putting the policies into effect.

She respected the Civil Service as an institution and valued the traditional virtues of integrity and impartiality. She liked and respected many but not all of the individual civil servants whom she had to deal with, and she went out of her way to be considerate and kind to those who worked in her office. But I think that she thought that civil servants in general were too set in their ways and had become too accustomed to the management of decline.

In discussing appointments with her, she never once asked, "Is he one of us?" She wanted to know whether someone was a doer as well as a thinker, and whether he or she had what it took not just to advise cleverly on policy but to manage a department or division effectively.

As many have remarked, she expected her colleagues and those who worked with her to work very hard, and she set us all an example in that respect. She was a glutton for work and took an infinity of trouble to master the detail of every subject that she was called on to consider, often to the discomfiture of those with whom she was going to discuss it.

That was all made easier for her and more challenging for the rest of us by her capacity to manage on three or four hours of sleep a night, not just for a night or two but seemingly indefinitely. For her, the working day was two or three hours longer than it was for any of the rest of us weaker vessels. There was no cat-napping during the day. There were times when it seemed like a very unfair advantage. She kept up the pace throughout my time, although I believe that there were some slight signs of weakening towards the end of her time in office.

One of my duties was to advise her on issues about the organisation of the machinery of government. I do not think that she was ever much interested in those issues: she thought that they were of secondary importance. What mattered to her was having the right policy and having the right person in place to put the policies into effect. Tinkering with organisations diverted energy from what really mattered and was a waste of time, energy, and money.

As has been said, she was a conviction politician with skill and determination in expressing her convictions. But she was also, as I very often saw, a shrewd, cautious and pragmatic political operator in government and adept at adopting and presenting pragmatic outcomes in a framework of principled conviction.

In 1982, the Government committed themselves to a policy of "rolling devolution" in Northern Ireland. The policy made little progress and after the election of June 1983 the Prime Minister was persuaded to explore the possibility of an agreement with the Government of the Republic of Ireland, which might give that Government, as a surrogate for the minority community in Northern Ireland, the opportunity to have a say in aspects of the governance in Northern Ireland without compromising-and this was very important for Mrs Thatcher-the sovereignty of the United Kingdom Government in Northern Ireland.

After nearly two years of negotiation, closely supervised and negotiated by the Prime Minister and her colleagues, as the noble and learned Lord, Lord Howe, and the noble Lord, Lord Hurd, will remember, we achieved a draft agreement. The draft was never going to set the Thames on fire-or the Liffey for that matter-and it could not be expected to go down well with the unionist community in Northern Ireland. It cannot be claimed that Mrs Thatcher was enthusiastic about it even at the time, but she clearly preferred an outcome that she could proclaim as a success, and which would certainly be welcomed in Washington, to a breakdown of negotiations and a failure of the policy that it expressed and represented. So she signed the agreement and so long as she remained Prime Minister she unwaveringly defended and adhered to it. After her retirement she was apt to say that she wished it had not been made. I believe that she was mistaken in that. Unlike the noble Lord, Lord Trimble, I think that the agreement, which has certainly been of lasting benefit to relations with the Irish Republic, was one of the foundations for the subsequent developments in Northern Ireland's affairs brought about by Sir John Major and Mr Blair.

[Lord (Michael) Howard of Lympne was born 7 July 1941 and educated at Peterhouse College, Cambridge. He served as an MP and in the Cabinets of Margaret Thatcher and John Major and was Leader of the Conservative Party 2003-2005 entering the House of Lords in 2010 when he stood down from the Commons.]

3.25 pm

Lord Howard of Lympne

My Lords, in order to understand the true greatness of Margaret Thatcher it is necessary to remember the state of our country and our continent in 1979 when she became Prime Minister. Our country was in decline — a decline that many thought was permanent and some thought was terminal. I remember listening — I think it was in 1978 — to one of the great gurus of the time. He saw no answer to our predicament. He said: "After the next election, we shall either have a Government that doesn't try to do the things that are necessary, in which case failure and decline will inevitably continue, or we will have a Government that tries to do the things that are necessary, in which case it will become so unpopular that it will be bound to lose the election after next". Margaret Thatcher proved him wrong and in doing so, as the Prime Minister said, saved our country.

It has been said many times, including this afternoon, that she was a divisive figure. She was. She had to be. There was no consensus on the right thing to do for our country. If she had waited for consensus, nothing would ever have happened. She saw what needed to be done and she did it with clarity, courage and conviction. It is also true that her divisiveness on occasion extended to members of her Administration. On one occasion, a Minister sent a paper to her that she rejected. He had the temerity to send it back with the words, "Prime Minister, this is government policy". She replied: "It may be government policy but I don't agree with a word of it".

In 1979, as we all know, Europe was divided in two. The eastern half was subjugated to the yoke of communist tyranny. The part that Margaret Thatcher played, in partnership with Ronald Reagan, in freeing those countries, has been well documented. However, there is one aspect of the story that is less well known. In 1990, as her Employment Secretary, I went to Poland. My noble friend Lord Fowler, my predecessor, had set up something called the Know-How fund to help establish small businesses in the newly free countries. My opposite number was Jacek Kuron, who had been imprisoned for his opposition to communism. He took me to see Marshal Jaruzelski, the man whose regime had imprisoned him. Marshal Jaruzelski told me about the part Margaret Thatcher had played in the rise of Solidarity. He said: "She visited Poland during one of Solidarity's strikes in the shipyards of Gdansk. She said to me: 'You know, this isn't an ordinary strike and you ought to talk to its leaders'. Until then, I had had no more intention of talking to them than I had of flying to the moon. But she persuaded me, so I began to talk to Lech Walesa — and you know what happened after that".

All of us who have stood for elective office have hoped to make a difference. That has become rather a cliché but, like most clichés, it is true. There are very few people who have made a difference on the scale that Margaret Thatcher achieved. She saved our country; she helped bring freedom to half our continent. The light of her legacy will shine as a beacon down the generations.

[Lord (Paddy) Ashdown of Norton-sub-Hamdon was a Royal Marine Officer; Liberal Democrat MP 1983-2001; Leader of his Party 1988-1999; and a Peer from 2001.]

3.30 pm

Lord Ashdown of Norton-sub-Hamdon

First, in a life that has, I suppose, had some small excitements, nothing that I have ever experienced so terrorised me as having to stand up as a young, inexperienced, wet-behind-the-ears leader of my party to question her in the House of Commons when she was at the full plenitude of her powers, with the inevitable result that I would be ritually handbagged (*hit over the head by Lady Thatcher's handbag*) twice a week in front of the microphones of the nation. Thank God there was no television in the Chamber then.

My second remembrance illustrates the point made by the Leader of the House about one of Lady Thatcher's best qualities and most formidable weapons. My wife and I had been invited to one of those Downing Street events to mark the visit of some foreign leader; I honestly cannot remember exactly who it was. Afterwards, as we came down the stairs of No. 10, we met the Prime Minister coming up. My wife, who, I should explain, is much more rampantly left-wing than I am, hated her policies with a passion. The Prime Minister stopped and talked to us for a few moments. As she moved away, my wife hissed through gritted teeth, "She's absolutely bloody charming, damn it". So she was — to everyone, except of course those who happened to be in her Cabinet, as this row of wholly unextinct volcanoes sitting in front of me will no doubt attest.

This was only one of her many paradoxes. As the noble Lord, Lord Armstrong, pointed out, she was not at all the straightforward, black and white, no-nonsense, unbending warrior leader that she latterly liked to portray. She knew, at least until the very end, when to compromise and did so, perhaps most significantly when, although relishing her anti-Europeanism, she nevertheless signed Britain up to the single European market.

In my view, three qualities set her apart as something different but each of them had its drawbacks. The first was a passionate commitment to freedom. As a Liberal, needless to say, I mostly welcomed that, although perhaps not as much as I should have at the time. Later, in Bosnia, when I tried to get a stagnant economy moving, I found myself putting into practice many of the very things that I had opposed when she introduced them: aggressive liberalisation of the markets, stripping down the barriers to business and lowering taxation. In these things she was right at the time, even if today we find that, taken to excess, some of these attributes have not led to greater prosperity for all but to near ruin and a disgusting climate of greed for the few. In this, I suspect that revolution she started has perhaps somewhat run its course. Our challenge today is to find a kinder, less destructive, more balanced way of shaping our economy, but that is today. At the time when she did those things, they needed to be done.

However, her belief in freedom was, one might say, strangely partial. She did much to enhance individual economic freedom, and our country was much the better for it, but she did far less to enhance the political freedoms of, for instance, the gay community or the people of Scotland, or perhaps most markedly and paradoxically-and this has been commented on, too — the standing of women in society. She was — and arguably, given the context at the time, this was one of her very greatest achievements — Britain's first woman Prime Minister. However, her influence and power came not from the exercise of the female principles in politics but from the fact that she was far better than any man at the male ones.

Her second defining quality was her patriotism. David Cameron, the present Prime Minister, recently called her the "patriot Prime Minister". It is a good phrase and an apposite one. However, her patriotism too, though so powerfully held and expressed, was more about the preservation and restoration of Britain's past position than it was about preparing us for the challenges of what came next. She used her formidable talents to give our country a few more years of glory, and for that we should be eternally grateful. However, that legacy means that Britain today still finds itself uncomfortable and undecided about its true position in the world, not least in relation to Europe, where the infection that she planted still has the capacity to rip apart her party. There can be no doubt that she restored our country's position in the world but in a way that perhaps today makes us even less able to answer Dean Acheson's famous challenge that, having lost an empire, we have yet to find a role.

Her final triumphant quality was of course her courage. This, I think, is the pre-eminent quality of leadership and she had it in abundance. Yet this, too-her greatest asset-had its dangers. I used to have a principle in distant, more robust days that I would never take on operations anyone who was not at least as fright-ened as I was, but she was frightened of nothing. She could see the risks but she ignored them if she believed she was right, and paradoxically this, in the final analysis, was what ended her long term as Prime Minister. Is it not always hubris that gets us in the end?

She was complex, extraordinary, magnificent, fallible, flawed and infuriat-ing. One thing, however, is certain and cannot be denied except by those so sunk in bitterness that they will not see: she won great victories for what she stood for at home and huge respect for our country abroad. If politics is defined-and I think it can be-by principles, the courage to hold to them and the ability to drive them through to success, then she was without a doubt the commanding politi-cian and the greatest Prime Minister of our age.

[Lord (Robert) May of Oxford was born 8 January 1938 in Australia and was educated at the University of Sydney. He was inter alia former Chief Scientific Adviser to the UK Government, President of the Royal Society, and a Professor at Sydney and Princeton. Today he holds Chairs at Oxford and London and was made a life peer in 2001.]

3.37 pm

Lord May of Oxford

My Lords, among the many tributes that Lady Thatcher received in her life-time, she especially valued her election as an honorary fellow of the Royal Soci-ety, and I think that she would be very cross if that were not mentioned on this occasion.

Lady Thatcher was, of course, a science graduate from Oxford, studying under, and doing research with, the Nobel laureate Dorothy Hodgkin. (*Nobel Prize for Chemistry 1964*). At the Royal Society event celebrating her election, with uncharacteristic self-deprecation, she observed that this validated her career choice, because she doubted whether she would have been elected a fel-low of the Royal Society for her research in chemistry.

Over the past two centuries, the Royal Society has elected very few Prime Ministers as honorary fellows, but Lady Thatcher richly deserved this recogni-tion for the way she promoted and enlarged the voice of science, and science advice, in government. It is easy to forget the huge importance in the immediate aftermath of World War II of having good science and the voice of science influencing the Cabinet. The presence in the Cabinet Office of a first-rate scientistdistinguished and effective — as Chief Scientific Adviser had declined. In the 1970s, the office of Chief Scientific Adviser had declined to an informal one-ortwo-day-a-week meeting with the policy unit in the Cabinet Office.

Lady Thatcher turned that around. She appointed a distinguished scientist and industrialist from Pilkington glass, Sir Robin Nicholson, and reversed that trend. She also valued, and indeed established, ACOST, the Advisory Council on Science and Technology, and frequently chaired it, which no subsequent Prime Minister has done.

In summary, we all know what a remarkable woman Lady Thatcher was, but we need more commonly to include and recognise her interest in and commitment to science as one of her remarkabilities, if I may coin a word. It certainly should be so recognised.

[Lord (Norman) Tebbit was born 29 March 1931, was an MP 1970-1992, and served Margaret Thatcher in Cabinet 1981-1987. He was seriously injured and his wife very badly so (permanently disabled) in the Brighton bomb at the Grand Hotel in 1984 and he gave up front line politics to help care for her leaving the Commons in 1992 to become Baron Tebbit of Chingford. Before entering politics he was an RAF pilot and then flew commercially.]

3.41 pm

Lord Tebbit

My Lords, I take my mind back to before I was elected to the House of Commons, when I spent a great deal of time abroad. Like so many of us at that time, I was constantly embarrassed at the sympathy that was offered to me by foreigners for the state into which Great Britain had descended. A few years later, I again spent a lot of time abroad, as the Secretary of State for Trade and Industry. The change could not have been greater in the admiration that was expressed for what had been done in this country. It was sometimes, I thought, slightly over the top. I could never quite get my mind around the remark made to me in Italy: "Oh, if only we had a Thatcher here!". Can one imagine the concept of an Italian Margaret Thatcher?

We should also come to some kind of consensus here today that there were two quite remarkable Prime Ministers of post-war Great Britain: two Prime Ministers who actually changed the country and did so in the way they wanted to change it. They did not sit as change happened round about them. They were Clement Attlee and Margaret Thatcher. We have accommodated ourselves to many of the things which Clement Attlee did, although many of us would have opposed them at the time. Even some of those in his party, of course, opposed his policy on British membership of NATO and possession of nuclear weapons, for example; and we, on our side, for much of what he did in the social services area.

We should also recollect that Lady Thatcher came into office in 1979 somewhat against the odds that would have been offered a year or so earlier, because of the winter of discontent. The trades union generals had brought down Ted Heath's Government. They brought down Jim Callaghan's Government. They brought into office the Government of Lady Thatcher. They expected, particularly Master Scargill, to bring down her Government, too. What would have become of our democracy had they succeeded?

How many Prime Ministers could have defeated them and preserved our democracy? How many of those who saw her in her early days as Prime Minister would have dreamt that in partnership with Ronald Reagan she would have precipitated the end of the Cold War and the bringing down of the Berlin Wall? It was she, of course, who observed that Prague was not in Eastern Europe but at the centre of Europe. That is a geographical fact. One of my regrets is that her successors did not sufficiently exploit what she had done, and that we have left those other Europeans-the Russians-still rather outside the European family and compact. There is still much to be done.

It is often said of her, and we have heard it again today, that she was divisive. However, there were two great influences in her life. One was her scientific training-and I am particularly glad that the noble Lord, Lord May, mentioned that aspect of her life. The other, of course, was her religious belief. If I may observe to right reverend Prelates, there is a precedent for being divisive: there are sheep and there are goats. The noble Baroness was aware from both her scientific training and her religious beliefs that there are things that are right and things that are wrong, technically, scientifically and morally. She pursued that which she believed to be right. I must say that as her party chairman I found that my life was made much easier by my understanding of the certainties of her beliefs. She never asked me to commission a focus group. Had I been asked I would have resisted manfully, I hope. What is more, if I woke in the morning, turned on the radio and heard the BBC's version of the news of the day I would know what her reaction would be to the news because of the certainty of the construct of her beliefs. It made life very much easier for me.

I should also like to say how grateful I will always be for the fact that she gave me the opportunity to serve in high office the country that she, I, and I believe all of us here, love. I am also grateful to her for that other side of her character, for the support that she gave to my wife and me after we were injured. No doubt somebody in this House will correct me, but I cannot think of a precedent for a Secretary of State remaining in office as Secretary of State although absent from the Cabinet for over three months. She allowed me to run my office from my hospital bed. Admittedly, I had the support of two splendid civil servants in particular who ran my private office, both of whom have appeared again in other roles: Mr Callum McCarthy, and another fellow who I believe has achieved high office somewhere more recently; he was the Secretary of State for Health not long ago. They were quality people, but it was she who backed me and allowed me to continue.

I did not always agree with her, because I have some rather strong convictions and views, too. I recollect one occasion when I left her office at No. 10, walked back to Victoria Street, got into my office and asked my Private Secretary if there had been any calls from No. 10. "No, Secretary of State", he said, so I knew then that I was still the Secretary of State while I was walking back.

Of course, she was brought down in the end not by the electorate but by her colleagues. Not only is it quite remarkable that she won three elections running—someone else has done that since — what was remarkable was that she polled slightly more votes on the occasion of her third victory, when she had been in office for eight years, than on her first. I regard that as a triumph for her.

My regrets? Because of the commitments that I made to my own wife, I did not feel able either to continue in government after 1987 or to return to government when she later asked me to do so. I left her, I fear, at the mercy of her friends. That I do regret.

[Lord (Clive) Soley was born 7 May 1939 and educated at the University of Strathclyde and the University of Southampton. He was an MP 1979-2005 and Chairman of the Parliamentary Labour Party 1997-2001, becoming a Life Peer in 2005.]

3.51 pm

Lord Soley

In a way one of Margaret Thatcher's achievements was that she forced the Labour Party to reinvent itself. Following the comments of the noble Lord, Lord Tebbit, I should say that it was also what Clement Attlee, later Lord Attlee, made the Tory party do after its reputation in the 1930s. Both those people had very different personalities but had a similarly dramatic effect on changes in the country. We need to remember that.

I also recall Jim Callaghan saying to me in May 1979 that the people he felt most sorry for were those of us who had just been elected, because, he said, "You will be in opposition for about 10 years". Well, we were 18 years in opposition, which was when we forced ourselves to change. It is an important impact in British politics that our system forces political parties to change. If you do not listen to the electorate, the electorate ignores you, and you pay a very high price for that.

I want to say a few other things. Jim Callaghan also said to me at the time that he had hoped with North Sea oil that we would be able to make some changes to the economy that we needed to make. That was really where he was at. He felt that the economy needed to change, and that with the advantage of North Sea oil we could do it. Margaret Thatcher took a different view. She felt, as has been indicated a number of times, that you had to force change on people. This is where I part company, and it is a fundamental difference between the two parties. There were ways of bringing about the changes that were necessary then without some of the conflict that we experienced. You need only look at what Germany did, particularly with East Germany, to see how change of that type can be brought about differently. That is an important lesson. It is a powerful one.

Margaret Thatcher also had, as the noble Lord, Lord Tebbit, knows, a strong suspicion if not dislike of trade unions. He and I debated that on one or two privatisations. I noted the good comments made by Matthew Parris in the *Times* yesterday about how she hated the closed shop, and hate was underlined by Margaret Thatcher. That is one of the ways in which she made some of the negative aspects of the trade unions change. I have never taken the view, and still do not take it, that trade unions are not a very important defence in a democracy; they are an important right for people. But I also acknowledge what we were blind to in the 1980s: that some of the practices within the trade union movement were not only doing us damage but were bad practices that needed to change. That is another message we should emphasise.

This may sound patronising but it is not intended to: when I questioned Margaret Thatcher in the House I sometimes felt that she was very much on the right track but was somehow missing the big opportunity. Council house sales are one such example. In my view, selling council houses would have been a brilliant policy if she had done what Hugh Rossi, I think, had suggested: reinvesting all the money from the sales of council houses into the building of new houses. Margaret Thatcher took the opposite view. If she had not, that would have been a truly brilliant policy. As it was, it was the right policy, but it was not followed through in the way I would have liked. Most people here have said that she followed through all her policies with determination. However, I should have liked her to have pushed over to the other side a bit on that policy so that we could have had the investment in housing that would have saved us a lot of the problems we have today.

I certainly did not like some of the language that was used. It has to be said that the language used about the trade unions was deeply damaging to the fabric of Britain, particularly in the north and the west. I was shadow Home Office Minister at the time and I looked at what the police were doing during the miners' strike, the print union strikes and others. What troubled me was that when the phrase "the enemy within" was used, you had to know that the police officer facing the picket line was often a relative or close friend of the miner on the other side of the line, particularly in south Wales but also elsewhere in the UK. The phrase "the enemy within" began to fragment society in a deeply unsatisfactory way. In a way, her love of an argument and pushing it through with a passion and fury of her own made her enemies, which perhaps need not have happened.

I agree entirely with the comments made earlier about the Anglo-Irish agreement, although, as I think I have said in this House once before, we owe an awful lot to Jim Prior for that and for his strategic thinking on the Anglo-Irish agreement. That was absolutely right.

Fairly soon after I was elected, the Falklands issue came up. I have heard the quotes from Enoch Powell, and they were absolutely right. What interested me and taught me a lesson was that, as a result of defeating General Galtieri, the dictatorship in Argentina fell. It might be beneficial if the people of Argentina think about that. Although it might not have been the intention in the first instance, it was the outcome. It might be contentious to say this, but it also is my belief that that helped to bring about the end of the juntas in South America, which we all took for granted at that time. One after another they fell. One of the messages was that you need to stand up to dictators. Again I might regret some of the language that was used-not least in the *Sun* at the time, which played on the worst aspects of nationalism — but the reality was that standing up to a dictator like that had benefits for the Argentinean people as well as being the right thing to do.

In a way, what saddens me the most is the divisions between the north and south of Britain and with Wales. If the policies in Scotland had been different, the Tory party would still be significant in Scotland. I for one as a Labour politician often prayed for the Tory party to recover in Scotland. If it had not been destroyed, the SNP would not be where it is today: namely, a threat to the union, which Margaret Thatcher would have been appalled by. In part, it came about because of the assumption that Scotland could be taken for granted. It cannot, and the same applies to Wales and other parts of Britain, including the north of England.

I think that history will judge her well. She was a major political figure by any standards. She argued dramatically and with great passion, but in doing so at times she sowed the seeds of bitterness. She loved an argument, she loved a challenge and she loved change. In that way, she was a Tory radical, not a one nation Tory. It is an important lesson for us all that you can be a great leader in a democracy but that no great leader changes things without hurting people. I say this not as any criticism of Margaret Thatcher, but I think that we should be careful about going down the road of military involvement in funerals, because there is danger in linking that to political parties. That might cause us problems in future.

Margaret Thatcher was an extraordinary performer as Prime Minister and very influential. That taught me a lot, but it is important that we recognise that there is a balance. People who are doing what are to my mind foolish things, such as having parties in the street, are totally wrong, but we need to recognise that in a democracy minorities have to be heard. No Prime Minister can govern entirely compassionately-Prime Ministers have to take tough decisions and hurt people-but in doing that they need to try to get some balance in the community. That requires compassion as well as conflict.

[Lord (John) Wakeham was born 22 June 1932 and qualified as an accountant. His wife Roberta was killed in the Brighton bomb of 1984 when he was trapped in the rubble for many hours. He was an MP 1974-1992 and served Margaret Thatcher in many capacities. He later married his secretary Alison Ward who had previously been Margaret Thatcher's secretary.]

4.02 pm

Lord Wakeham

My Lords, I sense the mood of the House and shall be as brief as I can. I do not intend to say anything about the great issues surrounding Margaret Thatcher, but I was her Chief Whip for the whole of her second term in office, and I want to say one or two little things about what I would call the human and personal side.

Frequently, late at night, I would have a long talk with her about the events of the day. I am afraid that the things that she said on those occasions will go with me to the grave, but anybody who had the slightest doubt about her sense of humour had only to be there on one of those evenings. She had a very agreeable sense of humour, even if, on some public occasions, she managed to conceal it.

Secondly, I have to say to my noble friend Lord Tebbit how much I appreciated what he said about the kindnesses that we received after Brighton. The kindnesses and support that we got were way beyond the call of duty, to the point where I held my wedding reception at No. 10: the first time, I think, that anybody had been married in No. 10 since Lloyd George's daughter when he was Prime Minister. It was very special that we were allowed that.

My last point has a degree of topicality. I remember when the chairman of the Procedure Committee in the Commons came to see Margaret Thatcher to say that he had a wonderful idea for improving Prime Minister's Questions. He had the bright idea that instead of Questions being on Tuesday and Thursday, they should be on Wednesday for half an hour. She looked him steely in the face and said, "What do you think the House of Commons would like?" That was the end of it. Things stayed as they were.

She had more madness-not madness, more reason-than she admitted. Of course she knew that every Tuesday and every Thursday, she had to be, as she put it, match fit for Prime Minister's Questions. That was a great advantage. However, there was a second great advantage in that her whole Government knew that on Tuesdays and Thursdays the boss was in the House of Commons defending the Government. If any department had not sent a note as to what issues were coming up, I used to get the message and would very tactfully ring some fellow who was towards the end of his political career, although he did not know it at the time.

We have heard great things from all noble Lords, but all I would say about her is that she was an extremely human person to work for and that to do so was of course the greatest privilege.

[Baroness (Shirley) Williams of Crosby was born 27 July 1930 and educated at Somerville College, Oxford and as a Fulbright Scholar at Columbia University. During a long career in politics she served in Cabinet as Education Secretary 1976-1979. She was a member of the "Gang of Four" which in 1981 split from the Labour Party to found the Social Democratic Party, later folded into the Liberal Party today known as the Liberal Democrats. She is an emeritus professor at Harvard University's JFK School of Government.]

4.05 pm

Baroness Williams of Crosby

Mrs Thatcher and I followed one another at Somerville College, Oxford. She became the first woman president, I think, of the Oxford University Conservative Association, (*I believe the first was Rachel Willink, just a few terms earlier. She was daughter of Henry Willink, Churchill's Minister of Health, and thus had high connections that Margaret did not enjoy.*) and I came, nearly five years later, to be the first woman leader of the Oxford University Labour Club. Somerville was the cradle for Prime Ministers, including Mrs Gandhi, and it very much embodied and understood Mrs Thatcher, who, above all — this is the first serious point I want to make-had the most incredible single-mindedness, determination, dedication and self-discipline. I do not think in my entire political life that I have ever met anybody who combined those four qualities in the way that she did. From the very beginning, she knew what she wanted to be and what she wanted to do, and managed to overcome virtually every obstacle one can think of.

So far in the speeches that we have heard, including the very moving one from the noble Lord, Lord Tebbit, we have not heard quite enough about the extraordinary patriarchal nature of British politics in the 1960s and 1970s. It was not easy to put yourself forward as leader of the party or, later, as a Prime Minister in those days. Our society was still a deeply masculine one, where any woman who stood up opened herself to patronage, to the assumption that she was of a second level of intellect and to all the rest that went with that. It is important to say-hopefully with respect but with some memory of what things were really like -that, for example, the then Prime Minister, Mr Heath, was clearly not too happy to have that particular woman in his Cabinet and rather cleverly seated her five seats away from him, so that she could not be seen if she got up and tried to speak. We remember that she had an extraordinary capacity to overcome-and even not notice in some ways — the objections that were raised to her as a woman. The assumption when Airey Neave took over her campaign for the leadership was that she would be most unlikely, on those grounds, ever to succeed.

In that context it is perhaps worth my telling one anecdote. According to Sir Denis Thatcher, at one stage he was sitting at home in Flood Street while Mrs Thatcher was ironing his shirts, which she was very keen on doing, and getting breakfast. She said, in a sort of rather casual way, "Denis, I am thinking of running for the leadership". To which he responded, "Leadership of what, Margaret?" That somehow sums up the wonderful balanced detachment and humour of Sir Denis. I cannot underline too strongly the extent to which I think Mrs Thatcher began to lose her life when he passed away. He was absolutely central and key to her whole personality and her ability to become what she was.

The second, very important, thing that I want to stress is something mentioned by my noble friend Lord Ashdown, which is her astonishing courage. Many people, including not least of course the noble Lord, Lord Tebbit, will recall the courage that she showed, and then sustained on their behalf, throughout the whole of the Brighton episode. Let us pause for a minute and notice the courage and daring that it took to take on the Falklands, 8,000 miles away, with the likelihood that we were going to be badly beaten. She knew that she had, in a sense, nothing to lose and everything to gain but it was still an extraordinary decision to make for a woman who was leading, to some extent at that point, a divided Cabinet.

I want to say one other thing. There is a great danger that we will sanctify Mrs Thatcher. She would not want that at all. She was always a great warrior. When she and I were in opposite positions — we were both Secretaries of State for Education, and sometimes opponents — she did not try to pretend that there was no difference between us. She loved it. She relished argument. She relished confrontation. She would not relish it now if this House failed to refer to that as an aspect of her personality and being.

There was another side to it, and I share the views of those who have expressed that. Her policies were terribly hard on the industrial north and Midlands. Her policies did not completely reflect the common ground that we were beginning to develop as a multicultural and multiracial nation. To me, that is an important part of what we are today.

It was interesting, however, that she was essentially a deeply pragmatic politician, as the noble Baroness, Lady Royall, pointed out. I will make two points on that. She never, ever, took on those things which were essentially, fundamentally accepted by the British people. She never attempted to roll back comprehensive education; she approved more comprehensive schools than I ever did. She never attempted to take on the National Health Service and turn it into a privatised service, because she knew where the British people stood and never forgot the reality of politics.

In conclusion, she was unquestionably one of the most remarkable Prime Ministers of her century, and in the world at that time. She also found it hard to get her mind around globalisation. Do not forget that she opposed, for example, the unification of Germany, which was key to the creation of a truly democratic Europe, west and east, in the period after the Cold War. We should not go too far in saying that she and Ronald Reagan brought that about; they made a major contribution, but there was of course somebody called Mikhail Gorbachev who showed astonishing courage in attempting to change the nature of the Soviet Union.

I do not want to take any more time up. There are many great speeches to be heard, and we have heard already some outstanding speeches. However, for courage, for single-mindedness and determination, there are few who matched Mrs Thatcher. History will certainly see her representation change in some ways — that always happens in history — but I do not think that she will ever be forgotten.

[Lord (Norman) Fowler was born 2 February 1938 and educated at Trinity Hall, Cambridge. After a career in journalism he served in the Commons 1970-2001 and in the Lords since then. He held many senior positions.]

4.12 pm

Lord Fowler

My Lords, listening to the radio and watching television in the Isle of Wight, I was struck by the number of Conservatives at Westminster who said that Margaret Thatcher had brought them into politics. Some even suggested that they had been Thatcherites long before she even came to power.

Although I served with her in opposition and in government for 15 years in succession, I make neither claim. Mine was rather a different journey. In the leadership election of 1975 I voted for Ted Heath, and then followed that by voting for my noble and learned friend Lord Howe. It is fair to say that that was rather an exclusive campaign. We had 25 definite promises and pledges and we ended up with 19 votes, that being entirely par for the course in House of Commons elections. We had some good quality, however, in my noble friend Lord Brittan and my right honourable friend Kenneth Clarke. As we chewed over the result in a small room upstairs, none of us was convinced that the party had made the right choice. It was then, to my total amazement, that Margaret Thatcher put me into her first shadow Cabinet; it is fair to say that that amazement was widely shared. I had never done a Front-Bench job before. I was put in charge of health and social security against Barbara Castle; I think that is known as a baptism of fire.

However, that proved a point about Lady Thatcher. Margaret was sometimes seen as surrounding herself with known supporters and yes-men. She had the confidence and the self-belief not to do that. As the noble Lord, Lord Armstrong, said, you did not have to be "one of us" to be in her Cabinet. All three of us at the time were doubters, but all three of us became members of her Cabinet, and our very good candidate — who sadly got only 19 votes-became her excellent Chancellor of the Exchequer, to whom she owed so much.

The second point is that she was personally kind and generous, and much concerned that her Ministers should not lose out in any way. I learnt about that in a roundabout way. After about 18 months I was moved from health and social security to transport. It was not the move that I was looking for. "What? Transport?", I said to Margaret indignantly. She said, "Norman, I did transport. You can do transport". That is exactly what happened. It proved to be a lucky move, for when the new Government were formed I went into the Cabinet, never having been even a junior Minister. Margaret Thatcher had a lengthy apology to make. She said, "I'm afraid we can pay in full only 22 Cabinet Ministers and you are the 23rd, so we will have to pay you at the rate of the Chief Whip" — my noble friend Lord Jopling, who is somewhere around. She said, "I am really very sorry about that". I thought it best not to say that I would probably have done it for nothing had she asked, and we moved on.

I was fascinated by what the noble Lord, Lord Armstrong, said about the visit of President Mitterrand to Downing Street. The noble Lord was lucky to face a socialist. My opposite number was a communist, M. Fiterman. The great thing was that after all these great events, you need a communiqué. It was a very genial meeting but there was nothing much we could agree on. The one thing we could agree on, at least in principle, was the need for a Channel Tunnel. The communiqué became about the Channel Tunnel. It ceased to be just an aspiration of the Department of Transport and from that moment became a proposal of No. 10 and went onwards.

My third point, on looking back on those momentous years, is that there were undoubted tragedies such as the Grand Hotel bomb. I remember as Health

Secretary going back to Brighton the next morning — I had been there the night before-to visit some of the wounded. If I may say so, I remember the courage of many people, not least my two noble friends here today. There were other undoubted crises, such as the Falklands. That was the only time I remember Margaret Thatcher going round the whole Cabinet table and asking each Minister, one by one, whether they were in favour of sending a task force. Virtually everyone agreed; there was only one exception. (*Not mentioned in Margaret Thatcher's own memoirs*). However, I am bound to say that I at least agreed with my fingers metaphorically crossed because I joined the Army for my national service in 1956, at the time of Suez. That was not our greatest time. It seemed to me that if we could not get our forces efficiently from Cyprus to Egypt, it would be very difficult to get them to the other end of the world in the way that we did. The success of the Falklands was a tribute to our totally professional Armed Forces and to the consistency, determination and courage of Margaret Thatcher. My lesson from that was that the MPs who had voted for her as leader in 1975 had been proved absolutely right.

Above all, serving with Margaret Thatcher was always exciting. It was sometimes also great fun. Some say that she stamped all over her Ministers. It is true that if you were prepared to be handbagged she would oblige. She did not respect Ministers who came in with a proposal that they immediately withdrew when they heard the initial response from the Prime Minister. I learnt very early on that she really did enjoy an argument. Sometimes you actually won that argument as well.

She was an activist, she was a radical and she was, above all, a leader.

[Lord (David) Waddington was born 2 August 1929 and was educated at Hertford College, Oxford. An attorney he served in the Commons 1968-1974 and 1979-1990 and for Margaret was Chief Whip 1986-1989 and Home Secretary 1989-1990 when he was elevated to serve as Leader of the House of Lords 1990-1992 and Governor of Bermuda 1992-1997.]

4.21 pm

Lord Waddington

I shall try to be brief, my Lords. I will not add to the catalogue of Lady Thatcher's great achievements: I merely wish to indulge in one or two rather personal reminiscences, which throws some light on her character.

Margaret Thatcher came out to help me in the Clitheroe by-election in February 1974 (1ˢᵗ *March 1979*). It was a very cold day and after an hour or two we repaired to a place to have lunch. I sat the constituency chairman on her left. He was so intimidated by the occasion that he could not think of anything to say for five minutes. He then burst into song and said, "Leader of the Opposition. Don't you think it's time we went for PR?" I thought that the Leader of the Opposition would explode. She choked on her prawn cocktail, gave a great gulp and then said, "Well, of course, if you never want the Tory Party to win another election that is a very good idea". The constituency chairman slumped into his seat and never said another word.

Margaret did not suffer fools gladly but she could be immensely kind-somehow very tolerant of ordinary human failings. The other day I read a book written by Carol Thatcher. In that book about her father, Carol said that she asked him one day what was his idea of the perfect afternoon. He said, "It is sitting in a deck chair on a hot afternoon with a bottle of bubbly by my side reading a good book, and Margaret in a reasonably calm frame of mind".

You have to say that Margaret was not always absolutely calm when you were working with her. She was always challenging, always relishing a good argument. Sometimes, when you had endured the flame and the fire, you came out of it thinking you might have won but you were never quite sure. She was a towering figure, but I saw signs of human frailty. I was with her behind the stage in the conference hall in Brighton in 1984. She was waiting to go in front and make her great speech. She was slumped on a sofa and I think it was Gordon Reece sitting on the arm of the sofa. Margaret was saying, "I don't think that I can go through with this". He said, "Of course you can, of course you can. When you get out there, the whole world will be cheering for you", and so it was. She went in out front of that audience and gave one of the most marvellous speeches of her whole life.

Margaret was absolutely free of side and self-importance. Once, I had an argument with her as to whether the BBC licence fee had been discussed in various committee meetings that we had had on the Broadcasting Bill. I said that I was absolutely sure that the licence fee had never been mentioned; she said that she was sure that it had. The minutes were called for; a man came into the room with a great bundle of documents. She seized the documents, threw them on the floor and flung herself on the floor to read them, bidding me to join her. After three or four minutes of fruitless search, someone knocked on the door and came in. Seeing that extraordinary sight, they might have been quite embarrassed. Margaret was not at all embarrassed. She got to her feet full of bad temper, not embarrassment. She flounced out of the room saying that the discussion would soon be resumed and that she would soon prove how pathetic was my memory.

She was a great person, a great person to work with, and I am immensely proud to have had the opportunity of serving under her.

[Lord (David) Williamson of Horton was born 8 May 1934 and educated at Exeter College, Oxford. He was a senior civil servant.]

4.26 pm

Lord Williamson of Horton

My Lords, I have been invited by the Convener of the Cross-Benches to join all the tributes to Baroness Thatcher, as I worked closely with her for some years. My memories of those years are vivid-not surprisingly, as Margaret Thatcher was never in the half light but always in the full light of events. My admiration for her is as strong as ever.

There are many noble Lords whose political responsibilities and political careers were very closely associated with Margaret Thatcher, and their tributes are weightier than mine. My tribute is from the point of view of a civil servant who briefed her and accompanied her to many summits and high-level meetings in the often tense and frequently contentious area of European affairs. It was both a pleasure and a challenge to work with her. It was a pleasure because, contrary to the popular impression, she always listened carefully to briefing and did not make up her mind until she had heard the facts and arguments. It was only after that stage that she became the Iron Lady. It was a challenge because she, rightly, judged the issues on the overriding criterion, "Is it in the British interest?", and so did I, not on other factors such as pressure from other EU states or other institutions.

Among the issues, arguments and, indeed, rows, during my time with Margaret Thatcher was the battle to obtain, and the process of obtaining, the budget rebate, which I believe has so far brought home about £70 billion to the United Kingdom taxpayer. In the light of later events, which are not relevant to our Sitting today, you cannot imagine how strongly she argued for two objectives-not one but two-which were, first, money and, secondly, the requirement of unanimity, so that the UK had a veto if there were any later attempts by others to take away or reduce the rebate. Both those objectives she obtained.

In the course of that, I learnt a lot about disagreements. It is therefore also a pleasure to me that, although all my papers are lost deep in the archives, I still have somewhere a piece of torn green blotting paper, on which, after a discussion between Margaret Thatcher and me, in the margins of a European Council, she wrote: "I agree. Margaret Thatcher", and then, again, "I agree. Margaret Thatcher". In the field of European affairs, that may not be unique, but it is certainly rare.

[Lord (Leslie) Griffiths of Burry Port was born 15 February 1942 and educated at Fitzwilliam College, Cambridge and the School of Oriental and African Studies, London. A leading Methodist minister, he was made a life peer in 2004.]

4.29 pm

Lord Griffiths of Burry Port

If I may draw your Lordships' attention to an entirely different aspect of the life and character of the noble Baroness, Lady Thatcher, it would be to mention her origins as a good Methodist. This has already been mentioned by the right reverend Prelate the Bishop of Oxford. Lady Thatcher was born in Grantham in the county of Lincolnshire, and of course, John Wesley was himself born in that same county, at Epworth. She was born into a very devout Methodist home, and the pieties and religious practices of that home, as well as the values and principles, were early learnt. I believe she had them processed into her very being, and I shared my views about that with her later on in her life.

I want to register where she comes from in terms of the primordial energies that shaped her character. She came down to London to pursue her career, although while at Oxford, as well as pursuing her scientific career, she was part of a preaching team that went around the villages near Oxford to take the Gospel and pronounce good news. Some of those who were in the team with her are still alive and will tell you their own tales. If only we can get the Appointments Commission to bring them into your Lordships' House they would regale us with many a tale.

I believe therefore that I should not just introduce an element that is artificially drawn in, granted the grand themes that have already been adumbrated in previous speeches, but that I should describe something that was essentially her. She and Denis were married at Wesley's chapel, where I have the privilege to be the minister, and Carol and Mark were baptised there a little later. She had an enduring fondness for the chapel and came back regularly. I say to many visitors who come our way that if they look at the handsome communion rail that was given to us by Margaret Thatcher, it is the kind of evidence that everybody needs that, despite all those who say the opposite, she did actually help some people to their feet. It is worth noticing that as a vice-president of the Friends of Wesley's Chapel she was a faithful friend, although, of course, as many Methodists do, she was translated into the other place, namely the Church of England, and made that her spiritual dwelling place on a regular basis.

I would have loved to have shared with her my feelings about her quotation of a sermon by John Wesley when she was in Edinburgh. It was a sermon on money, and of course, she was well known to have her own views about that. I think that she wanted to draw John Wesley very much into her own thinking and to make him suit her purpose. She quoted two points of Wesley's sermon, that it was the responsibility of all Christians to earn all they can — that is all right — and to save all they can, although I can personally attest that with a 0.5% interest rate there is not much point in doing that these days. However, she omitted the third point of John Wesley's argument, that having earned, and having saved, good Christian people should be altruists, spending and giving all they can for the common good.

As I say, she was a great friend. It is interesting that as well as being the minister of the church where her marriage service took place, I happen to be an honorary canon of the cathedral where her funeral service will take place. I shall be there next Wednesday in that capacity.

There are many points upon which I disagreed fundamentally with her. When she came, for example, to open one of the two museums that we have on our site — it was in 1981 and things were not going well for her at that time — many of us who championed the cause of the poor and were very radical young Methodists were out there, shouting the odds and sounding a different music from what was inside the building she was opening. She was as well briefed for a humble visit to the Methodist chapel as she ever was on matters of policy in the ways that have been alluded to in previous speeches. She knew the answers even though we who were there all the time often did not. It is strange that God, or whatever noble and secular Lords want to substitute for God, has put a sense of humour at the heart of things. This young Turk who was asking for this chapel to be pulled down and for the money raised to be given to the poor is now the minister of the very chapel that he wanted to be destroyed and disposed of.

However, she was a friend to the end. She wanted to come to church the week after their 50th wedding anniversary. Unfortunately, she suffered a stroke in the course of a short holiday that she was then taking in Madeira and was not able to come. I count it a great privilege to have known her just a little. She exchanged some opinions with me, for example about South Africa at a crucial stage in its life. She said "The chief's the man", meaning of course Chief Buthelezi of the Inkatha Freedom Party — and she could not have been more wrong, could she? At the same time, she did things which I suspect we on our Benches would be glad of because they were things that we would have liked to have done, but perhaps did not have the right positioning to do.

Hers was a very complex character. History will tell, but she was larger than life. The inhabitants of the county of Lincolnshire are known popularly as yellowbellies. She was not one of those. (*There are at least ten competing explanations for this phrase not one of which connotes the cowardice implied here.*)

[Lord (Tom) King of Bridgwater was born 13 June 1933 and educated at Emmanuel College, Cambridge. He served in the Commons 1970-2001 and in Cabinet 1983-1992 and was elevated to the Lords in 2001.]

4.36 pm

Lord King of Bridgwater

In the discussions already, I noticed that the noble Lord the Leader of the House referred to Britain being on its knees. I have brought with me my prop, which I used in successive elections in 1983 and 1987. Some noble Lords may be familiar with it. It is Sir Nicholas Henderson's "valedictory dispatch" from Paris, which he sent under the impression that he was retiring from the Foreign Office on 31 March 1979. He did not actually retire because no sooner had he got back to this country than the noble Lord, Lord Carrington, who was the new Foreign Secretary, invited him to go to Washington. He was a very successful ambassador for us there and very important during the Falklands War.

Perhaps I may read just a few extracts from what Sir Nicholas then said. It is entitled *Britain's Decline; Its Causes and Consequences*. Incidentally, it was written to the right honourable David Owen MP — I am sorry that the noble Lord is not now in his place — who was Foreign Secretary at that time before the 1979 election. He wrote:

"Sir — since Mr Ernest Bevin made his plea a generation ago for more coal to give weight to his foreign policy our economic decline has been such as to sap the foundations of our diplomacy".

He went on to say that, "[I]n the mid-1950s we were still the strongest European power military and economically ... It is our decline since then in relation to our European partners that has been so marked, so that today we are not only no longer a world power, but we are not in the first rank even as a European one ... We are scarcely in the same economic league as the Germans or French. We talk of ourselves without shame as being one of the less prosperous countries of Europe".

Sir Nicholas went on to say that "anyone who has followed American policy towards Europe closely over the past few years will know how much our role as Washington's European partner has declined in relation to that of Germany or France".

He ended with this statement: "Viewed from the continent" — he was our ambassador in Paris at the time but would be retiring — "our standing at the present time is low. But this is not for the first time in our history, and we can recover if the facts are known and faced and if the British people can be fired with a sense of national will".

Is that not what we are discussing here today, and is that situation not now remarkably transformed?

If I have one criticism of a great Prime Minister, it would be that in showing the leadership for that national will she worked far too hard. The one thing that I remember at Cabinet meetings-and one or two of my colleagues may recall this-was the occasional stifled yawn because it was such an extraordinary time. I remember walking out of a reception at No. 10 that she gave one evening. She was saying goodbye to various guests and just ahead of me was a BBC producer from the World Service. She said, "I do like the World Service. I listen to Radio 4 at 11 pm and midnight, and then I switch to the World Service and listen to that at one o'clock, two o'clock and three o'clock". Anyone who worked with her will know that she displayed commitment and knowledge, whatever subject came up. The amount of background work that she had done was clear, as the noble Lords, Lord Williamson and Lord Armstrong, will remember better than me.

Bearing in mind all the pressure that was on her, we have heard a number of tributes today to her personal approach to people and to her kindness. I recall a wonderful incident which, as noble Lords will understand, made a great impression. I came into the Cabinet at the very beginning of January 1983. My mother died two weeks later. I think that the first Cabinet meeting we had was when Parliament came back. She took me to one side and asked, "Did your mother know, before she died, that you had come into the Cabinet?" I said that she did and she replied, "I'm very pleased". It was that sort of personal interest in people that made such an impact on us all.

I do not blame her for landing me with some of what I think were the nastiest jobs in government. (*Tom King became Margaret's Mr Fix-It*). That would not be quite fair. I was Secretary of State for Employment through the miners' strike and I agree with everything that my noble friend Lord Tebbit said. Afterwards — I think this applies also to the comments about the Falklands — it may have looked as though the decisions that were taken were easy. However, both events were close run. They could easily have gone wrong and, if they had, it would have been the end of the Conservative Government and the end of her as Prime Minister. They were close-run things and very tough, and I say that having been closely involved not only with the Falklands but with the miners' strike, together with my noble friend Lord Tebbit, with whom I sat on the emergency committee throughout. However, they came right, and there is no question that her determination was the crucial factor with regard to both the Falklands and the miners' strike.

Then, for a quiet life, I went to Northern Ireland, where I had the pleasure of inheriting the plan that had been laid by the noble Lord, Lord Armstrong. It did not meet with universal approval from the Unionist party and we had some interesting times. I recall one moment when both Margaret Thatcher and I looked suitably nonplussed. We had the signing ceremony in the large drawing room in Hillsborough in front of all the television cameras and then she made a suitable speech, saying how she hoped that this would be the beginning of a good relationship, and that it would establish more security and confidence in Northern Ireland and a better relationship with the Government of the Republic. She then turned to Garret FitzGerald and invited him to speak. He started off in Gaelic. Margaret looked at me as though I would know what he was saying. I had been Secretary of State for only two months and had not learnt Gaelic in that time.

Neither of us had any idea about what he was saying and a bit of a shiver went through the room until we got back to the English language, which was a relief.

Her courage showed throughout that time. At the very beginning, I happened to have a flat on the same landing as Airey Neave. The bomb was placed in his car outside our block of flats and the tilt switch did its deadly work when he came out of the House of Commons car park. This was when Margaret was just embarking on a terrifically demanding election campaign. I do not think that any of us will forget the speech that she made as a new Prime Minister two weeks later at St Martin-in-the-Fields in memory of her great friend, who had had so much to do with her success as leader of our party and had been her spokesman on Northern Ireland.

Then of course we had the Grand Hotel and, sadly, Ian Gow. I remember that through all the difficulties — I agree entirely with the noble Lord, Lord Armstrong — and whatever comments and reservations come out now or later, she certainly backed me to the hilt all the way through as we sought to ensure that the Anglo–Irish agreement would bring benefits to Northern Ireland and the United Kingdom.

I will refer to an event that noble Lords may remember: the bomb outrage at the Remembrance Day service in Enniskillen. The event shocked everybody in Northern Ireland, right across the communities. It was a really difficult time when the confidence that one needed to maintain was slightly wobbly. I said, "The British Legion aren't going to allow their Remembrance Day service to be destroyed. We're going to have another service in two weeks' time". I talked to the noble Lord, Lord Powell, who was then her Private Secretary, and asked, "What is she doing on Sunday week?" He said, "Oh, she's got a meeting with President Mitterrand in Paris". I said, "What time is that meeting?" He said, "It's in the afternoon". So I said, "Look, if we organise it, do you think she'd come to Enniskillen to give the lead, reassurance and comfort that is so important?" Without hesitation, and in spite of the fact that she was a prime target for the terrorists all through her time, she came. It was wonderful cover. The press said,

"What's she doing on Sunday, with this big parade in Enniskillen?" We said, "She's got a meeting with Mitterrand". With the help of the RAF, she came in the morning and we had a great service. She got lashed and drenched with Fermanagh rain in the square of Enniskillen, but she did not let that put her off, and it was hugely appreciated.

Then of course I moved to defence for a quiet life and was able to see for myself the extraordinary respect in which she was held in Eastern Europe. I think I was the first NATO Defence Minister to go to a Warsaw Pact country. I went to Hungary. I knew already of the extraordinary respect in Poland for what she had done, which has already been referred to. In Hungary they gave me a piece of rusty old barbed wire. It was part of the 200 miles of the iron curtain that had stood for almost 50 years on the border of Hungary to keep back people who wanted to move away for a better life. The image throughout Eastern Europe at the time was that she above all was the person to whom they felt enormous gratitude.

Then we had the Gulf War. I sympathise in one way with Saddam Hussein. He was not to know that on the day that he invaded Kuwait, Margaret Thatcher would be in Aspen, Colorado, to receive the Medal of Freedom at the Aspen Institute, and that President George Bush was flying down the next morning to present her with the medal. That was Saddam Hussein's bad luck. As I travelled round the Gulf after the first Gulf War, there was no question that the belief of the leaders of the Gulf countries that they owed a debt to Margaret Thatcher for the speed of response of the United States at that critical moment. Contrary to Nicholas Henderson's valedictory report, such was her standing that George Bush invited her to attend a Cabinet meeting in Washington. Undoubtedly, her determination assured the speed of response that we got.

That determination and respect led to some problems in government. It was almost impossible for anyone to get elected in any country in the world without including in their election address a picture of them shaking hands with Margaret Thatcher. I remember that on one occasion the Cabinet meeting had been brought forward. She said to me, "I'm sorry this is happening a bit earlier, I'm going to the Derby". Somebody said, "You're going to the Derby?" She said, "No, I've got to meet Mugabe". That was an indication of the extraordinary range of people who wanted to be seen to be associated with her.

I suppose this is the ultimate endorsement. Some may remember the interview that she did in the United States with Walter Cronkite, which showed that the standing of Britain under Margaret Thatcher had changed completely. At the end, Walter Cronkite turned to her and said, "Mrs Thatcher, will you accept a nomination for the presidency of the United States?"

That leadership and will transformed our country. Her courage, humanity, good will and friendliness to anyone who went with her are things that we will never forget. It is a great privilege for anyone to have the opportunity to pay tribute to a very remarkable person.

[Lord (John) Birt was born 10 December 1944 and educated at St Catherine's College, Oxford. A television man, he rose to become Director General of the BBC.]

4.50 pm

Lord Birt

My Lords, over a long career in broadcasting, I had many encounters with Mrs Thatcher, as she then was. Some were surprisingly endearing, even tender, and some were extremely challenging, as noble Lords might expect, especially when I was at the BBC. I see the noble Lord, Lord Turnbull, is with us today. When Mrs Thatcher left No. 10, the staff in her private office clubbed together to give her as a parting gift a shortwave radio. The noble Lord said, "Prime Minister", as she was for another day or so, "this is so you can be angry with the BBC all over the world".

I first encountered Mrs Thatcher almost 40 years ago when, as a young television producer at ITV, my colleagues and I, several of whom I see here with us today in the Chamber, chronicled the deepening crisis in the UK in that grimmest of decades to which many of your Lordships have already referred-the 1970s. It was a decade of stagnating state-run industry, of accelerating inflation touching almost 30%, of three-day weeks, of the *Times* unpublished for a year, of widespread industrial strife and thrombosis. It was a decade in which the UK had to turn to the IMF for a standby credit.

On "Weekend World", where I worked at the time, we canvassed proposed solutions to our dire circumstances on both left and right. We took a particular interest in the ideas of Keith Joseph, not mentioned yet today, and his then protégé Margaret Thatcher. She did not emerge as Leader of the Opposition fully formed. I recall her as a tentative and nervous interviewee under Peter Jay's intense and rigorous cross-examination. Her fiery conviction would come later.

When Mrs Thatcher became Prime Minister in 1979, the country was anxious for all that to end-but the resistance that she had to overcome was still enormous, including, as others have said, from within her own party. But as we know, her conviction intensified, her determination grew and her courage proved formidable. Mrs Thatcher set out single-mindedly to address her toxic inheritance, and in due course she did indeed eliminate inflation. She introduced discipline to our public finances, she privatised the nationalised industries and she brought the trade unions under a new system of law. All that reform was unavoidable, but it also, as others have suggested, came at a high social cost.

In other ways, her premiership was not clear cut. Mrs Thatcher was an economic but not a social liberal. She was viscerally uneasy about Europe yet embraced the single market. She hated communism, but she championed détente. As we all do, she left behind unfinished business-in her case an underresourced, underperforming public sector. While she liberated markets and inspired a new spirit of enterprise in the UK, we would in due course learn that without strong and effective regulation we would suffer gravely from untrammelled market excess.

However, if Churchill saved us from Nazi domination and if, as the noble Lord, Lord Tebbit, has already mentioned, Attlee was the architect of a benevolent social state in the UK, it was Baroness Thatcher who reversed our post-war economic decline and restored Britain's confidence and standing, and who offered her successors a chance to build a new Jerusalem.

In an interview for the series on her premiership that she recorded for the BBC after she left office, Lady Thatcher declared,

"The Prime Minister should be intimidating. There's not much point being a weak, floppy thing in the chair."

She was never that — she was a very great Prime Minister indeed and truly the right person at the right time. The nation is deeply grateful to her.

[Lord (James) Mackay of Clashfern was born 2 July 1927 and educated at the University of Edinburgh and Trinity College, Cambridge. An attorney, he became Dean of the Faculty of Advocates, Lord Advocate, and Lord Chancellor 1987-1997.]

4.55 pm

Lord Mackay of Clashfern

My Lords, reference has already been made to Margaret Thatcher as a scientist and to her strong religious beliefs. However, there is yet another aspect to her experience that we should have in mind. She was a member of the Bar, having been a pupil to Lord Brightman, who many of your Lordships will remember from when he served here as a Member of this House and did tremendous work in committees of the House in various ways and in various subjects. She was a trained barrister.

My first personal contact with Margaret Thatcher was when she phoned me in Edinburgh on the Monday after the election in 1979, inviting me to become the Lord Advocate. A period of intense legal activity followed. At that time, the Lord Advocate was a member of the UK Government, but now, of course, he no longer is. He is a member of the Scottish Government, and the office of the Lord Advocate is to a great extent replicated in the office held by the noble and learned Lord, Lord Wallace of Tankerness. I was invited by Michael Havers, the Attorney-General, to co-operate with him in advising the Government on a lot of different matters. The ones that stick particularly in my mind are the European matters, because it was a time of great struggle in Europe in relation to the contribution that the United Kingdom had to make, which many thought was excessive. There were suggestions that we could refuse to make our contribution, and a lot of advice was sought about that.

The thing I remember particularly about Margaret Thatcher was that she was most careful on no account to do anything that was contrary to the legal advice she had received. From time to time, of course, she probed the soundness of that advice but, assuming the probing had been unsuccessful in dislodging it, she never went beyond it. Although that work was, in a sense, just legal work, it had an effect on the way in which she was able to negotiate, without the need to stop paying, the reduction in our contribution that she achieved. Many people thought that it was with the handbag; I believe that it was with really strong arguments that had been developed in the months before she went.

By 1987 I had become a Lord of Appeal in Ordinary. I was sitting in this House listening to a debate about extradition when I received a call to come over to see the Prime Minister on Monday afternoon at about 5 pm. To my intense surprise, the Prime Minister told me that Michael Havers had resigned earlier that day for the reason of ill health, and she invited me to become the Lord Chancellor. She said that she was very anxious to have it on the news at 7 pm, so the time for decision-making was not ample, but that is what happened. Her decision in that respect must be regarded as very courageous.

Her courage in other fields has been spoken of, and it was beyond any question, but her courage in this field was pretty remarkable because a very highly placed legal authority said that if he had been asked to take on the controlling of the Scottish legal system, he would have liked to have known something about it before he did it. I think your Lordships will know what was intended by that.

In those days, the position of Lord Chancellor to which I was appointed had a certain priority and protocol. Shortly after my appointment, my wife and I were invited to a state function at Buckingham Palace. At that time, the protocol was — it may still be, for all I know — that the first couple to greet the Queen and the royal guests from the other country was the Archbishop of Canterbury and his wife. The second couple to go in was the Lord Chancellor and his wife, and the Prime Minister followed. My wife could hardly contain herself at the idea of going in front of Margaret Thatcher into the royal presence. Mrs Thatcher just said to her, "This is what you have to do. On you go". My wife had to do what she was told. Her character did not allow for much debate on that kind of thing.

While I held office, I was completely free from any interference whatever in the work of the Lord Chancellor's Department from Margaret Thatcher. She never interfered. As your Lordships will remember, in those days the nominations for senior judicial appointments were made to the Queen by the Prime Minister on the advice of the Lord Chancellor. It has changed now, but that was the rule then. In no case did Mrs Thatcher ever interfere with any recommendation that I made for a judicial appointment. That was a sign of extraordinary confidence, which I very much cherish.

In those days, protocol gave the Lord Chancellor a status that sadly has been somewhat affected by recent changes. By the time Margaret Thatcher resigned as Prime Minister, it fell to me as a senior member of the Cabinet to express on behalf of her Cabinet our tribute to her. I have to say that I was greatly assisted in the preparation of that tribute by Sir Robin Butler, as he then was, because we did not have a lot of time in which to prepare this document, which we thought had some importance. She began to respond but, as those of your Lordships who were there will remember, she had some difficulty in controlling her emotions. Someone suggested that I should read her response, which of course she had written out. I said, "No, not at all", which was enough to encourage her to carry on, because she got immediate control of her emotions and finished what she had to say. Your Lordships will also remember that later that day in the House of Commons, she made possibly one of the best parliamentary speeches of her life. I am glad to think that she was prepared by the earlier experience.

As I have said, my wife and I are very conscious of the tremendous support and kindness we received. I have just illustrated our experience at Buckingham Palace, but that is just one from a great number. I know that many people here and outside have experienced extraordinary kindness and thoughtfulness from a woman who was extremely great.

[Baroness (Jean Barker) Trumpington was born 23 October 1922 and was educated privately to her mid teens. After a career in local government she was made a life peer in 1980.]

5.05 pm

Baroness Trumpington

I had to speak today because I owe Margaret Thatcher everything. In 1980 she delivered her first Honours List. There were six men and me — rather like today.

I was so lucky to come here and to have worked for her and with her, and fought with her. The fighting was part of the process. She liked to have something to fight against. It gave her ideas and helped her make up her mind later. I remember a poor man who sat between us at a dinner. I said, "The *Daily Mirror* is quite right about the mentally handicapped". She said, "The *Daily Mirror* is never right". (The Daily Mirror *sides with the Labour Party*). That started us off. I think the poor man thought we were going to hit each other, and probably him, in the middle of the dinner. That was the way it was.

The alternative was the incredible kindness. On one occasion when in terror I had to attend a full Cabinet meeting simply because my boss was unable to get there. I only had one remark, which was, "Professor So-and-So should get the job. The Department for Education agrees". In terror, I said it three times. I also had not had the opportunity to see how the Cabinet worked. It was quite a revelation. When the meeting was over and she was leaving, she came up to me, patted me on the shoulder and said: "I'll see that your professor gets the job". That was the way in which we operated. It was either death to the end or eternal friendship — and I know which I would choose.

[Lord (Kumar) Bhattacharyya (Labour) was born in Dhaka 6 June 1940 and educated at the University of Birmingham. An engineer, educator, government advisor, and founder of the Warwick Manufacturing Group, he was elevated to the Lords in 2004.]

5.09 pm

Lord Bhattacharyya

My Lords, the tributes paid to Baroness Thatcher demonstrate the huge impact she had on our national life-and rightly so. No matter what our political views today, so many of us are Thatcher's children. I will be very brief and simply share my memories of witnessing first hand Baroness Thatcher's famous drive, conviction and determination as she worked to save and revive Britain's industries.

Margaret Thatcher was that rare creature, a scientist-politician, as many noble Lords have just mentioned. She liked to get the facts and most definitely did not like waffle. Those of us who worked with her witnessed some memorable hand-backings, conducted with a very British, forensic politeness. Sadly, there was much to be forensic about when Baroness Thatcher became Prime Minister. Manufacturing dominated the economic landscape but in both government and private hands, our industries were underinvested, uncompetitive and unsustainable, which made them dependent on life support from government. Our manufacturers were industrial basket cases, yet it seemed a political necessity to protect the jobs that they represented. Our shop floors, such as Longbridge, had become global symbols of industrial anarchy.

Baroness Thatcher knew that this was not merely the fault of the workforce. British managers were poor. They had no understanding of global competitiveness, product development or design. They spent their time not managing companies, but managing their unions. By the 1980s, Japanese technologies and products starkly demonstrated the fundamental uncompetitiveness of British industry. As Britain's first professor of manufacturing, I had the honour of having my advice sought as the Government searched for solutions to this crisis. It was pretty bleak at times. I remember when it was first proposed to privatise Longbridge, nobody even wanted to buy it. However, there was a solution: hard work for British pride. British businesses had to start working with foreign companies. Some resisted that, but not Baroness Thatcher. She always understood the importance of working better, working smarter and then working harder.

Baroness Thatcher was never anti-worker, as people think she was. She certainly hated restrictive practices, barriers and compulsion, but she truly wanted to give workers a chance to achieve and improve their lives. That is why she came to encourage us to connect with industry, support advanced technology and give industrial workers new skills and opportunities, which we did.

What is Baroness Thatcher's legacy to British manufacturers? Through some very tough times, and despite much criticism, she built a framework for prosperity by giving British businesses the freedoms they needed to manage, invest and trade. The removing of the shackles made a huge difference. What we did not do, after she left, was capitalise on this. From Birmingham to Sunderland, British and foreign companies which invested in the future demonstrated what could be done. For example, as a result of Baroness Thatcher's reforms, we now have a thriving automotive industry. Yet too rarely have we seized the chance of industrial success that Baroness Thatcher's reforms gave us. For Governments and business alike, the lure of easy, unearned money was perhaps too great, and that happened for two generations. It is perhaps ironic that the freedom that

Baroness Thatcher so cherished meant that we suffered from the financial specu-
lation that she personally regarded with distaste. She preferred older, purer values: hard work, getting on and earning your place in the world.

The whole world heard those values. Everywhere I travel, from China to
India to Singapore and to this very Chamber, I hear echoes of Baroness Thatcher.
The voice is familiar and firm. I suspect that the noble Baroness would know
exactly what to say to those responsible for our industries and leave them in no
doubt what they needed to do to get Britain growing. We talk about rebalanc-
ing the economy; she would have done this 20 years ago. That polite, insistent,
forensic voice will be long missed by all who heard it.

[Lord (Norman) Lamont of Lerwick (Conservative) was born 8 May 1942
and was educated at Fitzwilliam College, Cambridge. Inter alia he served as
Chancellor of the Exchequer 1990–1993 and was elevated to the Lords in 1998.
He served Margaret Thatcher as Financial Secretary to the Treasury 1986–1989
and as Chief Secretary to the Treasury 1989–1990.]

5.14 pm

Lord Lamont of Lerwick

My Lords, I will follow directly on from what the noble Lord, Lord Bhattacharyya, has just said about manufacturing. However, before I do so, what a
wonderful treasure trove this session had been. It is going to be of great value
to historians and people who write about Margaret Thatcher, because so much
material has been produced in the period that we have been here.

I will not go over the economic points. I agree with the things that have been
said about how she saved our country and how her name is synonymous with
courage. I, as a huge admirer of her, of course accept that there was bound to
be argument after her death. However, I have been somewhat shocked and saddened by some of the comments made outside the House. I was so pleased that
the noble Baroness, Lady Royall, was so direct in her condemnation of those
today.

I do, however, understand some of the anger that was felt in some communities that were impacted by our industrial policy. I want to comment on that
because I was in the Department of Trade and Industry under the noble Lord,
Lord Tebbit. I was in charge of all the state-owned, loss-making industries.
When Mrs Thatcher appointed me, she said, "Your job is to work yourself out
of a job" — that is, I was to try, with Norman Tebbit, to make them profitable
and then privatise them. There was, as the noble Lord said, a real problem of
competitiveness and the cost to the taxpayer of sustaining those industries at a
time when we were desperately trying to reduce borrowing. There was the fact
that the jobs in so many of those state-owned, loss-making industries were not
real jobs-they were supported only by the taxpayer.

I always remember discussions with Ian MacGregor, the chairman of the
British Steel Corporation. In one instance, he told us that it was necessary to
make tens of thousands of people redundant in order that other people could

keep their jobs later on. He said that all the jobs would go if we did not grasp the nettle and take the firm, painful decisions that were necessary. It was indeed, as the noble Lord, Lord Bhattacharyya, said, because of inadequate management that people such as Ian MacGregor, Graham Day and Michael Edwardes were asked to take charge of industries to try to improve their productivity and move them towards profitability.

The problem of the one-industry or one-firm town was always in Margaret Thatcher's mind. Special measures were devised but, of course, when an industry goes, it goes quickly; it takes much longer to get new investment in. Sometimes it happens, as with Corby, but it is a difficult process. Some people said that Mrs Thatcher and Sir Keith Joseph were going too fast and that we should go slower, but to her and to her Ministers it appeared that those who said "Go slower" did not really want to make the changes at all.

It will be for historians to judge, but I think that when they look back, they will be struck by the fact that so many other European countries saw a similar decline in manufacturing to us during that period and that things that were blamed on her were really an inevitable progression of European economies.

One thing that Margaret always did when there were factory closures in a constituency was to agree to see the local MP. I know that she had innumerable meetings with Labour MPs representing some constituencies because there were frequent closures. Some very improbable and unlikely friendships were struck up between Margaret and people who opposed her and her policies on the Floor of the House.

Much has been said, and I support it, about how she was really a person of compassion and concern. The stationer Smythson once told me that Margaret Thatcher was the biggest purchaser it ever had of little notelets, because she was always writing personal notes to people when they had hard luck or bereavement or illness in the family. I have a little collection of notelets that I received. She was extremely loyal to people. I always remember when one of her PPSs, Fergus Montgomery, was accused of shoplifting. (*He was an MP and close aide to Margaret Thatcher in the 1970s*). It was all over the *Evening Standard* that the Prime Minister's aide was accused of shoplifting. What was the first thing she did? She took him into the tea room and went around the House of Commons with him, showing that she thoroughly supported him. Of course, the charges were all subsequently dropped.

I remember hearing of a meeting at which Ferdy Mount in the policy unit was present, an important Cabinet sub-committee. He had a terrible cold and kept coughing. Margaret said to him, "You've got to do something about that cough. What you need is this". She named a particular medicine. He said, "No, no, no, no". She said, "Just a minute", and disappeared out of that important meeting, went upstairs for about 10 minutes and came back with a whole packet of capsules which she then insisted that he took there and then. Of course, colleagues were thoroughly annoyed that that very important meeting had been disrupted, but she was so informal in that way.

I remember once helping her to host a party in Downing Street. I do not remember quite what it was for but after it was all over she invited the waiters who had been pouring the wine to sit down with her on the sofas and chairs. She poured them all a glass of wine and carried on chatting to them, discussing the party.

It was sometimes said that she was compassionate and concerned about drivers, secretaries and doorkeepers but not at all about Ministers. That is not true, although on one occasion I protested to Keith Joseph about how she had handled a particular colleague during a meeting. He looked at me in utter astonishment and said, "Oh really? You know her method. She deals in destructive dialogue". Then he said, "She gives me the lash. They send a stretcher for me".

She could sometimes be very unpredictable in meetings. I remember one occasion when she had been on a plane coming back from the United States. She sat next to the head of MGM — "More Gutsy Movies" — a man called Lew Wasserman, who was the chief executive. Somehow on that journey he persuaded her that her crowning glory as Prime Minister would be the state financing of film studios in Rainham Marshes in Essex. I was Chief Secretary to the Treasury at the time and this was revealed to me. I expressed some bewilderment and astonishment at this proposal and said to her, "But I thought we believed in controlling expenditure". I received a glare. I said, "I thought we believed in low taxes. I thought we didn't believe in subsidies to inefficient industries". I got more and more desperate and said, "Prime Minister, there's no unemployment in Essex. We would have to build the roads in order to get to Rainham Marshes". I remember her glowering at me very fiercely and in desperation I said, "You do know, Prime Minister, that we'll have all the environmentalists against us because there's a very rare bird" — I knew about these things — "called the Brent goose that breeds there". She looked at me and said, "You are utterly hopeless. All you ever say is 'No, no, no'. You do not have a constructive idea in your head. If you had been in my Government since 1979, I would have achieved nothing". I said, "Well, Prime Minister, you're always right about everything but there's one thing you're wrong about. I've been in your Government" — [*Laughter.*] I went back to the department and said, "The Prime Minister's made a very strange decision but we must get on with it". A few hours later, a call came through saying that she did not wish to pursue the matter. I saw her the next day, beaming. She congratulated me on something but there was no reference whatever to that matter.

Dealing with Margaret Thatcher was always unpredictable. She used to say, "Thatcher's law is that the unexpected always happens", and she made sure that that was the case. She was a wonderful person — someone whose name will, as I said, always be synonymous with courage. She was a person who always did things for the right reasons. It was a huge privilege to have known her and an even greater privilege to have been in her Government.

[Lord (Michael) Forsyth of Drumlean (Conservative) was born 16 October 1954 and was educated at St Andrews University. He was MP for Stirling 1983–1997 and Secretary of State for Scotland 1995–1997. He famously led a group of students to Margaret's then home in Flood Street, Chelsea, when she was the newly elected Leader of the Opposition to present her with 50 red roses on her

50th birthday, a media event that flashed around the world and helped his career enormously!]

5.23 pm

Lord Forsyth of Drumlean

The shadow Leader of the House, the noble Baroness, Lady Royall, was kind enough to point out that from time to time I helped Lady Thatcher as she attended the House of Lords. However, it was becoming something of a burden. I found that trying to keep going with my job and being here to look after Margaret was quite difficult, so I thought that I would tackle this problem. I said, "You know, Margaret, you've been Prime Minister and you've done a great service to our country. You don't need to come here as often as you do". She turned to me and said, "Michael, when we accept appointment to this place, it is our duty to attend here. How many times have you been here in the past two months?" That illustrated her love for Parliament and her devotion to it. Someone said earlier that she was scared of nothing. She was quite scared of the House of Commons. I remember seeing her knees knocking when she was making speeches. That was because she respected the House of Commons. When you were discussing policy she would often say, "What do we do about telling Parliament?" This was always central to her, and she had great respect for our constitution.

I first met her through Keith Joseph, as a young man in my early 20s, at the Centre for Policy Studies, now so ably chaired by my noble friend Lord Saatchi, where they were trying to build the building blocks to turn around our country. As a young man I was told that Britain had no future-that it was best to emigrate. Somebody wrote an editorial in the *Times* saying that it would be impossible to govern without the support of the trade unions. I thought, "I'm going to have to get involved here". I never wanted to be a politician, but I ended up becoming one because of Margaret Thatcher, Keith Joseph and the battle of ideas. Ideas fascinated her. Whenever you had an issue or a policy discussion, she would always start by saying, "What are the facts?", and then you would work out how you were going to sell this particularly difficult policy.

She was quite forgiving of mistakes, and I made a few. As a young man I was involved in her leadership campaign as chairman of the Federation of Conservative Students. We produced literature to encourage people to vote for her, which was aimed at young people. I made the mistake of sticking one of the stickers on the party chairman's door in central office, and there was the most almighty row, because the slogan was, "Put a woman on top for a change". I thought, "She will never speak to me again", but typically, she pretended not to understand the double entendre.

It is said that you can judge people by their opponents, and that has been used in the context of the disgraceful minority of Trots and socialist workers who have behaved so badly in recent days. I will mention one thing about Gordon Brown. As Prime Minister, Gordon Brown invited Margaret to No. 10 on several occasions but on one occasion she was invited for the unveiling of a portrait-a portrait of Margaret that had been commissioned and paid for privately.

In his tribute to her, Gordon Brown said that there were only three other oil portraits of Prime Ministers in No. 10 Downing Street. One is of Walpole and was the first portrait of a Prime Minister to hang in the Cabinet Room; another was of Wellington, who saved us from Napoleon; and the third is of Winston Churchill, who saved Britain and Europe from the Nazis. He went on to say, "And I think it is entirely appropriate, Lady Thatcher, given what you have done for our country, that the fourth should be of you". I was astonished by that, and then I thought, "Well, actually, it is possible in politics to recognise brilliance and achievements while still disagreeing". Gordon Brown deserves considerable credit for recognising that.

The noble Lord, Lord Griffiths, mentioned Margaret's Methodism. Her religion was very important to her. However, she could be pragmatic about it. In her latter years a number of us tried to get her involved in social occasions. It is often said that she was not interested in the arts and music and so on, but that is nonsense. She was just so busy sorting out the country that she did not have time for it. I invited her to Ascot, and she said, "Well, I was brought up as a Methodist and we're not really keen on this gambling, but I understand there are six races". She opened her handbag and said, "I've got £5 for each race. Is that all right?" The first race was run and she lost, and she looked extremely glum. I had seated her next to someone who was a racing expert, and I said, "What's happened?" She said, "We've lost". I said to this chap, who was called Dominic Burke, "Dominic, if you lose the next race you'll go the way of Michael Heseltine". She said, "That's quite right". She won every single subsequent race. She had all this money and said, "I'm not sure the Methodists were right about this gambling", and was so pleased that she stood on the balcony and joined in the singing of "Roll out the Barrel". I thought, if only people could see the real Margaret Thatcher, and not the Margaret Thatcher that has been painted as an image.

A number of people have pointed to her having a feel and affection for, and an easy way with, ordinary folk. My noble friend Lord Lamont talked about this. When I worked for Flemings investment bank, we had a fantastic collection of pictures. She asked to see the pictures, so I arranged a dinner and a number of prominent people from the City came to it. They all sat down while we finished looking at the pictures. I was taking her up and everybody was waiting for her. Then the lift door opened and a cleaning lady came face to face with Margaret Thatcher and said, "Oh, Mrs Thatcher, I like you". Margaret said, "My dear, what are you doing here at this time of night?" She said, "I'm just finishing my shift, but I'm such an admirer of yours". They got chatting and Margaret said, "Do you do the whole place yourself". The cleaner said, "No, I've got all my friends downstairs but they won't believe that I've met you". Margaret said, "We'll go and meet them". I said, "But Margaret, we've got a dinner going", but she went down and talked to all the cleaning ladies while everybody else had to wait. That was very typical of the way in which she operated.

Since 1990, she has been supported by a magnificent team of people. Of course, Denis was her main support until his sad death but Mark Worthington, her political secretary, really did work seven days a week and 24 hours a day. He did a brilliant job and sometimes dealt with very difficult issues which came up from time to time. I would particularly like to mention Cynthia Crawford, who was with her from the start. Crawfie organised her wardrobe and I can tell your Lordships that she was very careful about how she used her clothes and how they could be recycled.

However, Margaret always turned out absolutely immaculately, down to the last day that she was here, for a lunch just before Christmas.

I went to the last lunch that she held in No. 10 before she left as Prime Minister, when Keith Joseph paid a handsome tribute to her. He had been the architect of so many of the ideas that she, with her pragmatism and clarity of mind, had gone on to implement. He said that she was a beautiful giant who had achieved more than any of us ever dreamt would be possible. I cannot add to how he put it. He is, sadly, not with us here today but made such a tremendous contribution quietly to the Conservative Party and its philosophy.

[Lord (William) Waldegrave) of North Hill (Conservative) was born 15 August 1946 and educated at Eton College, Corpus Christi College, Oxford, and Harvard University. He served in the Cabinet 1990-1997 and became a peer in 1999.]

5.32 pm

Lord Waldegrave of North Hill

I was her last appointment to the Cabinet. In the run-up to the first Gulf War, I was going across two or three times every day as Minister of State at the Foreign Office until she said, "Come in, William, I want a word with you. You are to be Secretary of State for Health". This was unexpected news to me, as it was to the rest of the country and certainly to the health service. She looked at me and said, "I think you need a large whisky. I will have one too. Now, Kenneth has stirred them all up" — that was my right honourable friend Kenneth Clarke — "and I want you to quieten them all down".

She was extremely pragmatic, in the best sense, about the health service. She made it perfectly clear to me that if I thought that the reforms which had just been launched were not well based, it was up to me to stop them. As a matter of fact, I came to believe that they were the right thing to do and tried to follow them through. However, that showed that although she was often described as an ideologue — this is a point that has been made today — she was not. She did not fall into the mistake of thinking that there were grand theories to explain everything. She stuck to common, decent morality and then looked at the facts.

I want to make two small points in relation to that. It has been said already by the noble Lord, Lord May, above all, and by others that her science training was crucial to her. I think that it was; she was the first and only woman to be Prime Minister and the first and only scientist to be Prime Minister. I hope that there will be more of both. As the noble Lord, Lord May, said, she played an extremely important part in a number of crucial scientific issues, of which perhaps the most famous was the work to take action to stop the production of CFCs — chlorofluorocarbons — which were damaging the ozone layer. It did no harm, of course, that some of the crucial science which led to the proof of the damage to the ozone layer had been done by British scientists, by the British Antarctic Survey, so it was respectable science. She acted.

It was not always so successful. As a Minister in the Department of the Environment, I tried to persuade her to impose flue gas desulphurisation on the power stations to stop acid rain. She did not want to do it, partly because she did not want to put the price of coal up and damage the coal industry even more, although this may sound paradoxical to some. I plotted with Horst Teltschik, who ran Chancellor Kohl's office, and said to him ahead of a bilateral summit in Bonn, "Will you get your man to really put some pressure on over this, because I think she might move". She obviously saw me coming a long way in advance. We arrived in Bonn in helicopters and got out. There was a local inversion — a local hot day — and therefore smog. "Now Helmut", she said to the cowering Chancellor — he was always a little nervous of her, as were others — "I will tell you what you have here. You have got an inversion and a smog. If you had proper clean air laws, like we do in England, that would have put paid to all that. I will explain the chemistry to you if you like". He did not want to know the chemistry and no more was heard over that weekend of my plot. She was not an ideologue, she was somebody who looked at the evidence.

The noble Baroness, Lady Williams, said of course that we must not forget the towering contribution of Gorbachev to the reformation of Europe. But who was it who first spotted that Gorbachev was the person with whom we were going to be able to "do business"? As a footnote here, we should pay tribute to a brave man, Oleg Gordievsky, who briefed her that Gorbachev was going to be a man you could do business with, but then she sold Gorbachev to Reagan, and the rest was history.

As another example, where she is often misinterpreted, she understood that FW de Klerk was something different and that all the clamour about sanctions was irrelevant. She preserved Britain's position, so that when things began to move in South Africa, well briefed by a formidable ambassador in the noble Lord, Lord Renwick, we had leverage and she could say to de Klerk, "We will help you do this". That is what Mr Mandela himself recognised. He paid tribute to her role in the final transition days from apartheid in South Africa. It is a crude and completely ignorant caricature to say that she was on the wrong side in South Africa — when it came to it, she played a crucial part.

The House deserves one apology from someone like me, who is a member of the University of Oxford, which she loved. I was present once when she was at a dinner at Somerville, my mother's college, and spoke so movingly about what Somerville had meant to her, a grammar school girl coming into the world, and how passionately she supported the equality of opportunity that those colleges provided. It was a disgraceful example of the perennial ineptitude of the collectivity of the University of Oxford, which has nearly always managed to get these issues wrong-it got it wrong over Asquith and it got it wrong over her. It remains a disgrace and I only wish that there were some way of putting that right posthumously, but there is not.

In 1973, my then boss, Lord Rothschild, made a speech — or at least he gave a lecture which was then leaked — saying that in the year 2000 Britain would be half as rich per capita as France, which caused displeasure to the then Government of Mr Heath. It did not happen and instead we just overtook France. What had happened in between? Lady Thatcher had happened.

[Lord (Hugh) Thomas of Swynnerton (Conservative) was born 21 October 1931 and educated at Queen's College, Cambridge. He served in the Civil Service and was a novelist and a very distinguished historian. He was elevated to the Lords in 1981.]

5.39 pm

Lord Thomas of Swynnerton

My Lords, I had the pleasure and drama of being the chairman of Margaret Thatcher's favourite think tank, the Centre for Policy Studies, referred to so warmly by the noble Lord, Lord Forsyth, a minute or two ago, for all her time in power. It was a great privilege and great fun. (*No doubt but history judges the Institute of Economic Affairs (IEA) to have been far more important.*)

When she asked me to undertake this, I said, "But Prime Minister I do not know about economics". She said, "Economics doesn't matter: history matters and you know history". I think she believed that. She thought that the historical background to events was more important than anything else. For example, when she went to the Soviet Union for the first time, she arranged a meeting of historians of the Soviet Union of great distinction such as Leonard Shapiro, Hugh Seton-Watson, Isaiah Berlin, George Urban and others to discuss the historical legacy of Russia and how far Russia could be said to be influenced by its own history even in Soviet days. The same thing was true about Argentina. She was interested in the history of the countries to which she went.

Once I summoned up my courage and wrote an analysis of the different dynasties of China, which I hoped would help her when she went to Peking for the first time. I gave it to her and I saw the surprised eyebrows of that great Sinologue Sir Percy Cradock rising in laughter. Incidentally, Sir Percy was one of the many people in the Civil Service whom she greatly prized and appreciated.

It is worth mentioning something that has not been mentioned hitherto-her historic position in foreign policy. It was remarkable that by the late 1980s, she was on the closest possible terms with Mr Gorbachev, the secretary general of the Soviet Union and at the same time a great personal friend and ally of President Reagan. To have been great friends with the Soviet Union and the United States was a remarkable and unique achievement. I do not think that we ever had that, even in the days of Sir Winston Churchill, when the doubts about Stalin were always present and lurking behind.

I happened to go to a dinner in Downing Street the night that the Argentines surrendered. The historian present, Sir Michael Howard, pointed out that the victory that we had had over the Argentines had not really had an equivalent since the Battle of Agincourt in terms of number of people killed on our side as opposed to those killed on the enemy side. "Not since Agincourt", said Margaret Thatcher, who appreciated the allusion vigorously.

Margaret Thatcher was always concerned with things other than economics and it was a pleasure to work with her for such a long time and to have had such an interesting and moving time working at her disposal as I did for 10 years.

[Lord (George) Robertson of Port Ellen (Labour) was born 12 April 1946 and educated at the University of Dundee. He was Secretary of State for Defence 1997-1999 and Secretary General of NATO 1999-2004.]

5.43 pm

Lord Robertson of Port Ellen

Some three years ago, I was looking after Baroness Thatcher at the annual ball for the British Forces Foundation, where she was the patron and I serve as a trustee. I said in casual conversation, which was actually very difficult with Baroness Thatcher, "I saw Carol on television the other night". She said, "Oh yes. Carol was on. She speaks too much sometimes". I said, "I wonder where she got that from?", and she said, "From her father of course".

I was a foreign affairs spokesman on the opposition Front Bench for 11 years-probably a world record for anybody in that position. I saw 29 Foreign Office Ministers come and go but only two Prime Ministers. I had that specialised vision of seeing her go from the Euro-enthusiasm of her speech at Bruges, which still reads well as an epistle to Britain's strong position in Europe, to the famous day in the House of Commons when she quoted Jacques Delors and said, "No, no, no". My memory was not of the "No, no, no", emphatically delivered, but of watching the face of the noble and learned Lord, Lord Howe, the Deputy Prime Minister, as she said the words. It was as if he had been slapped across the face with a dead fish. Clearly it had a major impact, and perhaps that was the beginning of the end of the Thatcher era.

On the day I was appointed Secretary-General of NATO in 1999, I received hand-written letters from both Jim Callaghan and Margaret Thatcher congratulating me on the job that I was about to take and offering me their best wishes for what I was about to do. It was a remarkable thing to get two such letters on the same day. I had a lot of experience in foreign affairs to take with me to NATO. A lot of what I had to do in opposition was to agree with the Government over the Falklands, Hong Kong and the rest of it. I also had to attend a series of functions held by the Government. I used to think that Lancaster House was my works canteen. I went to one lunch in Downing Street with Russell Johnston, representing the opposition parties, in honour of the King of Tonga. He was a very large gentleman with a very small voice. Russell Johnston and I were very keen to get back to the House of Commons for Question Time at 2.30 pm but recognised that we could not leave before the principal guest. We waited until the last second when Mrs Thatcher walked out of the room with the King of Tonga to escort him to the lift. Russell Johnston and I shot down the stairs but were overtaken by the Prime Minister. She said, "The king is in the lift". Clearly, if the King of Tonga was in the lift, nobody else could get in. I said, "Yes, he's quite a sizeable guy, but very difficult to hear at the back". She said, "Oh, wasn't it fascinating what he said?" Her eyes were glowing. "He said he's probably the first Prime Minister in history to go on to become king". Russell Johnston and I had the same thought at the same time, but neither of us had the courage to say it.

She was a remarkable person. As I travelled both as Defence Secretary and Secretary-General of NATO, I realised that she was a very significant figure outside the country. As her popularity declined in this country and indeed in her own party, there was absolutely no doubt that the pioneering instinct that she had had, especially in Central and Eastern Europe, was well registered and recorded, and will be there for a long time to come. I have had a lot to do with Russia. I was the first chairman of the NATO-Russia Council. I recognise that the Russians saw in her somebody who was strong in her beliefs and in what she stood for. They respect strength. The collapse of the Soviet Union that occurred-I remind the House-30 months after its exit from Afghanistan was a seminal moment in world politics. However much we disagree with her in other areas, we cannot underestimate the role that she played in that tectonic shift.

During my time in the House of Commons as MP for Hamilton, I had a different view. Hamilton, the county town of Lanarkshire, overlooks the River Clyde. Beyond it are the towering industrial cathedrals of Ravescraig, Gartcosh and Dalziel, the great steelworks of the west of Scotland. They do not exist any more. Maybe they were going to go anyway. Heavy steel, engineering and the coal industry are perhaps in decline all across the Western world, but it was, as some of her former Ministers have said, the way in which it was done which left the lasting impression and which will cloud the memory of somebody who made such an impact on British life.

That is something that we have to register and remember. She was a mixed blessing. Of that there is no doubt. I have got a feeling that some of these distasteful and disgraceful demonstrations that have taken place in the streets might well have pleased her. She was not somebody who expected acclaim and unanimity, whether it was in the European Council or in the country as a whole. I remember the night that my friend the noble Lord, Lord Forsyth of Drumlean, organised a special dinner after 9/11 in memory of the employees of JPMorgan Chase who had died in the attacks on the World Trade Centre. Margaret Thatcher was there with Denis at the table. She made some comments about me speaking at the dinner; anyway, she was quite cordial. At the end there was a toast, the loyal toast to Her Majesty the Queen, followed by a toast to the President of the United States of America. I leant in across and said, "What if there was a toast to the President of the European Commission?" She looked at me and said, "The words will never pass my lips".

She was a great lady. There will be mixed feelings about her, but there is no doubt about the impact that she had on this country.

[Lord (David) Young of Graffham (Conservative) was born 27 February 1932 and educated at University College, London. An attorney, he had a very prominent business career before serving Margaret Thatcher as Minister without Portfolio, Secretary of State for Employment, and Secretary of State for Trade and Industry after his elevation to the Lords in 1984.]

5.51 pm

Lord Young of Graffham

My Lords, it is a great privilege to be able to pay tribute to the memory of Baroness Thatcher. I was her creation. The noble Lord, Lord Tebbit, put me in the Manpower Services Commission; she invited me into Cabinet. For five years, I had the privilege of working closely with her. I do not want to talk about those. Much has been said about the trials and tribulations of what happened over that decade. However, taking the words of Premier Chou En-Lai, when asked whether the French Revolution had been a success-"It is too soon to say"-I believe that the perspective on Margaret Thatcher will change as the decades go by and that her reputation will grow.

However, there is one aspect that has not really been covered which I would like to mention. It has been covered partially. I refer to her compassion and her greatness as a human being. Much has been said about the Falklands, but a little known fact about the Falklands is that every night during the six weeks of the campaign she would have a list of the casualties and every night, before going to bed, she would write a long, hand-written letter to the parents or partner, explaining how they lost their lives and in what a good cause it really was.

I was to experience this myself two or three years later. My young brother, Stuart, who was chairman of the BBC, died. On the day he died, by the time I got home, there was a three-page letter from Margaret, condoling me and talking about Stuart. An hour later, I got a phone call from Shirley, his widow. She had just received a similar letter, entirely different in content. Later on that day, my mother rang me. She had also received a letter from Margaret. How many serving Prime Ministers would take the trouble actually to do that?

One other little story shows that side of her character. After she had left office, my wife and I took her and Denis out for dinner. We were sitting at the Savoy when a waiter spilt something over my wife's dress. Margaret grabbed my wife's arm and said, "Don't say a word. If you complain, he'll lose his job". How many people would actually think that way? With all the talk about the Iron Lady, I pay tribute to a very human lady who accomplished so much for us all.

[Lord (John Selwyn Gummer) Deben (Conservative) was born 26 November 1939 and was educated at Selwyn College, Cambridge. He served as Secretary of State for the Environment and as Chairman of the Conservative Party.]

5.54 pm

Lord Deben: My Lords, I was chairman of the Conservative Party on that terrible night in Brighton and I was with the noble Lord, Lord Butler, and Margaret Thatcher at that very time. It was very late. We were writing the speech. Those occasions went on for ever. I thought I had the final bit. I knew I had not, of course, because there used sometimes to be speeches where I would be in the cellar writing on the autocue as it was moving and as she was speaking a bit that she decided she did not like. However, on this occasion, the noble Lord, Lord Butler, was finishing some work with her and I had just walked across the corridor to get the final speech photographed when there was a terrible bang. Automatically, the girls working in the office running off the speech and I all got to the floor. There was a second bang because the roof lifted off and then dropped again. It sounded like another explosion. The dust began to fall.

On my knees, I moved towards the door, opened it and put my head around it. On the other side of the corridor, the door to Mrs Thatcher's room opened and she was on her knees looking around the door. Tragic comedy are the only words that I can say to describe what was happening. It was a mixture of, "What has happened? What should we do? Don't we both look silly?" She got up, brushed herself down and said, "Right, we had better get on with something". But what should we get on with, because we had no idea? She knew that things had to go on. She never said, "The party conference will continue". Everyone assumed that it would because we knew-that was the point made by the noble Lord, Lord Tebbit-exactly how she would react and precisely what we would be expected to do. So we went off and organised the continuance of the conference. No one asked the question, except for the local chief of police. We soon told him that he had better not ask her that or he might be in even worse trouble than he clearly was going to be. The conference continued, although it was a harrowing and difficult time.

I was lucky enough to help write a lot of Mrs Thatcher's speeches. She kidnapped me after a speech I had made at a wedding. I was not in Parliament at the time. She said, "Would you come and help me write speeches?" I was surprised because I did not come from the same part of the party and I would not automatically have been thought of as a natural writer. But once she knew that you were loyal and that you cared about her, the relationship was absolutely one of trust, confidence and support. Occasionally, she would say, "Don't listen to this John, I am going to say something nasty about Europe." She would say it and then she would say, "You can listen again now", and we would move on.

I could not understand why I was seated next to her on the day we went with the Queen to open the Channel Tunnel. I was the Secretary of State for the Environment. We were both sitting there and I could not understand why. Then I realised that I was the foil. As we moved out of the station, she said, "This has got nothing to do with the Germans, you know. It is entirely the French. But I do not see why we import all that food from France. Why should we buy French cheese? We have perfectly good cheese of our own." I realised that she wanted an argument; so an argument we had. The argument went terribly well and we were half way through before either of us recognised that we had gone into the tunnel. It was absolutely a typical part of what she loved, which was to discover where she wanted to be by saying something to which she demanded a response. Her only demand was that you were rigorous in your argument. I have watched her destroy people, although never her unequals. She never set people down if they were in a humble position. However, she destroyed people who pretended that they knew the facts but came ill prepared. You never went ill prepared to a meeting with Margaret Thatcher.

I support the comments that have been made about her amazing kindness. You grew to have a very deep affection for her, even though you often disagreed. That was a very unusual ability on her part, and it was, as the noble Lord, Lord Young, said, down to her kindness to us all. If you had not had anything to eat, there were late-night meals in her flat. The first thing she would ask if you were late was, "Have you had something to eat?" I have eaten more coronation chicken produced by Margaret Thatcher than I have at any other place or at any other time. I think that she did know how to cook other things but that was the staple diet. She also always knew about your family. She always asked about them and was interested in them. She knew their names and never forgot any of those things. When you think of the number of people she had to deal with, that was remarkable.

Of course, she could make terrible mistakes. She came to my constituency during the campaign for the 1979 election, which she won. She did so as a favour, because I was fighting a seat which the Conservatives had always won, but she made time to come. We decided that it would be very good if she went to a farm. She arrived and there was a rather ill calf, which she was not supposed to touch. We had a nice fluffy lamb for touching. However, she walked up to the calf, put her arms round it and picked it up. It was very heavy. For the photographers, it was fantastic-wonderful. Holding up the calf, she said, "I'm going to call it Victory". However, the calf was ill and we got every vet in Suffolk to attend to it. We hid the calf from public eye and kept it alive until after the election. We were terrified that this blooming calf would die on us.

I want to say two very serious things. First, I echo the comments of the noble Baroness, and my very much loved friend, Lady Trumpington. Margaret Thatcher was a very beautiful woman. She had beautiful hands and lovely ankles, and she knew precisely how to use both. Any woman who is stupid enough to think that there is something unsuitable about using the gifts that God has given her should be ashamed of herself. She knew perfectly well that she used them not because she was not as good as men but because she was better than men, and she also wanted to have a bit of an advantage. It was a pleasure to see how she turned herself out and how she never forgot that she was a woman.

Secondly, I think that history will remember a rather special thing about her. She was a very cautious woman. She did not take on things lightly and she took them on one at a time. She recognised that you could not have a whole plethora of interventions, initiatives, new ideas and headline-grabbing ideas. She knew that you won things only by taking them one and one, by fighting them through and succeeding with them one at a time. Caution is something that does not normally go with a charismatic leader, but one reason that she stayed for so long and was so successful was that she did not go ahead with the abolition of the dock labour scheme until she had dealt with the problems of the mining industry. She did not move to privatise water until she had made sure that people recognised that it was the only way to pay the bills. She had a quality of caution, which is something that very few people of her strength have ever evinced.

It was a privilege, a pleasure and enormous fun to work for her. Things were always unexpected and changed utterly all the time. You never knew what she was going to say or how she was going to receive a carefully crafted few paragraphs, but you did know that you were in the company of greatness. She was a star, and stars rarely come. When they do, we should recognise them without rancour and certainly not say, "It is not quite as bright as we would like it to be", or that it fell in a different way than we might have liked. We should just say, "Thank goodness that our lives have been enlivened by that star".

[Lord (Maurice) Saatchi (Conservative) was born 21 June 1946 in Baghdad and was educated at the London School of Economics. He co-founded the eponymous advertising agency with his brother and served as Chairman of the Conservative Party 2003–2005. The Saatchi brothers created Margaret Thatcher's 1979 political advertising campaign which included the famous line 'Labour Isn't Working' next to a long line of people queuing for benefits.]

6.05 pm

Lord Saatchi

My Lords, the words party loyalty and love of party are often derided. They can lead to tribal politics, too much adversarial behaviour, tit for tat, Punch and Judy, and so on. But those words in the hands of Margaret Thatcher had a magnificence which only she could have achieved. I will explain how I know that.

After she was deposed, the view arose in our party that it would be a good thing, as there was much tension in the party at the time, obviously, if the former Prime Minister was invited to our party conference. It would be cathartic. She would not speak-that would be too dangerous-but she would go on to the stage to receive the applause of the party and that would be a cathartic moment. That was the idea.

I was with her in the green room in Blackpool and, in the course of making the kind of conversation that one does in the green room at party conferences, she said, "What did you do last night, Maurice?" I said, "I had a lovely dinner with Professor Anthony King", whom she knew. She said, "Where did you go?" I said, "We went to a lovely restaurant, but a funny thing happened". She asked what. I explained that we were upstairs; the downstairs was absolutely packed, as all restaurants in Blackpool are during party conference week. I explained that, upstairs, there was only our table for two and the rest of the room was empty. A long table was laid out for dinner for about 16 people. Professor King and I had the room to ourselves, as I explained. I also explained to her that when it came to pay the bill, I asked the woman who owned the restaurant: "What happened to those people?" It was a shocking moment and I remember it vividly. I have never described it before, but I am doing so now. She said, "You did this. Your party did this. Don't you realise that my husband and I can't keep this place running. Party conference week is the most important week of our lives. Without the money from party conference week, this restaurant would close". I said that I was very sorry; I paid the bill and we left. It was very upsetting. She was in tears.

I explained all that to Margaret and then-this is exactly what happened-she said, "Maurice, pass me my handbag". I did not know what she was talking about. I passed her handbag to her and she started to rummage inside and took out her pen. She continued to rummage inside and took out a cheque book. She said, "Maurice, what was the name of the restaurant you went to last night?" I said, "I think it was the Blackpool Brasserie". She wrote the words Blackpool Brasserie on the cheque and said, "How much do you think they lost as a result of those people not coming?" I said, "I don't know, £300 or £350". She made out the cheque; she signed it "Margaret Thatcher". She tore it out of her cheque book, gave it to me and said, "I want you, Maurice, to take this cheque to the restaurant, give it to the man or the woman who owns it and tell them, 'Conservatives don't behave like that'". What a woman.

[Baroness (Brenda) Dean of Thornton-le-Fylde (Labour) was born 29 April 1949 and started her career as a union member as a teenager rising to lead the print union SOGAT.]

6.09 pm

Baroness Dean of Thornton-le-Fylde

My Lords, Mrs Thatcher, as she then was, was a truly remarkable woman. She was elected in 1975 as leader of the Conservative Party. We need to take into account the fact it was not just the fact that she was elected the first woman leader of the Conservative Party, and what she had to overcome, but her very humble background and beginnings. I can remember quite clearly the impact that had on women in Britain. Whatever your political views at that time, we realised that she had made a huge achievement in a party that we had always regarded as male-dominated: the old boys, public school and all the rest of it. From the side came this woman who succeeded in being elected as leader of the Conservative Party. At the time, one of my heroines, Barbara Castle, wrote-and I paraphrase-"Having listened to the lass, she deserves to be elected. She is head and shoulders above any of her opponents, but I don't think they know what they're getting". How true that was.

However, 1975 also held another important landmark. It was the year that the United Nations declared International Women's Year. It was also the year that Barbara Castle's Equal Pay Act and the Sex Discrimination Act became effective. Many of the women in Britain, of all political parties and none, felt that this was a turning point for us: this really was good news and women would start to make their mark more than they had been able to in the past. It would be down to ability rather than a whole host of other criteria.

It is regrettable that the legacy of this quite remarkable woman, who was the dominant politician in the 1980s, did not much encourage the growth of women coming forward and taking positions of authority. I have heard today many warm stories that I have never heard before from Conservative Peers in this Chamber which, it seems to me, are stories of the family of conservatism. However, we must also remember that the public perception was not that. It was one of a Prime Minister who, whatever political party a Prime Minister comes from, has a responsibility to try to generate within the nation a feeling of one nation, consensus and being able to move forward together. Yet that public persona of conviction and confrontation held back much of what might otherwise have been achieved.

We have heard today about the trades unions. It has become a mantra, one of her huge achievements. It is just as dangerous to sweep all trades unions into one pocket of description, as it is to do so to any political party or group. There are trades unionists who recognise that change needed to take place. There are some sat on these Benches today, and I like to think that I was one of them; certainly, my noble friend Lord Young of Norwood was another, and my noble friend Lord Brooke of Alverthorpe. We were trying to make changes. Unfortunately, that statement about "the enemy within" was probably one of the most polarising statements against any change that we would have been able to achieve, and made consensus difficult. Had Mrs Thatcher, as Prime Minister, taken the same view with a number of the trades unions in Britain as she had with the President of Poland, in suggesting that he should talk to Lech Walesa and his fellow workers, maybe the outcome would have been different.

The trades unions achievement of Lady Thatcher is something with which history will deal. It will also be for history to judge her, but I think that we can all agree today that none of us would either support or condone, whatever our political views, the small number — we need to keep it in perspective — of demonstrations against Mrs Thatcher, bizarrely celebrating her passing. That is not something with which any of us identify or would condone.

One of the other strong memories I have of Mrs Thatcher was that many on the Conservative Benches in the Commons did not want her elected. She won. She deserved to win. Yet her last day in office as Prime Minister was marked by the brutality with which people in her own party treated her, somehow forgetting all that she had achieved for them. That was a disgraceful day, in my view, and did not recognise her achievements for the party. To hear all the support, warmth and memories that are being given today, there are some members of her party who have perhaps forgotten the role that they played in that very brutal downfall. It is something that my own party have never done to a leader in the past and I hope will never do in the future.

[Lord (John) MacGregor of Pulham Market (Conservative) was born 14 February 1937 and educated at the University of St Andrews and King's College, London. A merchant banker he served as an MP 1974-2001 and in Cabinet 1985-1994 becoming a life peer in 2001.]

6.17 pm

Lord MacGregor of Pulham Market

Shortly after I was elected to the House of Commons in 1974, I became a member of the Committee on the Finance Bill, which in those days went on interminably and at great length for many days, through the night in the upper

corridors of the House of Commons, going line by line through the various proposals in the Finance Bill itself. Baroness Thatcher was at that point our opposition Front-Bench spokesman on economic affairs, so led on the Finance Bill in
the Committee stages. On the day of her election as leader, we were meeting in
Committee that afternoon and evening. As some others will recollect, none of
us on the Committee expected her to be with us at all that evening, given the
many interviews that she had to give and the many celebration drinks and so
on with all of her supporters. Robert Carr, later Lord Carr, who was then her
Front-Bench deputy (*surely Robert Carr was the Shadow Chancellor and Margaret his
junior. Carr served as such 4 March 1974-11 February 1975*) on economic affairs, took
the lead in Committee. I happened to be on my feet, dealing with a very abstruse
and technical point on some aspect of the Finance Bill, in full flow at about half
past ten, when to my astonishment the door opened and in walked Margaret
Thatcher. She proceeded to sit on the Front Bench for the whole of the rest of our
session, through the night, leading from the Front Bench. I was so astonished at
her arrival, and so obsessed with my technical details, that I am afraid I mumbled
a rather inadequate congratulation on her victory. However, we were all absolutely amazed that she stayed to see the session through. That demonstrated in
a remarkable way her dedication and very strong sense of public duty, and her
commitment to her duty in the House of Commons.

Secondly, as Minister for Agriculture, I was very much involved in the first
full-blown reform of the common agricultural policy. We had many sessions in
Brussels on that front. We had got to a point in the middle of the night where
we were near to reaching agreement, but it went beyond the negotiating brief
agreed for me by the Cabinet. I had to refer back to the Prime Minister for her
agreement and authority to go ahead in the way that I wanted to. If I remember
correctly, this was at about three o'clock in the morning, so I agonised long and
hard about when I should ring her to get her approval. I rang at about 6 am, got
straight through and heard her response in a very clear voice. Clearly she had
been up for some time, working on her briefs — I very much take the point made
on this by the noble Lord, Lord Armstrong. I got her agreement and we were able
to go ahead. That demonstrated her indefatigable energy, her immense capacity
for work and her decisiveness when convinced.

I will add two separate points. On one occasion in Brussels, I collapsed with
a burst ulcer in the middle of the night and had to be carted away briefly to
hospital. I was astonished the next morning to receive a very large bowl of flowers and a warm sympathy note from Baroness Thatcher herself. It was another
example-we have heard many today-of her kindnesses in so many ways. I was
greatly touched.

I very much support-because I had experience of this myself-the points made
by my noble friend Lord Fowler and others in relation to the way in which she
absolutely tore into you if you were not a master of your brief and in full com-
mand not only of the facts but of the arguments. This was a bit disconcerting
at first. You thought that she was basically disagreeing and that you would get
nowhere, but if you persisted and knew the facts of your brief, she would agree.
It took me some time to realise that this was her style, because I recognised that

it was what I did to civil servants who put forward briefs to me. I always looked overnight for the points that I was not happy about or did not agree with, and started off with those before in the end agreeing with the conclusions that the paper had made. That was a great feature of all the negotiations that we as individuals had with Baroness Thatcher.

My last example is her final speech in the House of Commons on her resignation. As Leader of the House, I was sitting next to her during the speech. It was obviously an immensely difficult occasion and I was very nervous for her. I need not have worried. She defended her record and achievements with great clarity, power and eloquence. Half way through she was questioned by some opposition Back-Benchers-in particular, if I remember correctly, Dennis Skinner-to whom she responded with great gusto, drawing a huge response from her own Back-Benchers. At the end of the put-down she said something like, "Now, where was I? You know, I'm enjoying this". It was absolutely typical of the way in which she approached these speeches. It was a remarkable speech, and a performance that displayed the qualities of great courage and conviction that have been referred to frequently today and by which I will always remember her.

[Lord (Archie) Hamilton of Epsom (Conservative) was born 30 December 1941 and educated at Eton College. He served as MP for Epsom and Ewell 1978-2001. Between 1987 and 1988 he was Margaret Thatcher's Parliamentary Private Secretary.]

6.24 pm

Lord Hamilton of Epsom

My Lords, I joined my noble friend Lord Jopling's Whips' Office in 1982. The highlight of our year was when the Prime Minister came to have dinner with us, which normally ended with a question and answer session when her praetorian guards of Whips were treated rather like backsliding leftists. However, it was always a very invigorating occasion. It was a great honour for us when she then suggested that she might return the favour and that we might come with our wives to have lunch at Chequers. Unfortunately, that never happened because the Brighton bomb came in between, so instead dinner was laid on in Downing Street for both the Lords and the Commons Whips.

That meal ended in the same way, with the Prime Minister saying, "Right, does anybody have any problems or concerns they would like to raise?" I remember that my noble friend Lady Trumpington asked the first question, about pensions. She got slapped down pretty swiftly, and then John Major, who was the Treasury Whip, piped up and said, "Prime Minister, there is deep concern in the country on the following issues". She went for him such as I have never seen. A row erupted of such seriousness that it ended on a very sour note. At one stage, we thought that John Major might even walk out of the room, and we were very concerned that he may have completely destroyed his political career. As we walked from the dining room to the drawing room in Downing Street, Denis Thatcher came up to him and said, "Don't worry, dear boy, she gets like this sometimes". The next day, she reconciled the position with John Major, and three months later he was a junior Minister in her Government. That story is becoming better known and is very significant, because it indicates the sort of woman that she was. She loved the row but never had any feelings of bitterness. She respected people who stood up to her and never held it against anybody at all.

I came to get to know her much better in 1987, when I was made her PPS. If I am brutally frank, I was not terribly good at the job. I did very badly when Alan Clark came to see her as Minister of Trade, and I totally failed to tell the Prime Minister something. I do not think she was aware that Alan Clark always rather prided himself on having two attributes of Adolf Hitler, namely that he was a vegetarian and hated foxhunting. His pitch to the Prime Minister was that he considered it a very good idea if labels were to be put on furs saying, "The fur being sold here has been caught in an extremely inhumane trap". It would have been rather like having a health warning on cigarettes. The Prime Minister was absolutely appalled by this and said, "Alan, what on earth makes you so concerned to do this?" He said, "Prime Minister, didn't you know that I'm a vegetarian?" She looked at him and said, "But Alan, you are wearing leather shoes". He drawled, "I do not think you expect your Ministers to wear plastic shoes, Prime Minister". Needless to say, the pleas got nowhere because the calculation that Alan Clark had not made was that because the Prime Minister was MP for Finchley, many of her Jewish constituents were furriers and the last thing she was going to do was ruin their business.

She was very interesting. She never read the daily papers. I remember taking that up with her at one stage and asking why she did not. Every morning in Downing Street, we used to get the most wonderful summary of absolutely everything that was in the daily papers from Bernard Ingham's press department. I would give my eye teeth to get hold of that today; it was a brilliant piece of work. However, she used to say, "I never read the daily papers because they write such harmful and personal abuse about me and my family that I could never get the job done that I have to do". Later, when John Major was Prime Minister and having his problems with the media, I raised this with him. I said that she had never actually read the daily papers, and he looked at me as if I had gone slightly weak in the head. Certainly, part of her thing in life was that you have to do the job you are faced with and that it really was not good enough to be reading the papers every day, or you just could not get on with what needed to be done.

I always remember a meeting, held at Downing Street at five o'clock in the evening, to discuss a policy paper. I thought that it would all go quite calmly; I knew that the Cabinet Minister who was presenting the paper was a friend and somebody she supported. He had no opportunity to present his paper as such.

She launched into him and said, "It strikes me that the problems with this are the following", and so forth, and another furious argument took place, leaving us all looking at our feet and wondering, "Goodness, where is all this going to go?" She always kept to the timescale, which was half an hour for the meeting. We were coming to the end, and she summed up by saying, "Of course, I agree with absolutely everything you are trying to do here. I just thought I'd play devil's advocate and make sure that you'd thought out all the arguments". That is just one of the reasons why she was a very great Prime Minister.

As the leader of the Conservatives she was always terribly bored that the socialists had something called "Socialist International". She thought that this gave a lot of respectability to left-wing parties, and she could not quite understand why the Conservatives should not have the same thing. She was, therefore, very much party to setting up something called the European Democrat Union, which later moved on to be the International Democrat Union. Although she never took me, as her PPS, on foreign trips, this was a party political occasion, because the IDU meeting was being chaired by Chancellor Kohl. We sat in the most enormous room in the Reichstag building — this was, of course, before the wall came down-and Chancellor Kohl gave a speech to welcome everybody that I strongly suspect was written by somebody else. She just made a few short notes, and when it came to her opportunity to speak she pointed through the window and said, "People tell me that the building that we can see over the Berlin Wall, out through this window, is the headquarters of the East German intelligence service. People also say to me that they are probably listening to every word we are saying here today, in which case I would like them to know — ", and she then went into a great tirade about how freedom was what we were all fighting for, and that freedom would conquer in the end. How right she was; the wall came down not very much later.

The right reverend Prelate the Bishop of Oxford alluded to the fact that she was brought up as a Methodist, but she was always very much an adopted member of the Church of England. When I was sitting with her in the House of Commons, waiting to vote late in the evening, she was going on about the worrying question of women priests. She said that she did not think that there should be women priests in the Church of England because she thought it would split the Church of England. I took issue with her and said, "I don't think, Prime Minister, that as a woman Prime Minister you can really take objection to women becoming priests. Anyway, I don't know what you're so worried about; I think women are capable of greater spirituality than men, and they are also less prone to sexual temptation". "Oh, I don't know about that!" she said. As always with Margaret Thatcher, she never agreed that you had won the argument, but some weeks later Bernard Ingham would put out a very small press release, saying, "Thatcher backs women priests", and so forth. So she came round in the end.

The noble Lord, Lord Armstrong, referred to the fact that she could survive on three or four hours' sleep. I had to spend quite a bit of my time travelling in an armour-plated Daimler, whose roof was of course lowered to make it more bomb-proof. It had a very inadequate air-conditioning system, and we usually had very large policemen and drivers sitting in front. The heat used to accumulate massively, and I have to say that both she and I used to nod off quite regularly. It became rather embarrassing when my wife went around saying, "Archie spends much of his time sleeping with the Prime Minister in the back of her car".

Margaret Thatcher first came to stay with me in the country shortly after she stood down, in January 1991. It was interesting. We were sitting there in the evening and the telephone rang. It was John Major ringing her up to say that the hostilities were about to begin in the Gulf. Needless to say, she stayed up the whole night listening to the wireless to hear what was going on. I was Minister for the Armed Forces but went to bed and listened to the news the next morning. That might be one of the reasons why she was Prime Minister and I never was. It was an indication of her extraordinary determination to be involved, and, of course, it was a war that she had been very much involved with in the beginning.

The Thatchers came to stay with us quite regularly from that moment. We even had them to stay twice for Christmas. Shortly after Denis died, she came to stay with us down in Devon. At that stage, she still thought that Denis was alive. There was a period of her life, which was quite short, I think, when she was not really reconciled to the fact that he had died. It is regrettable that so much of that film, "The Iron Lady", should have been on the period in her life when she thought that her husband was still with us. She was never really the same again after he died. It knocked her very hard. He was a great companion to her and life was extremely difficult for her from that moment on.

She was a very great lady. She was an evangelist. She was not like most modern politicians. She had a mission. But everything that she stood for will survive her. From my point of view, it has been a very great privilege to have served with her and to have served in her Government.

[Lord (John) Gilbert (Labour) was born 5 April 1927 and educated at St John's College, Oxford, and New York University. An MP from 1970-1997, he held some junior positions and is best remembered for introducing the legislation to make the wearing of seat belts compulsory.]

6.35 pm

Lord Gilbert

My Lords, I would like to begin, if it is not an impertinence to speak from this side of the House on this subject, by associating myself as vigorously as I can with the remarks of the leader of my party in this House, my noble friend Lady Royall, and my noble friend Lady Dean in condemning some of the things that are happening in other parts of the country today. I was brought up, like many of your Lordships, under the rubric and golden rule "De mortuis nil nisi bonum". (*Of the dead, nothing unless good*). I dissociate myself from what is going on. It has no part of my party's support.

Secondly, I want to say how deeply I feel for noble Lords opposite who served closely with Mrs Thatcher in her Cabinet and at No. 10. I know what it is to lose a friend and a leader, even when they have left the leadership. I remember very vividly how desperate I felt when Harold Wilson died. I understand that colleagues opposite must feel terrible emotions at this time and I want them to know that they are understood on this side of House.

I am now, not unnaturally, going to talk about something a little unfashionable about the late Baroness — her luck. She was a very lucky Prime Minister and a very lucky politician. There is nothing wrong with that. I am sure that I will be corrected by the historians among us, but I am told that whenever a name was put to Napoleon Bonaparte for promotion to general, his first question was, "Is he lucky?" It is a very good question indeed. Baroness Thatcher was very lucky. To say that is in no way to diminish her achievements and accomplishments. I want everyone in the House to understand that.

But look what happened at the beginning. It was only because not a single man was prepared to stand against Mr Heath, whether on the grounds of reticence, gentlemanliness, loyalty or timidity, that she was the only one. That was luck. She could not have arranged that in advance, so what brilliant luck. I remember when it happened. I was in the same committee as the noble Lord, Lord MacGregor, when the news came through. I remember rejoicing with my noble friend Lord Barnett, who was leading for the Government. He was Chief Secretary and I was Financial Secretary to the Treasury on that occasion. We rejoiced and said, "That's marvellous. The Tories will never win a seat north of Watford from now on". It just shows how wrong and stupid one can be.

Then we get to the 1979 election. Who could have lost the 1979 election against a Government where the dead were going unburied, the garbage was piling up in the street and the country was in a state of utter shambles? She could not have lost. Anybody leading the Tory party would have won the 1979 general election. We created Margaret Thatcher, in that sense.

As for the next two general elections of 1983 and 1987, I have to be rather careful. I know that it is said that you make your own luck in this world. I do not know whether Margaret Thatcher had a big part in the choice by the Labour Party as to who was to lead them into the 1983 and 1987 general elections, but she could hardly have done a better job, in my view. If I say any more, I will probably get the Whip removed from me, so I must be very careful.

She really did not have it that difficult in those two general elections. As for some of the other people whom she was up against — Arthur Scargill; I ask you. Would you not love to have Arthur Scargill as your opponent in any debate going, a man who is frightened to go to his own members to get them to vote for a strike that he called? I cannot find parliamentary language to use to describe Arthur Scargill. Mrs Thatcher did not create Arthur Scargill; the National Union of Mineworkers, or certain branches of it, did, although not in my part of the world, I am glad to say, not in the West or East Midlands.

After (*Before. The battle with the NUM came after the Falkland Islands war.*) Arthur Scargill, she was up against a bunch of fascists from a tinpot banana republic in South America. It was a gift. I am told that it was a very close run thing: that we might not have won in the Falklands. I do not share that view, although I know that that is an unorthodox view. I know that certain things happened down there that should not have happened and that there was a certain amount of military bungling, which was our fault-not Mrs Thatcher's fault. As far as world opinion was concerned, to be up against a bunch of tinpot fascists was absolutely brilliant. She was lucky. She did not decide that the Argentines were going to invade the Falklands. She did not decide what a bunch of so-and-so's they were to have running their country. That was all her good luck. Good luck to her, but do not let us forget that she had an enormous amount of luck right through her career from beginning to end.

I assure noble Lords that that is in no way intended to diminish her achievements, because the important thing in this world is that if you get your luck, you use it and take advantage of it, and she did, ferociously, without any quarter given. I admire her greatly for that.

I have said enough this evening. I feel honoured to have served in both Houses when Margaret Thatcher was a Member.

I have just remembered a little story. I will let your Lordships into a secret that no one in this Chamber will know until I describe it, not even the noble Lord, Lord Wakeham. I was once present at a conversation between Mrs Thatcher and Ted Heath. I was the only other person present: beat that. She had only recently become leader of the Conservative Party. It was an extraordinary event that brought that to pass.

I had gone to a memorial service for Hubert Humphrey. It was held on a day when the Cabinet was meeting. The Cabinet was going to come, but had not showed up because the meeting had overrun. The first three rows on the left-hand side of the aisle were left empty, and I parked myself in the middle of the fourth row. I had not been sitting there long before a figure came up and sat down next to me on my left. It was Margaret Thatcher. She was looking sparkling and effervescent. Needless to say — do I regret it? No, I do not — I tried flirting with her. I thought I was doing rather well, actually. Of course, I would, would I not? I complimented her on how her dress suited her, the colour of her eyes and all that sort of thing. We were getting on famously.

The rest of the pew was empty until, all of a sudden, a shadow appeared at the other end of the pew, escorted by the ushers, and was sat down next to me on the other side. It was Ted Heath. There then ensued a conversation between Margaret Thatcher, me and Ted Heath, which was a very unusual conversation in that nobody said a thing to anybody from start to finish. Considering the personalities involved, I think that is probably unique. That is enough of that story.

We have lived in the shadow of greatness. We shall never see her like again.

[Lord (Michael Morris) Naseby (Conservative) was born 25 November 1936 and educated at St Catharine's College, Cambridge. He was an MP 1974-1997 and Chairman of the Ways and Means and Deputy Speaker 1992-1997.]

6.45 pm

Lord Naseby

My Lords, in paying my tribute to Margaret Thatcher, I can now share with the House a little piece of history. I was Airey Neave's unofficial PPS in 1975, and chief bag carrier. My job was to help him organise the future leader of the Conservative Party. In the initial stages, we met in Room J3 in the House of Commons; it was my job to book it, et cetera. The first person that the Neave team supported was not Margaret Thatcher; it was Edward du Cann. That campaign produced 80 or 85 supporters; it was around those sorts of numbers. However, Edward came to that group and made it clear that he did not wish to stand as the future leader, because he had recently married and he and his wife had discussed the situation and he was withdrawing his candidature.

We had an immediate meeting of the group and went through the others forecast to be running, and the consensus was that we should ask Margaret to join us. At that point, the information was that Margaret had precisely two supporters. I was asked to make contact, which I did, and Margaret came to address our meeting in Room J3. It was clear from the way that she addressed that meeting that this was a woman of considerable potential. Several Members this afternoon have mentioned "strategy"; she had a very clear strategy at that meeting, and had sensed what the party wanted in a new leader. Airey turned to me when Margaret had finished and said, "We'll have no questions now. Would you be kind enough, Michael, to take Margaret to the room next door and come back?", which I did. We had a fairly lengthy discussion. The unanimous view of the people present, except for three, was that we should support Margaret Thatcher. Most of the rest is history, other than that I was in charge of trying to persuade the 1974 intake to support Margaret.

The second example I give of Margaret and her ability and understanding of people and countries was after we took over in 1979 and I was on the Back Benches as a PPS in Northern Ireland. Even then, I had an interest in Sri Lanka. Judith Hart had commissioned something called the Victoria Dam in Sri Lanka. I knew about the dam-it would cost about £100 million-and I asked to see the Prime Minister to suggest to her that the project should go ahead. I had an audience with her, and with the then Overseas Development Secretary of State, and Margaret said, "Michael, there are two points I make to you: first, that if we as a country have an agreement with another country"-as the noble and learned Lord, Lord Mackay, said earlier today-"we stick to it. So the agreement is that the project will go ahead. Not only will it go ahead but, secondly, I wish to be there at the opening".

Some years later I was pleased to be there with Margaret and Denis, and we had a garden party before the formal opening at the dam. The big thing in Sri Lanka in those days was the President's elephant named Raja. Denis was asked whether he wished to give bananas to the elephant, and of course accepted. Unfortunately for Denis, he was not too good on the anatomy of an elephant. Denis decided that elephants took bananas through their trunks. Just as Margaret was about to tell him, "No, don't put it in his trunk", it was too late. Denis put half a dozen bananas in the trunk of the elephant, which then did a typical elephant snort and the rest of us were covered by bananas. Margaret said, "I thought I told you early on, 'Put it in his mouth, not in his trunk'. Did you not hear me?"

Those are my two personal memories. As some of you know, I take a great interest in history. If Cromwell was the catalyst of parliamentary democracy, then in my judgment Margaret Thatcher will go down as the person who was the catalyst to change our country into the country it is today.

[Lord (Michael) Spicer (Conservative) was born 22 January 1943 and edu-cated at Emmanuel College, Cambridge. He was an MP 1974-2010 and Chairman of the 1922 Committee 2001-2010.]

6.50 pm

Lord Spicer

My Lords, my noble friend Lord Tebbit said that his top two PMs — using the terminology of today's *Sun* — were Margaret Thatcher and Clem Attlee. Word has it that Clem Attlee was a very skilled sacker of Ministers. The norm when sacking a Minister would be something along the lines of, "Thank you very much for coming to see me, Michael. With your sophistication you will know that I've got to make room in my Government. You are a bit long in the tooth now, we've got younger men to look after and we would very much enjoy it if you would become Governor-General of the Bahamas and, with your wife, enjoy the rest of your life". It is said that Clem Attlee would say, "Look, I've got to get rid of you by the time of the one o'clock news. Do you know why you've got to go?" "No, sir". "Because you're no bloody good, that's why". The fact is that he, like Margaret Thatcher, was a strong Prime Minister.

I intend to intervene for a very short time, but I feel bound to do so. I was her PPS, although not for as long as my noble friend Lord Hamilton, and I was Deputy Chairman of the party at the time of the Brighton bomb, when my noble friend Lord Deben — he probably does not remember this — rang me from the police station where he and the Prime Minister had gone after the bomb exploded and said, "She's got two things she wants you to do. One is to get the show on the road and the other is to open the shop at nine o'clock for the conference". (*Many caught in the bombing lost all but the clothes in which they were dressed. A local depart-ment store, Marks & Spencer, opened early so that delegates could be appropriately dressed.*) Those are my two credentials for joining the debate.

One memory I will share with the House goes back almost to her last day in government. I was Minister for Housing and she summoned me to the Cabinet Room. It was a one-to-one meeting — I was on my own with her — and she said the words that will always be in my mind. We had had our meeting and I was packing up my papers when she said, "Michael, you know we've failed to destroy the dependency culture". That stuck with me. A lot has been said today about her caution, and I will say a word about it myself. What has not been said is that she did in some cases regret that caution. That is something that has not fully come over. It was not just the dependency culture, although she did regret that she had not done anything to make sure that the welfare state was focused on those who really needed support. In the modern idiom, she would have "done her nut" had she realised that it would be a Conservative–Lib Dem coalition Govern-ment who would be the first to do something about it.

On privatisation, there were all sorts of things that she would have liked. She did not privatise coal, the railways, the nuclear industry or the Post Office. With the really difficult one, electricity — as it happened I was the Minister who took the Bill through the Commons-I believe that it was very much the powers of persuasion of my noble friend Lord Parkinson against the advice of Walter Marshall, her great friend and mentor in many ways, that created the Bill that we eventually put through Parliament. It was very much touch and go as to whether we went ahead with that privatisation, because of her caution.

I stress her caution only because others have emphasised her sense of direction and the wonderful things that she achieved. Her caution stretched beyond privatisation to Europe, which has been mentioned already today. She did, I think, regret the Single European Act and how far she pushed the Maastricht treaty before it came into being.

All that is something of an antidote to some of the more critical things that have been said about her extremism and her desire to do things in a hurry. Far from it-I think that sometimes she felt that she had not done things in enough of a hurry. I want to put that to the House because I think her impetuosity has been much misinterpreted, and that has come across in several speeches today. She was a very cautious and very wise person, and that is why she was so effective. It was a great honour to serve with her in that context.

[Lord (James Douglas-Hamilton) Selkirk of Douglas (Conservative) was born 31 July 1942 and educated at Eton College, the University of Edinburgh, and Balliol College, Oxford. He was an MP 1974–1997 and a Member of the Scottish Parliament 1999–2007.]

6.55 pm

Lord Selkirk of Douglas

I endorse the view of several noble Lords that Margaret Thatcher was prepared to go the extra mile on small, non-political, non-party matters last thing at night when she returned to her office in Downing Street. I remember being told that by the late Ian Gow, who took me into her office and showed me the kinds of letters that were sent to her, as well as bottles of whisky for charity fetes and the like. Just like an old trooper, she would settle down and sign the lot.

If I may say so, being a Minister in her Government was challenging, interesting and never dull. In Scotland, home ownership went up from about 30% to about 60% under her premiership, which was a massive change. Lady Thatcher believed very strongly in expanding home ownership, and one episode is extremely vivid in my memory. The Prime Minister was in Uphall, West Lothian, for the first rent-to-mortgage sale in Scotland to former public sector tenants. As we stood in their sitting room in that small house, a girl who was the editor of the local school magazine asked Mrs Thatcher, as she then was, what her favourite sport was. The Prime Minister immediately made the surprising revelation that it was skiing. She then went on to say that neither she nor any of her Ministers would be doing any skiing at all, as none of them could afford the time off if they broke a leg. As it happened, I looked across at Michael Forsyth — now the noble Lord, Lord Forsyth of Drumlean — who was Secretary of State for Scotland and was standing just beside her. I knew for a fact that both he and

I had just completed our arrangements to go skiing within days, if not hours. We gave each other a smile but said not a word.

After the ceremonial transfer of ownership, I was invited to go with her in the Prime Minister's car and, as we left, a protestor hurled an egg straight at us. The driver accelerated and the egg landed harmlessly in the road. The Prime Minister looked as though absolutely nothing had happened, and it was then that I realised that she was not called the Iron Lady for nothing.

She may not have made a farewell address to this House but she certainly summed up what she believed in in two sentences in her book on statecraft, showing all her continuing zeal and cutting edge. She wrote:

> The demand that power be limited and accountable, the determination that force shall not override justice, the conviction that individual human beings have an absolute moral worth which government must respect-such things are uniquely embedded in the political culture of the English speaking people ... They are our enduring legacy to the world.

She was very much at home in the House of Commons. She was a standard-bearer for parliamentary democracy, and that is something of which her own family can be very proud, as can we as parliamentarians.

[Lord (Robin) Butler of Brockwell (Crossbencher) was born 3 January 1938 and educated at Harrow School and University College, Oxford. He was a civil servant.]

6.59 pm

Lord Butler of Brockwell

My Lords, I have listened to all the wonderful tributes paid this afternoon and this evening, and I have asked myself whether there is anything which I can add. There are just one or two aspects which I should like to add. I was not going to speak about the Brighton bomb because her resolution and courage on that occasion has been widely dealt with. However, since the noble Lord, Lord Deben, who I am glad to see in his place, referred to it and to the tragicomic aspect of it, I should supplement the picture that he gave of his crawling to the door, opening it and meeting Margaret Thatcher's face on the other side. As he may remember, she was gorgeously attired in the blue evening dress that she had been wearing for the blue ball, which added to the absurdity of that tragic situation.

I am very pleased that reference has been made to the kindness shown to Lady Thatcher by the noble Lord, Lord Forsyth. I believe that another person should be added. He is a colleague of mine on the Crossbenches and was a colleague at No 10; namely, my noble friend Lord Powell of Bayswater. He and his wife have been splendid to Lady Thatcher in her latter days. Indeed, I think that on Sunday evening, he was the last person, outside her family, to visit her. About a month ago, my noble friend said that he had been with her on a Sunday afternoon. I asked him what he talked to her about because, of course, in her latter months, she found conversation difficult. He said, "We didn't talk. We turned on the television and we watched 'Songs of Praise' and we sung the hymns together". I think that that is a lovely picture of those two doing that.

The noble Lord, Lord Armstrong, has spoken splendidly about the support which Margaret Thatcher gave him as Cabinet Secretary, and her support for the Civil Service and the esteem in which she held it. I do not want to add to that, except to endorse everything that he said as being the case during my experience in the post which he occupied before me.

I should like to take up what the noble and learned Lord, Lord Mackay, said about her role as a lawyer. I am very glad he referred to that. I had a word with him outside the Chamber. Another aspect that needs to be emphasised was the way in which she upheld the rule of law, which was a very important principle in her life. I was travelling in a car with the Prime Minister when we saw on a newspaper hoarding that the High Court had found against the Government in the judicial review about the Government's banning of unions at GCHQ. She was going to the House of Commons that afternoon and it was clear that, quite understandably, the Labour Party would make a lot of this and would be jubilant about it because it had supported the trade unions in opposing the Government's action. She said,

> "Well, we must appeal but if the court rules against us, we must of course accept its judgment. We cannot ask the miners to accept the rule of law if we, the Government, are not prepared to accept it ourselves."

That is just one illustration of the principle that she held.

When judicial review was gaining force and I was head of the Civil Service, I suggested to Margaret Thatcher that we might arrange a seminar between senior civil servants and some of the judges so that the judges would know more about the way in which decisions were taken in government. "Absolutely not", she said. "I am not going to have any appearance of the Executive appearing to interfere with the independence of the judges. We must keep them strictly separate". That is an aspect of her principles and her Administration that I do not think has been much mentioned.

The noble Lord, Lord Armstrong, spoke of his experience working with her as Cabinet Secretary. Although the noble Lord, Lord Turnbull, was here earlier, nobody has spoken about the experience of working with her as a Private Secretary. Like the noble Lord, Lord Turnbull, I was her Principal Private Secretary, in my case between 1982 and 1985. Inside No.10, having the privilege of seeing her in that intimate setting, we of course saw a very different person from the one that the public saw outside. The public saw the bravura performances and the confidence. She has been charged with being overconfident, even arrogant, but you saw a very different picture, before the great public appearances, inside No. 10-somebody whose motivation and force was not built on overconfidence but was in fact built on lack of self-confidence. I say that because I heard her say it herself publicly, after she left office. She said it was something that the media never really realised about her. I believe that that was the driving force behind her perfectionism in her appearance, in her dress, in her speeches and in her grip on her briefing. All those things had to be perfect before she would appear in public. There was a reference earlier to the conference speech after the Brighton bomb and her sitting in the green room, saying, "I am not sure I can go through with this". Gordon Reece said, "Of course you can go through with it". I am absolutely certain that she was always going to go through with it. Many times, I saw her say beforehand that she was not sure she could do something and then go out and give a bravura performance.

When I was Principal Private Secretary, in briefing her for Prime Minister's Questions, I did not brief her on the facts-other people did that-but regarded my job as being to calm her down, usually by reassuring her that her case was good in answer to a Question and, just occasionally, if she was sleepy after lunch, to work her up a bit and say, "Prime Minister, I think you have to worry about this Question, this is quite difficult". It was about getting the horse to the starting gate with exactly the right amount of perspiration on the flanks, and then she would perform superbly in the House of Commons.

I was very glad that the noble Lord, Lord Jopling, said earlier that criticisms that she never listened were quite misplaced. She did listen, but talked at the same time-she could listen while she talked. It is true that she regarded attack as the best form of defence but she was also always willing to learn. Finally, I just offer an anecdote to the House which I think illustrates these three characteristics. It relates to a time after she had ceased to be Prime Minister and after I had ceased to be Cabinet Secretary. She very kindly came to my college at Oxford to talk. In the course of her remarks to the students, she said that one of the things that she worried about in modern life, and the life facing their generation, was the number of children born illegitimate. When it came round to questions, one of the students said to her, "Lady Thatcher, don't you think it is a little unfair to use the word 'illegitimate' of a child throughout its life when it has had no influence over the circumstances of its own birth?" Her eyes flashed and she said, "Well, what would you call them? I can think of another word but I think it would be even more unkind". I thought, "Goodness, what's going to happen?", but the moment passed. She came to dinner and chapel, and in the lighter part of the evening we were having a drink in the Master's Lodgings before she and Denis went back to London. We were talking about other things completely when she suddenly said, "You know, Robin, that young man who asked me this afternoon about the word 'illegitimate' had a point didn't he?" That was quite characteristic. I will wager that she never used the word illegitimate again. She was always prepared to learn, even from a student. She hit back immediately but then she thought about it and took the point.

Those are just three reminiscences I have out of a treasure house of memories. I never had any doubt while I was working with her as Private Secretary and Cabinet Secretary that I was a witness to greatness as well as to great events. Those are memories that I will treasure all my life.

[Lord (Roger) Freeman (Conservative) was born 27 May 1942 and educated at Balliol College, Oxford. An accountant he served as an MP 1983–1997 and in Cabinet 1995–1997. As Minister for Public Transport 1990-1995 he privatized British Rail.]

7.10 pm

Lord Freeman

My Lords, after that very powerful and moving speech by the noble Lord, Lord Butler, I want to talk very briefly about the late Baroness Thatcher's relationship with Parliament and the Conservative Party in the country.

I have two reflections and two comments to make, the first as the present chairman of the Carlton Club, preceded by my noble friend Lord Wakeham a few years ago. Baroness Thatcher was elected an honorary member in 1975, at a time when women were not members to the club. Incidentally, the Carlton Club, in 1922, broke the coalition, although I am in no way indicating that history is going to repeat itself. The Carlton Club has as members 65 Members of your Lordships' House and the other place, and has long revered and treasured Baroness Thatcher's involvement with the club. I am quite certain that her quiet determination and conversations with many ultimately led to the club opening its doors to women members. She did not argue the case, she just quietly and consistently encouraged it, and I think that all members of the club are in her debt. In 1990, some colleagues will remember that our club was bombed by the IRA, and we lost one Member of Parliament and several other members. She came almost immediately to the club and spoke to those who were injured and to the families of those who were killed. That was very much appreciated.

The second aspect is the wider party in the country, and I speak with modest experience as someone who had responsibility for the selection of candidates to my party. Baroness Thatcher made a tremendous effort to tour the country and encourage candidates. She always took the trouble to write to the candidate afterwards. I think that many of those who were subsequently elected to the other place still keep those letters. They were not just two or three lines; they were complimentary and encouraging words, which I think made a tremendous difference.

I will finish with a very brief anecdote. In 1986, which seems a long time ago, I was summoned to Downing Street to become a junior Minister. I said to the Prime Minister, "Thank you very much. This is a great day. My wife has just had a baby daughter". She said, "What's the hospital? What's the telephone number?" Fortunately, I could remember it. She dialled the hospital, and the receptionist answered. The Prime Minister said, "This is the Prime Minister speaking". I could hear the lady at the other end say, "Pull the other leg". The Prime Minister said, "I don't think I will, my dear. Just put me through".

[Lord (Peter) Palumbo (Conservative) was born 20 July 1935 and educated at Eton College, and Worcester College, Oxford. A property expert, he owns Kentuck Knob built by Frank Lloyd Wright in the Allegheny Mountains of SW Pennsylvania.]

7.15 pm

Lord Palumbo

My Lords, I have three very short, random stories. On one occasion, my wife asked Margaret what she thought of Tony Blair. "My dear", she said, "I do not think of him". That was all.

We have heard from the noble Lord, Lord King, about Margaret's support for Desert Storm, the first war in Iraq. We have heard that it was to some extent due to her that there was the backbone to go to war. I asked her some years later what she would have done if the second Iraq war had come on her watch. She said, "It is not sufficiently or fully realised that I was a scientist before I became a politician. As a scientist what we need are facts, evidence and proof. If we have the facts, and we have the evidence and we have the proof, we can check and recheck, and check as many times as is necessary before coming to a considered view. The answer to your question is that we had very few facts. We had no evidence and we certainly had no proof, so I would not have committed one single member of the armed services to a war from which they may not have returned. What I would have done was to give George Bush the sort of assistance that Ronnie Reagan gave me in the Falklands; that is to say, logistical support and intelligence support, but nothing more. And I would have told Bush so to his face". She was very definite about that.

When she offered me, some years before, the chairmanship of the Arts Council, she said to me, "Mr Palumbo, I want you to understand one thing very clearly, and you must not forget it. The Government has no money. You are being asked to supervise the distribution of a great deal of money, and you must spend it wisely and carefully because it is taxpayers' money, not government money". That is advice that I shall obviously never forget, no more than I shall forget a wonderfully kind and utterly magnificent lady.

[Lord (Terence (Terry) Burns (Crossbencher) was born 13 March 1944 and educated at the University of Manchester. An economist, he has had distinguished careers in both the public and private sectors.]

7.18 pm

Lord Burns

My Lords, like many other noble Lords, I owe Baroness Thatcher a huge debt of gratitude. Towards the end of 1979, on the advice of the noble and learned Lord, Lord Howe, I was appointed as chief economic adviser to the Treasury, a position that I held throughout the rest of Mrs Thatcher's time as Prime Minister. During that 10-year period, I had the privilege of attending many meetings with her. I had enormous opportunities to watch the particular style of debate and the method that she used when challenged, something that I had never seen before.

Apart from late-night speechwriting sessions which I occasionally got involved in, most of my experiences were of accompanying the Chancellors of the day, initially the noble and learned Lord, Lord Howe, and then of course the noble Lord, Lord Lawson. By their very nature, we were dealing with the major issues of economic policy and, even more so by their nature, they were usually very controversial. We normally had these sessions because there were some difficult issues to sort out. They were very tense and very often there were tricky issues to resolve. At times one did not expect to reach resolution. On more than one occasion when I left she said to me, "I just want you to look as you go out at what it says on that door", to remind me that it said First Lord of the Treasury. She was trying to indicate that, in the final analysis, it was going to be her word.

Of course, those people who did not work with Mrs Thatcher assume that by her very nature she began and ended with an entrenched position and refused to listen. The main point that I want to make today, like many noble Lords who have spoken, is that that is not at all how the process took place. Part of her enormous talent was her ability to question, challenge and press you on issues as a way of trying to find whether the views that she held herself could stand that stress-testing. I always felt that she was trying to test her own ideas and your ideas to see how they stood up to this process of questioning.

Like all very great leaders, she had a strong set of principles and values and a clear sense of what she wanted to achieve. But thinking back through some of the episodes and having spoken, sometimes at length, to people who have been writing biographies of Mrs Thatcher, the issues that we dealt with were looked at in enormous depth. The notion that these ideas were pulled off in a casual way and immediately pursued could not be further from the truth. They were issues that we went through time and time again, very often at meeting after meeting until all the aspects of the problem had been identified and she was satisfied that we had covered the issues. I often think that it was as a result of the extent of that process and the argument and debate that she gained strength in the end to make decisions and stick to them in the way that is well known.

As many people have pointed out, she was not always right. She often changed her position on issues. But whatever view you take of individual parts of it, I join with many others in thinking that her contribution in terms of the transformation of the British economy was enormous. I have little doubt that it came about by this combination of a very clear strategic mind and the ability to concentrate and look at issues in depth, stress-test them and go through them at great length before finally coming to a conclusion.

In recent days, I have heard it suggested that somehow the recent financial crisis has its origins in her approach to economic policy. Nothing could be further from the truth. Those who worked with Mrs Thatcher know that she disliked financial excess whether in the private or the public sector. In the early 1980s, when we were struggling with rapid growth of the money supply, she frequently asked why there could not be some limits to the leverage ratios of banks, even in a deregulated system. She was only very reluctantly put off this approach, which has now become much more fashionable after the events of recent years.

A surprised journalist said to me yesterday that after the events of recent years he had been looking at some of the things that Mrs Thatcher had said about the single currency and had been astonished to discover that most of the things that had occurred in the past few years were part of the debate that took place then and why she came to the view that the UK should not be part of the single currency.

Along with many others, I regard myself as enormously fortunate to have played a small part in those momentous years. As the noble Lord, Lord Butler, said, there was a real greatness about Mrs Thatcher and I feel very privileged to have watched that. I would like to hope that I learnt a great deal from those sessions and that extraordinary process of discussion, challenge and debate and really testing the ideas of the people you worked with.

[Lord (Mark Schreiber) Marlesford (Conservative) was born 11 October 1935 and educated at Eton College and Trinity College, Cambridge. He enjoyed a career in local government, as a journalist, political researcher and advisor.]

7.25 pm

Lord Marlesford

My Lords, I suppose that one thing that one thinks most about Margaret Thatcher is that she was the most courageous challenger. One reason why I think she will have an increasing part in the history books is that she presided over and contributed to the ending of one of the great political struggles in this country: the struggle between capitalism and socialism as economic systems.

Margaret Thatcher could always see the real point. For three and a half years, I was in Whitehall as an adviser and worked a certain amount with a think tank. I remember well that, on one occasion, the presentation made at Chequers by the think tank was to show where the Government were going, even if they did not want to go there. I remember that the noble Lord, Lord Butler, was demonstrating the way in which inflation would reach unthinkable double digits. There was a silence, broken by Margaret Thatcher thumping on her blotter at the Cabinet table in Chequers, saying, "If that chart is true, we have lost the next election". Then Tony Barber, who was the Chancellor at the time, waded in to say that it was not true — but of course it was. (*Anthony Barber was Chancellor of the Exchequer 1970–1974 so Margaret would have been Secretary of State for Education and her party did lose twice in 1974, paving the way for her to oust Edward Heath*).

I point out to the noble Baroness, Lady Dean, who said what a pity it was that Margaret Thatcher had not tried to talk more to the union leaders, that no one could have tried harder to talk to the union leaders than Ted Heath. Indeed, we had something called tripartite government, which was government, industry and unions. A fat lot of good that did.

After the 1974 election, I used, as a *fonctionnaire*, to attend meetings of the shadow Cabinet. They were very difficult meetings because Mr Heath did not accept that he had made mistakes and that things had to change. He and Sir Keith Joseph used to spar. I remember, on one occasion, Ted Heath saying to Keith Joseph, "I suppose that you'd let British Leyland go to the wall". Keith Joseph said, "Of course I would, if it could not put its house in order". Ted replied, "In that case, you would have blood on the streets". It was all awkward and difficult. As the shadow Cabinet left the room, I was following behind, when

Margaret Thatcher came up to me and said, "Mark, you know, Keith has nearly had enough, and the day he goes, I go". It was basically from that moment that she realised the need to make a challenge that had never previously been made.

I was struck by the speech made by the noble Lord, Lord Soley, about the unions. Of course there was huge variation. Some union leaders were people of great patriotism who did a wonderful job, but there were others, often in powerful positions, who used their position not in the interests of their members but to lead them over the economic cliff, often into economic suicide and unemployment. In British Leyland, Red Robbo was leading the union. It was a hopeless system. Now, as a result of restructuring, we once again have a great automobile industry in this country. We could never have done that if that challenge had not been made.

I would describe one of Margaret Thatcher's great contributions as being to what I call liberation politics. She liberated a lot of people who had had no prospects because they were in the proletariat herd. She hugely enlarged the middle class-the bourgeoisie-of this country. As a result of the structural changes that she introduced, we are a much more equal society than we were then. Far more people-tens or hundreds of thousands of people-now have the opportunity to run their own lives in a way that they did not have before she was around and was Prime Minister.

[The Earl of Caithness (Malcolm Sinclair – Conservative) was born 3 November 1948 and was educated at the Royal Agricultural College. He is an hereditary peer.]

7.29 pm

The Earl of Caithness

My Lords, this has been a fascinating afternoon and early evening of paying tribute to an extraordinary lady. I am sure that history will be more accurate as a result. She has been shown to be not only an iron lady but a caring and sensitive woman.

She changed the lives of many of us. I remember sitting in the Lords' Gallery in another place in 1979 at the vote of no confidence, watching some left-wing Labour MPs singing the "Red Flag" and thinking, "Who is going to be able to change this?" Mrs Thatcher stopped the rot of what politicians had been doing for so long and what they started to go back to once she had been unceremoniously removed from power. They used to agree to take firm action but, by the time they had got back to their desks, their resolve had started to wane and the condition of the country, as so many have said, deteriorated. She gave not just herself but all of us a belief and a confidence that things could change. It required a woman to give us men and other women that backbone and inspiration and the belief that a country could be changed if you had the commitment.

She changed my life through the kind offices of our great Chief Whip at the time, my noble friend Lord Denham. I was asked to become a member of her Government in 1984. My noble friend Lord Hill of Oareford referred to her small, thoughtful actions. I had never met my Prime Minister when I was invited to a reception in Downing Street. I was taken by my kinsman by marriage, the late Earl of Swinton. I said, "David, will you introduce me?" He did. There was a receiving line with many more important people behind me. Mrs Thatcher stopped, took me out of the line and spent five minutes showing me the pictures and other important things in Downing Street. For any chief executive to take time out with the newest employee of the company is extraordinary. We have heard other, similar tributes. How did that lady manage to find the time every day to make other people feel that they were important?

The noble Lord, Lord Armstrong of Ilminster, mentioned that she was a glutton for hard work and detail. After six months in the Home Office studying prisons day in and day out, I was summoned to a meeting with her and found that she knew far more about prisons than I did at the time. I came out of the meeting thoroughly chastened and realised that unless I learnt more and more I would be one of the next to be sacked from her Government — and rightly, because she was the chief executive. How did she know more about the one little section of the Home Office of which I was in charge, when she had a whole country to run? I thought that that was an amazing example of briefing and retentive memory, as well as of the experience by that stage of having been Prime Minister for a number of years.

There is one aspect that noble Lords have not mentioned. We have talked about how she changed her mind but not about how loyal she was when she had changed her mind. I remember this from my time as a junior Minister. Most of the speeches today have been from former Secretaries of State in another place. I am one of the diminishing band of people who have been elected to this House rather than appointed to it by a Prime Minister and have been part of the Government. When I was at the Department of the Environment, I had a discussion with her and she agreed to change a policy. It was a long and tough discussion that involved various other departments. When she grasped that the policy needed changing, she was the one who led from the front, leaving one carrying the standard behind her. I had never experienced a chief executive like that in all the jobs that I had done in the private sector. I had never experienced that sort of leadership. It was tremendous support for a junior Minister — not just for tea ladies and staff, or Secretaries of State, but for all levels of government. With a Government of 100 people, and given the number of times they change, it is a remarkable lady to whom we pay tribute today.

It is always an honour to be asked to serve your country as a member of a Government. To me it was a particular privilege to be the loyal lieutenant of an amazing lady who changed the way our country operates.

[Baroness (Detta) O'Cathain (Conservative) was born in Ireland 2 February 1938. She moved to England and had a very prominent business career with the Midland Bank, the Tesco supermarket chain, and British Airways.]

7.34 pm

Baroness O'Cathain

I am speaking because, of 49 speakers, only six are women. That is okay; it does not really matter and we should not feel that we have to speak. However, I want to speak especially for those who do not belong to the political Westminster village. I felt very honoured to come here. It was never on my radar. In fact, when I was asked to come to the House of Lords, I thought that I was being asked to have dinner here. What I mean is that I feel I should not be here, but I hope that I have contributed something.

I will not use the glass ceiling analogy but when Margaret Thatcher was elected as Prime Minister, there was a frisson among every woman in my peer group who, with qualifications, had been struggling to get up the ladder a bit, to do a bit more development study and to work that bit harder. We asked ourselves, "Will we ever get there?" Suddenly we saw this lady who was perfect in every way. No human being is perfect but she seemed to be perfect in every way and she was a role model for many of us. I am now going back to the 1970s, when quite an interesting thing happened. Suddenly-I am sure that the noble Baroness, Lady Dean, also experienced this-there was a burgeoning of women's networks. I am referring not necessarily to networks in which it was said, "You know somebody in that company. Do you think I can get a job?", but to networks in which women tried to see how they could, in turn, take their rightful place in this country.

I was president of the Women in Banking and Finance network for about four years. In fact, I took over from another Member of this House — my noble friend Lady Platt. She is the wonderful woman who, ever since the 1940s, always had a screwdriver in her bag. She was an aeronautical engineer and a role model for me — not that I could do engineering, physics or chemistry. She set up the Women in Banking and Finance network, whose members are remarkable people. A lot of them have senior positions in accountancy and consultancy firms, and they have done very well. How do they do it? They do it by meeting frequently, networking, going on development courses and playing golf together. It is not equivalent to a men's club — it is nothing like that — nor is it a sorority, as they have in the States. There are groups in all sorts of industries. The retail sector has them, and there are professional groups such as lawyers. Just because the word "Women" is in the title, men say, "Oh, you're off doing this", but men have been doing it for years. We have a lot of catching up to do.

I have been listening avidly for the past four or five hours — I am not sure how long we have been speaking; time passes quickly when you are interested — and it has been a marvellous history lesson. I know that history is becoming more and more fashionable. In fact, my right honourable friend the Secretary of State for Education is trying to highlight history as part of the curriculum, and that is very important. This is a zany idea but in about four or five weeks' time, or perhaps in the new term in September, why can we not have a copy of today's *Hansard* placed in every school so that they can learn from it? I have taken that idea from one put forward by Michael Gove — that of putting the King James Bible in every school. As I am a Bible follower, I do not want to suggest that there is an equivalence between the Bible and today's *Hansard* and that your Lordships are all evangelists or prophets, but I think that it is an idea to bear in mind. We have history here today which is alive. It is compelling and I think that people out there of any age would be prepared to listen to it.

I am speaking in this debate from my personal experience outside the West-minster village. I believe that, following the election of Margaret Thatcher, women suddenly got more spring in their step. We have a lot more to do, and we have had several debates in this House about women on boards, women in industry and women in the political sector. All I am saying is that we will miss her. We should benefit from her. We are all so grateful to have known her.

[Lord (Richard) Wilson of Dinton (Cross Bencher) was born 11 October 1942 and educated at Clare College, Cambridge. He was a civil servant.]

7.41 pm

Lord Wilson of Dinton

My Lords, I add my own tributes to the wealth of tributes which we have heard today — not, of course, at a political level, but as an official who served the Prime Minister, Mrs Thatcher, for three years, from 1987 to 1990, as head of her domestic and economic secretariat under the noble Lord, Lord Armstrong, and then under the noble Lord, Lord Butler. It was period of extraordinary and rapid change in so many areas: local government, with the community charge — I still cannot call it the poll tax; we were trained not to — the National Health Service; privatisation; education, with the introduction of the curriculum; the inner cities; and so on. The list felt endless.

Mrs Thatcher depended very heavily on briefing. She would use it once she came to the conclusion that she could rely upon you, and she did so very intensively so you had to get it right. There were occasions when she would disagree with one of her colleagues in a meeting. She would challenge them as to whether they were right or not on the strength of a brief. I can tell you, you learn things about the human body — your pores open in moments of stress — which I will not forget.

The other side of the coin was that she worked enormously hard; this, I am sure, is well known. We delivered lots of briefs to her in the evenings, and by the morning she would have mastered and be ready to use them to challenge with enormous skill. I remember saying to her on one occasion, "You must have worked very late to get all this into your mind". She said, "Well, I find midnight is the worst. By 12.30 I get a second wind". That, for me, captures it.

She was also very generous in the way in which she treated people who worked for her. She attributed to you qualities which you certainly did not have. I remember sitting down next to her at one meeting. She was deep in thought, and turned to me and said, "Now, can you explain to me what a put option is?" That is quite a difficult question cold, when a lot of other Ministers are coming in. On another occasion, when Ministers were discussing the national curriculum, she was passionate about the importance of schoolchildren learning poetry by heart. She launched unexpectedly into some Robert Browning, which she quoted at some length. Then she could not remember what came next, and turned to me as the secretary and said, "Now what happens?" Of course, I had not the faintest notion what happens next. It was very generous of her to think that one might know, but of course I did not.

She was also very kind, sometimes in a rather clumsy way. I was summoned on a Saturday to Chequers to explain to her a very complicated submission which I had put to her on the Friday night about how we might make the poll tax work or avoid some of the more difficult consequences which it seemed likely to have. It was really, really technically difficult. I was shown in to see her and she gave me a cup of tea. I had that in one hand and in the other she put an enormous cream bun, so covered in icing sugar that when we spoke there were clouds of it. We then had this very difficult and serious discussion while I held these two objects in my hands. It was a good meeting but it was slightly unusual.

We have heard from the noble Lord, Lord Spicer, about her caution. There were all sorts of sides to that quality. I used to be astonished by the certainty with which she felt that she knew and understood what the British people were feeling and thinking, and where they stood, whatever everyone else among her colleagues were saying or thinking.

One example which comes to mind was that a decision had been taken that the National Dock Labour scheme should be abolished. That was being planned in great secrecy and we had reached the point where Ministers were in a position to give the go-ahead. There was fear of a strike, and so on. When we met the Prime Minister, Mrs Thatcher said, "I can see that all the plans are ready but I should say that we are not going to go ahead with this decision today. We are not going to make the announcement. It is January and it is cold and foggy. The public are depressed and have had enough bad news. This is not the right time. We will wait until the spring, when the sun and the daffodils are out, and it will be all right". I found myself thinking, "How do we record this?", but we recorded it and lo and behold, the Government waited until the spring and the decision went exactly as she said. It was fine, but there was a sense in which she was certain about the timing. It was all going on in her head and it was very impressive.

The other side of Mrs Thatcher, which I hope does not get overlooked, was her interest in science. I remember No. 10 organising groups of PhD or post-doctoral researchers to come and meet her. She would grill them for an afternoon and they would emerge looking exhausted, while she would look hugely refreshed by the experience of having cross-examined them on their science.

I think it was in the autumn of 1988 that, having read over the summer about climate change, she decided that it was a really big problem which people had underestimated. I am not sure that the world remembers it but she made a speech to the Royal Society — way ahead of international opinion, or opinion in this country — in which she very clearly set the problem out in scientific terms. She drew attention to the threats that it had for future generations and the moral imperative that she thought that Governments had to act on it. That was a very important landmark in people realising that it was a problem. It illustrates the limitations of the power of even a great Prime Minister such as Mrs Thatcher that very little happened immediately because of it, but it is interesting that her scientific background led her into that insight. (*She later changed her mind*).

I hope that the noble Lord, Lord Butler, will not mind my remembering that when she had finally surrendered her office to Her Majesty the Queen, he gave a small impromptu party to enable some of us who had worked for her to say farewell. I remember two things about that occasion. One was that she was going round saying very intense things. I am not even sure that she entirely knew what she was saying to everyone. I remember her coming up and saying to me, "What I always feel about problems in government is that the important thing is to work out what is the right thing to do. You may not be able to achieve it, or not immediately, but that has to be your starting point. That has to be your goal". For me, that is what marks her out as an outstanding and extraordinary leader, perhaps above all.

The other thing I remember is the noble Lord, Lord Butler, himself saying in his speech to her, "Prime Minister, when we are old and retired the only really interesting thing about us will be that we worked for you". That was a lovely compliment and today we are all proving that compliment to be right. I certainly feel hugely privileged for having worked for her. Those are three years that I would not have missed for all the world.

[Lord (Howard) Flight (Conservative) was born 16 June 1948 and educated at Magdalen College, Cambridge. After a successful career in banking and investments he served as an MP 1997–2005 before being notoriously barred from restanding for Parliament by his then Party Leader Michael Howard for saying at a private meeting (secretly recorded) that an incoming Conservative Government would make more cuts than previously announced.]

7.50 pm

Lord Flight

My Lords, I pay tribute to Margaret Thatcher, who I believe was easily the greatest Briton of my adult lifetime. I will refer to six particular points, some of which have been touched upon by others. First, something which has struck me strongly has been the enormous loyalty, devotion and affection felt towards Lady Thatcher by all those who have worked for her, including the police who were responsible for her safety, and which she very much reciprocated. She was in many ways such a warm person, quite the opposite of her public image.

The second point, which is related to that, as many noble Lords pointed out earlier, is that she was a person of great kindness, compassion and modesty. Ahead of every general election she would pack her bags at No. 10 because she by no means took it for granted that she would win an election, even if she was ahead in the polls.

For millions of British people from all walks of life, men and women, she was their heroine. So many people who met her have said to me, "That was the highlight of my life". They realised greatness when they were in its presence.

Fourthly, and again, this is a point that was made by others but which comes out so strongly, she was someone of great integrity, honesty and principle, and she had a strong sense of duty both in national politics and in her own private life. She was also the key champion of personal aspiration and of equality of opportunity, and this was not only about enabling people to own their own houses, but about enabling them to start their own businesses and buy shares. She was the person who very much got rid of damaging old-fashioned class loyalties and turned a majority of this country into the broad, non-offensive label of middle class. What she achieved has led to that.

She was also the architect not just of our turning round the British economy after the problems of the 1970s but of a business revolution. I will give some brief quotes from leading businessmen, by no means all members of the Conservative Party.

The noble Lord, Lord Browne, formerly of BP, said that she, "breathed life into free enterprise".

The noble Lord, Lord Sugar, said that she created the "opportunity for anyone to succeed in the UK".

Sir Richard Branson said that she "understood what was needed to make business thrive and to turn the country into a country of entrepreneurs".

Many people forget that before her time even the terms venture capital and entrepreneur hardly existed in the English language, and certainly there was very little of it in practice. So much of what has been a success story in this country since then has been the growth of small businesses and new businesses, employing more than 13 million people. I cite, although it is perhaps a little specialist, the Cambridge cluster that has come up: 629 businesses with a turnover of more than £11 billion, employing 53,000 people, and in the key new areas of IT and technology, life science and physical sciences. Lady Thatcher would have been proud of that, and she would have seen that it promised a promising economic future for this country. Certainly, in the first 20 years of my own life, we never even thought about the ability to be entrepreneurs and to get new businesses up and running.

I was privileged to have got to know Lady Thatcher a little after she became Prime Minister, and the more I knew her the more I admired her. I echo the comments of others, even in the latter parts of her life, as regards her beauty, and those amazing eyes. I often think warmly of when I put her into her car after events which I had attended. If she had had a good conversation, particularly with young people, she showed even then how much she had enjoyed her evening.

[Viscount Bridgeman (Robin — Conservative) was born 5 December 1930 and educated at Eton College and as a Chartered Accountant. He is an hereditary peer.]

7.55 pm

Viscount Bridgeman

Shortly after Margaret Thatcher retired as Prime Minister, there was a meeting of the ACP to decide how her retirement would be marked. There was considerable navel gazing but in the end Lord Boyd-Carpenter was deputed to organise a dinner for her and Denis at the Cavalry and Guards Club. I had only recently arrived in your Lordships' House. We were mixed up career-wise and age-wise, and it was a very jolly event. At the end of the dinner, Humphrey Colnbrook, the then chairman of the ACP, said, "Margaret, this evening is not a time for speeches. I shall say just one thing: you took over the leadership of our party at a time when this country was sinking beneath the waves. Your abiding achievement as Prime Minister is that you restored its self-respect".

[Baroness (Peta) Buscombe (Conservative) was born 12 March 1954 and educated at the Inns of Court School of Law. She is an attorney, a regulator, and a businesswoman.]

7.57 pm

Baroness Buscombe

My Lords, this has been a most amazing debate but I felt absolutely compelled to say a few words as one who speaks of being, in a sense, of the next generation. I was not lucky enough, as many who have spoken today were, to have worked with her but I knew her a little. She had a profound effect on me and my generation, both men and women. For a few moments, perhaps I may share with noble Lords a little bit of a more distant perspective.

In 1979, I was in my mid-20s, a young barrister having fun and so on with friends, but we felt that the country was broke. The outlook was bleak. There was mass inflation, unemployment and terrible apathy as rubbish piled up around us and the strikes continued. The straw that broke the camel's back for me was that my father was mugged in broad daylight in St James's Park. His head and legs were smashed. No one came for hours. When someone finally came, he was taken to Westminster Hospital where they refused even to look at him because they were on strike. He was then taken to the Chelsea Hospital where they looked at him in a cursory way and then let him go home. He could not go back to work because his legs would not work. He was also embarrassed because his teeth had been smashed. He called the dentist who took one look at him and saw that his whole head had been completely smashed. No one had noticed because they were on strike.

Soon after that, thank God, the Conservatives won the election but my husband and I, as newlyweds, left for better climes to work in New York. It was amazing to have the perspective from New York. From 3,000 miles away, we saw her turn this country around. Her reputation grew exponentially in such a short time; it was extraordinary. We slightly felt that we were missing something by working in New York. The Falklands was extraordinary. The Americans were envious of us having this courageous woman as our leader. They would say, "God you're lucky having that person", and, "What leadership".

As others said today, and as my noble friend Lord Flight mentioned, what a difference she made in the business world. I have just returned from a parliamentary Commonwealth delegation to India. I still had business men and women and politicians there coming up to say how brilliant she was.

I have just a few brief memories as someone who was lucky enough to come into your Lordships' House. First, she emboldened me to stand for Parliament

— although, sadly, I did not win. I returned from America. I was jetlagged and in my car. I should probably not even have been driving. Prime Minister's Question Time came on the radio, with her just having flown overnight from Japan. She was amazing and I thought, "If she can do it, so can I". All this about her not helping other women is nonsense: she was the ultimate role model. She would have said to all of us, as indeed she said to me, "Women can achieve. Women can get there". However, of course, she wanted us to achieve on merit.

I remember when I first came into your Lordships' House I went to her for advice. I said, "Margaret, I don't understand this. What is the point of making a maiden speech unless you can say something that is worth saying? I do not understand all this business about not being controversial". She said, "Peta, you mustn't be controversial, but what you must do is stand up for what you believe". The other thing she said to me, which I think I have heard this evening, is never to start anything unless you are prepared to see it through.

A few years on, one evening in your Lordships' House I divided the House seven times on the Licensing Bill. I was determined and won seven times. Others were nudging me slightly, saying, "Peta, when is this going to end? Margaret Thatcher has a party. She is here and she's missing her own party". I went up to her and said, "I'm so sorry, Margaret, but I'm so glad you're here supporting my amendments". She said, "My dear, it's marvellous. I'm really enjoying myself. This is just like old times". This was her priority. It was her country and her belief in this nation.

Those were just a few thoughts that I wanted to share with your Lordships. Just being here today and taking part in these tributes to Margaret Thatcher is an enormous privilege. She was a truly extraordinary and remarkable lady and she will in many ways remain with us always.

[for biographical details see above]

8.03 pm

Lord Hill of Oareford: My Lords, we have heard many powerful and moving tributes this afternoon from all sides of the House. We have heard many examples of how Margaret Thatcher touched the lives of so many in your Lordships' House, both in public and private life. Noble Lords have added a lot to our understanding of this remarkable woman and there has been a lot of new material for historians to mine.

We are all fortunate to have been here as it has been a great parliamentary occasion for a great parliamentarian. But above all, I hope that Lady Thatcher's family will have the chance to read the tributes that have been made this afternoon about their mother and grandmother and all that she did, and feel very proud of what she achieved.

House adjourned at 8.04 pm.

A Summary of International Commentary

AFGHANISTAN
President **Hamid Karzai**: "One of the greatest leaders the world knew...a strong leader who had truly served her country, particularly in strengthening the UK's economy".

ARGENTINA
Andres Wolberg-Stok, who covered the Falkland Islands war as a young reporter for the *Buenos Aires Herald*: ""Thank you Maggie Thatcher, for catalyzing the return of democracy in Argentina."

AUSTRALIA
American female novelist **Lionel Shriver**, who lived in Belfast, Northern Ireland during Margaret Thatcher's third term in office: "Margaret Thatcher was a real feminist. Not for what she said but for what she did. She did not pursue justice for her gender; women's rights per se was clearly a low priority for her. She was out for herself and for what she believed in."
Comment in *Sydney Morning Herald*, 9 April 2013

John Warhurst, emeritus professor of political science at the Australian National University: "The judgments of Thatcher in death have been as diverse and as spirited as they were in life. While resident in London from 1983 to 1985, I witnessed them first-hand as a foreign observer. Hero above all heroes to some, like our former foreign minister Alexander Downer, she was a devil to others. Supporters and even some critics often rank her above all modern politicians on both sides."
Opinion in *Sydney Morning Herald*, 18 April 2013

BURMA

Po Thaut Kya, veteran Burmese journalist: "We were very interested when she became the British PM and we always followed her story very well. At the time, she was inspirational to Burmese people. She is a role model for women leaders and her death is a great loss to the world. We are covering the story and it will be our front page cover story tomorrow."
BBC Burmese service

CANADA

Statement from **Brian Mulroney**, prime minister for six years during Margaret Thatcher's time in office: "Some Canadians were unconvinced by her approach, but in a series of visits to Canada she won many friends here."

"By her final visit in 1988 she was recognized as the founder of modern Conservatism, a leader who had dragged her country from the brink of economic and social crisis, and a beacon of principled leadership to the world."
www.cbc.ca, 8 April 2013

CHILE

General Guillermo Garin, retired vice-commander in chief of the Chilean army: "During the military government, she was very brave.... She was a defender of the grand modernisations that Chile put in place and expressed her support versus a very hostile campaign run by the Soviet Union. President Pinochet always had tremendous admiration for her, they had a very close relationship highlighted by the visit she made to his place of detention in London ... They shared similar concepts of modernisation of the state."

CHINA

China's leading party paper, the *People's Daily*: "Faced with the weak economy, she launched a series of broad reforms from which the British are still benefiting today... Mrs Thatcher, the most distinguished female politician of the 20th century, has left the world with glory and controversy. An era has ended."

CROATIA

Natasha Srdoc, Co-founder and Chairman, Adriatic Institute for Public Policy: "In Eastern Europe we admired Lady Thatcher's courage and bold leadership in confronting communism and advocating freedom and the rule of law. Communism's fall was hastened through her principled leadership and close work with President Ronald Reagan. She then fought for Croatia's independence and understood the challenges that we still face today. When visiting Zagreb in 1998 Lady Thatcher stated: 'Corruption and gangsterism are scourges which afflict many newly developing economies and states. They should be ruthlessly and fearlessly expunged. Otherwise not just the free market but also freedom itself is in peril. These observations also highlight the fact that the system of freedom and free enterprise is, above all, based on the rule of law.'"

CZECH REPUBLIC

Vaclav Klaus, former president, prime minister and Thatcherite, told the BBC: "Thatcher was one of the greatest politicians of our time, in the Czech Republic she was our hero."

ECUADOR

Ricardo Nobos, Article entitled "El legado de Margaret Thatcher", published on April 14, 2013 in Ecuador: "God does something in the world so that at certain times in history, people come together to make great change possible. During the 15th Century, Michelangelo, Rafael, Bramante and many others came together and gave way to the Renaissance, leading the world out of the darkness of the lower Middle Ages...The 1980s decade brought together Reagan, Gorbachev, John Paul II and Margaret Thatcher. And the world changed. It was not the end of history as Fukuyama proclaimed, but it was the end of a story."

FALKLAND ISLANDS

Mike Summers of the Falkland Islands' legislative assembly: "She will be forever remembered in the islands for her decisiveness in sending a taskforce to liberate our home following the Argentine invasion in 1982."

Rosie King, resident of Port Stanley in the Falkland Islands: "She was probably the number one person in our history ... It was mind-blowing when we heard on the radio that Thatcher would send a taskforce. When she arrived afterwards, it was like a visit from the Queen."

"I met her on a street corner and we chatted very comfortably. It wasn't like she was a big world leader. She wasn't as harsh as she was portrayed and she was smaller than I imagined ... It was one of the most memorable moments of my life." *The Guardian*, London, UK, 8 April 2013

FIJI

Joel Anand Samy, Co-Chair, International Leaders' Summit: "Born in Fiji, a former British colony, I observed how India and other Commonwealth nations had embraced Keynesian economics. However Baroness Thatcher's principled leadership in upholding the rule of law and advancing economic freedom unleashed a global revolution reversing socialism. India followed in the 1990s by demolishing a legacy of British socialism, the License Raj, that onerous regulation and barrier for businesses. Baroness Thatcher's leadership in advancing economic freedom influenced the world and helped lift millions out of poverty as entrepreneurship was unleashed in emerging countries."

FRANCE

Comment in right-of-centre *Le Figaro* newspaper: "France needs a Margaret Thatcher A large part of the élite does not want it. However, it will come because of full international competition in social, fiscal and regulatory models. It is not an option. It is an obligation, if France wants to continue living."

GERMANY

Angela Merkel, German Chancellor, often called Germany's "Iron Lady" and voted the world's most powerful woman by *Forbes* for the third year running in 2013: "As a long-serving prime minister, she shaped modern Britain as few have before or since. She was one of the greatest leaders in world politics of her time. The freedom of the individual was at the centre of her beliefs so she recognised very early the power of the movements for freedom in Eastern Europe. And she supported them. I will never forget her contribution in overcoming Europe's partition and the end of the Cold War."

Bestselling daily newspaper, *Bild*: "One didn't love her, one admired her."

Frankfurter Allgemeiner Zeitung newspaper: "Icon of clarity."

Tageszeitung newspaper: "Britain has lost its best man."

GHANA

Ghanaian journalist **Elizabeth Ohene**, ex-deputy editor of the BBC's *Focus on Africa* programme, remembers losing her umbrella at Downing Street after a tough 1988 interview in which she challenged Baroness Thatcher on South Africa and apartheid: "I was leaving and I then realised that I couldn't find my umbrella — you know the British weather. I'm looking for my umbrella and then, suddenly, the prime minister was on all fours looking under the sofa to see if she could find my umbrella, which she did retrieve.

"It showed a part of her that I didn't think was there... she could have asked any of her minders to find my umbrella but she found it for me herself. That was the soft touch, I thought, of the Iron Lady."
www.bbc.co.uk, 8 April 2013

GUATEMALA

Giancarlo Ibárgüen, President, Universidad Francisco Marroquin (UFM): "Her privatization initiative produced a contagion all over the world, benefitting the poorest people in developing countries."

Eduardo Mayora, column published in Siglo 21, April 11, 2013: "Without minimizing the importance of other great judicial traditions, such as those of Rome and France, there is no doubt that the former Primer Minister Margaret Thatcher focused during the brief instants [that we spoke], as the great statesperson she was, on the circumstance of the political and civic life of modern States that, in significant fashion, distinguishes the civilized and prosperous nations on Earth from those that remain under rule of the arbitrary powers of some or even many personas, but not under the Rule of Law. Rest in peace, the Iron Lady."

Luis Figueroa, (UFM), blog entry April 8, 2013: "With the death of Margaret Thatcher, former Prime Minister of the United Kingdom, we lost one of the greatest figures of the 20th century, a giant in Classic Liberal politics and philosophy. During one term she not only arrested the decay of the United Kingdom, but also contributed greatly to slow that of the West at the hands of socialism."

Carroll Ríos de Rodríguez, article published in *Siglo 21* on April 10, 2013: "It just so happened that Margaret Thatcher, Ronald Reagan, Pope John Paul II and Mikhail Gorbachev coincided in positions of leadership. Each played their cards in such a way that together they put an end to the Cold War and demolished, without bloodshed, the Soviet empire. The Prime Minister forged a lasting friendship with the American president. Reagan wrote that Thatcher was a "tower of fortitude", while she thought that Reagan set himself apart from other leaders because he was not "plagued by bleak doubts". Thatcher, Reagan and Pope John Paul II consistently promoted the dignity of the person and individual liberty. For her exemplary life, a life of coherence, we are in debt with her, specially those women who devote themselves to politics."

INDIA

From an article in the **Economic Times:** "Thatcher's greatest achievement was to change economics in the face of toxic politics, and then change the politics of her country itself. Whenever anyone needs to find an example of what politics of conviction - the conviction informed by a faith in the market and in entrepreneurship - can achieve in a democracy, Thatcher would be a natural candidate."

ISRAEL

Prime Minister **Benjamin Netanyahu**: "Today I mourn the passing of Prime Minister Baroness Margaret Thatcher. She was truly a great leader, a woman of principle, of determination, of conviction, of strength; a woman of greatness. She was a staunch friend of Israel and the Jewish people. She inspired a generation of political leaders."

Shimon Peres, current president who was prime minister and foreign minister during Margaret Thatcher's premiership: "There are people, there are ideas. Occasionally those two come together to create vision. Lady Thatcher was an exceptional leader, a colleague in the international arena and a friend for me personally. She served as an inspiration for other leaders, as the first female prime minister of Great Britain she broke new ground. She showed how far a person can go with strength of character, determination and a clear vision."

LIBERIA

President **Ellen Johnson Sirleaf**, who became the first female president of an African country in 2005: "I admired her strength and tenacity. I admired her ability to make decisions, even when they were unpopular. And that's why she was called the Iron Lady, and I dare say that I'm also called the Iron Lady."

www.bbc.co.uk, 8 April 2013

MEXICO

Armando Regil Velasco, President and Founder of the Instituto de Pensamiento Estratégico Ágora (IPEA), April 9, 2013: "On June 11, 2009 I had the honor of awarding the Legion of Liberty to the former Prime Minister of the United Kingdom, Margaret Thatcher. The prize was a great occasion to thank and recognize the legacy of one of the greatest women in recent history. Today we remember her contribution to the cause of liberty in her country and the world.

Margaret Thatcher was not only the woman to occupy the highest political position in her country, but she also presided one of the longest and most effective governments in the history of the United Kingdom. Prime Minister David Cameron recognized that she did not only lead her country courageously, but indeed saved it."

NIGERIA

Ibrahim Babangida, former military leader: "[Thatcher] told us that it's about time that we engaged South Africa in constructive engagement, and that is perhaps the best way to get rid of apartheid. I took her advice and invited De Klerk to this country. I think she was a fine example of a very courageous political leader. She is admired greatly by a majority of countries in Africa."
The Guardian, London, UK, 8 April 2013

PARAGUAY

Victor Pavón, dean of Currículum UniNorte and author of an article published in *ABC Color*, Paraguay, on April 11, 2013.

"Margaret Thatcher's public policies were not populist. She did not try to befriend pressure groups. Nor did she vote at whatever cost, whether it be inflating the public budget or distributing money to maintain people in dependent misery on social populist programs directed by the politicians in power."

PERU

Mario Vargas Llosa (Nobel prizewinner in literature), Column published by *El País*, 2013, titled "La partida de la dama": "I spent almost all of the Thatcher years in Great Britain and what she did marked me profoundly. She is still present in things I believe and defend and that make me say I am a liberal. When the Lady ascended to power, Great Britain was sinking in mediocrity and decadence, a natural consequence of statism, interventionism and the socialization of political and economic life, even though, that is, it continued to hold on to and respect the institutions and liberty, something that is second nature to the British society.

"Few politicians have elicited the respect I felt for the Great Lady, because I have known few who, like her, always said what they believed and always did what they said. She believed in liberty, in the sovereign individual, in the Calvinist work ethic, in saving, in moral values as a basis for institutions and on a scrupulous respect for the law."

POLAND

Radoslaw Sikorski, Polish foreign minister, via Twitter: "Lady Thatcher, fearless champion of liberty, stood up for captive nations, helped free world win the Cold War. Deserves statue in Poland."

Lech Walesa, first president following end of Communist rule in Poland: "She was a great person. She did a great deal for the world, along with Ronald Reagan, Pope John Paul II and Solidarity, she contributed to the demise of communism in Poland and Central Europe. I'm praying for her."

Daily Telegraph, London, UK, 8 April 2013

"Observing her at work was a great opportunity to learn how to achieve goals. Once she gave me advice: 'Write down the 10 steps from where you are now to where you want to be.' It was a good lesson."

"The Margaret Thatcher I knew: 20 personal insights" in *The Guardian*, London, UK, 8 April 2013

RUSSIA

Leonid Kalashnikov, Communist deputy: "She is the greatest woman, the greatest politician. As an opponent, I always respected her. And how she, with the Americans, 'strangled' the Soviet Union is also worth quite a lot — because she did it correctly, logically and in their own interests."

www.guardian.co.uk, 8 April 2013

Former deputy prime minister **Boris Nemtsov,** recalling her visit to the city of Nizhny in 1994: "We went into [a] shop and Thatcher bought cheese and came out to see hundreds of city residents waiting for her. People were so amazed that they started to shout 'Thatcher for president of Russia!' The baroness asked me, what are they screaming? She laughed and said, when Gorbachev moves to London, they yell that it's time he became PM of the UK. They were similar. Neither one nor the other was loved in their motherland, but were respected abroad."

The Guardian, London, UK, 8 April 2013

Russian prime minister and former President **Dmitry Medvedev:** "One can have different opinions about her political views, but it is impossible not to respect her for her character and her political will."

Via Facebook, reported on www.bbc.co.uk, 8 April 2013

Mikhail Gorbachev, former Soviet leader and architect of Glasnost and Perestroika: "Thatcher was a politician whose word carried great weight. Our first meeting in 1984 set in train relations that were sometimes complicated, not always smooth, but which were serious and responsible on both sides. Human relations also gradually took shape, becoming more and more friendly. In the end we managed to achieve a mutual understanding, and that contributed to a change in the atmosphere between our country and the West and the end of the Cold War.

"Margaret Thatcher was a heavyweight politician and a striking person. She will remain in our memories, and in history."

Daily Telegraph, London, UK, 8 April 2013

"Her famous remark, 'I like Mr Gorbachev, we can do business together,' was later helpful to me. When I became general secretary of the Communist party, it made it easier to seek contacts and mutual understanding with Ronald Reagan and with leaders of other countries."

"The Margaret Thatcher I knew: 20 personal insights" in *The Guardian*, London, UK, 8 April 2013

SOUTH AFRICA

Statement from the **ANC** (the party currently in government): "The ANC was on the receiving end of her policy in terms of refusing to recognise the ANC as the representatives of South Africans and her failure to isolate apartheid after it had been described as a crime against humanity.

"However, we acknowledge that she was one of the strong leaders in Britain and Europe to an extent that some of her policies dominate discourse in the public service structures of the world. Long after her passing on, her impact will still be felt and her views a subject of discussion."

SPAIN

Spanish Prime Minister **Mariano Rajoy**: "Her commitment to democracy, to freedom and the rule of law together with her reformist vision, built up an extremely valuable legacy for current European leaders. Similar to the situation of the 1980s, the time during which Margaret Thatcher was prime minister, we are also facing huge challenges which require us to have political ambition and courage."

Ana Botella, Mayor of Madrid, Spain, in her blog: "Margaret Thatcher, a female pioneer...never shielded herself behind her gender to debate her adversaries in Parliament, she had a clear will to be an unabashed politician...With equal opportunity, women can go as far in politics as their effort, their merit and their courage allows."

José María Aznar, Former President of Spain, in an article entitled "Margaret Thatcher: una auténtica liberal-conservadora", reprinted by *Libertad Digital*. "Margaret Thatcher was an example of transformative leadership. She put an end to the tyranny of political correctness, gave battle in the field of ideas and did not accept the cultural dominance of the left. She believed in a nation of responsible indivdiuals, willing to earn their prosperity and committed to the defense of liberty, without surrendering to the State the responsibility for their lives. She was an authentic liberal-conservative. Her death leaves us a great void, but we retain the pertinence of her ideas, her goals and her political legacy."

Alvaro Vargas Llosa, Column entitled "Adiós a Margaret Thatcher", reprinted by *Libertad Digital*. "Another aspect of that international progressivism ought to value in her was her love of ideas. It is said, often, that she was an ideologue. She was not an ideological animal but rather a political animal who liked ideas, which is different. Before her, both conservatives and labourists had renounced to the world of ideas in British politics; all that mattered was represented by inertia, not by what they thought. Thatcher, who was nourished by the ideas of the Institute of Economic Affairs, who read a variety of authors ranging from Edmund Burke, the father of conservatism, to the Nobel Friedrich Hayek, always felt a deep respect for the intellectual realm that was not reciprocated. Some intellectuals — like Hugh Thomas, the historian and hispanicist — formed part of her circle of advisers at some point in time, but in few areas of social life was the hatred toward her so concentrated as in the academic world. However, again, the truth is she lent a service to the politics of her country, both right and left, because after the rebirth of a politics based on ideas, one and the other acquired a reflexive dimension they were lacking."

TANZANIA

John Malecela, ex-prime minister and high commissioner to London during Baroness Thatcher's time in power: "Although she liked adopting tough stances, which some of us did not agree with, we all agreed that she was a very principled leader and we respected her for that."
www.bbc.co.uk, 8 April 2013

USA

Former President **Bill Clinton:** "Like so many others, I respected the conviction and self-determination she displayed throughout her remarkable life as she broke barriers, defied expectations and led her country."

Barack Obama: "As a grocer's daughter who rose to become Britain's first female prime minister, she stands as an example to our daughters that there is no glass ceiling that can't be shattered. As prime minister, she helped restore the confidence and pride that has always been the hallmark of Britain at its best..."

"Here in America, many of us will never forget her standing shoulder to shoulder with President Reagan, reminding the world that we are not simply carried along by the currents of history — we can shape them with moral conviction, unyielding courage and iron will."

Dr Edwin J Feulner, Jr, founder and past president, The Heritage Foundation: "What do John Major, Tony Blair, Gordon Brown, and David Cameron have in common? Yes, they are all British Prime Ministers — the last four of them, to be precise. And yes, they represent conservative, labour and coalition governments. But more specifically, they succeeded Margaret Thatcher. None of them, no matter what their political beliefs have chosen to — or been able to — undo the revolution that is known throughout the world as Thatcherism. The fundamental relationship between the citizen and government was redefined by Margaret Thatcher's decisive decade as Prime Minister.

"She believed in the rule of law, equality of opportunity, and limited government. Margaret Thatcher held to her principles tightly and proudly and she did so for generations to come.

"She restored the Great in Britain and every conservative should be proud to follow her leadership role in the public policy arena."

Edward H Crane, founder and Preident Emeritus of the Cato Institute: "In the summer of 1999, my wife, Kristina, and I had the pleasure of spending four nights and five days on Steve Forbes' *Highlander* yacht with Lady Thatcher and Sir Denis, Steve and his wife and another couple, Walter Cronkite, Katharine Graham and other dignitaries joined us from time to time. Mrs. Thatcher was always the center of attention.

"One didn't really have a conversation with her so much as you provided an audience for brief (sometimes not so) lectures on a wide spectrum of issues. Always enlightening and always entertaining. Toward the end of the trip I said, "Lady Thatcher, you've been highly critical of U.S. policies, criticism I've mostly agreed with, but may we now criticize British policies?" Assuming a boxing stance, fist over fist, she replied, "Let's have a go at it!" Interestingly, she did defend the indefensible NHS.

"My wife asked what she thought her legacy might be. She responded that perhaps she positively changed the course of British history. 'A very slight rudder change on a large ship may take some time to have an impact,' she said, 'but the change can be dramatic'. Of course, few have ever had such an impact on Western civilization, not just Britain, as Margaret Thatcher."

Former First Lady **Nancy Reagan**: "The world has lost a true champion of freedom and democracy.

"It is well known that my husband and Lady Thatcher enjoyed a very special relationship as leaders of their respective countries during one of the most difficult and pivotal periods in modern history. Ronnie and Margaret were political soul mates, committed to freedom and resolved to end Communism. As Prime Minister, Margaret had the clear vision and strong determination to stand up for her beliefs at a time when so many were afraid to 'rock the boat.' As a result, she helped to bring about the collapse of the Soviet Union and the liberation of millions of people."

Meryl Streep, who won an Oscar for the Margaret Thatcher biopic, *The Iron Lady*: "To me, she was a figure of awe for her personal strength and grit. To have come up, legitimately, through the ranks of the British political system, class bound and gender phobic as it was, in the time that she did and the way that she did, was a formidable achievement. To have won it, not because she inherited position as the daughter of a great man, or the widow of an important man, but by dint of her own striving. To have withstood the special hatred and ridicule, unprecedented in my opinion, leveled in our time at a public figure who was not a mass murderer; and to have managed to keep her convictions attached to fervent ideals and ideas - wrongheaded or misguided as we might see them now - without corruption - I see that as evidence of some kind of greatness, worthy for the argument of history to settle. To have given women and girls around the world reason to supplant fantasies of being princesses with a different dream: the real-life option of leading their nation; this was groundbreaking and admirable."

— The Hollywood Reporter, 8 April 2013

Sir Mick Jagger (former London School of Economics student) interviewed on tour (Daily Mail, 11 June 2013): "[She] didn't change to anyone. I was slightly surprised by all these people that were still so anti-her and had all this residual resentment. In the '80s or early '90s I met her a couple of times. I don't want to talk about what we talked about, especially now that everybody else is blabbing about her. But I reminded her that her first attempt at entering Parliament was in Dartford, where I grew up. I remembered her when I was ten or something and she was campaigning. She was called Margaret Roberts then, she struck me as a peculiar politician. She was quite brittle. Most other politicians like to be liked. Most of them, even if you don't like them before you meet them, are still likeable when you meet them, because that's their gig — to be liked, and by people like me. And I know she had lessons to make her voice less strident, which is fine, but I don't really think she changed for anyone."

US-based British writer **Andrew Sullivan:** "I was a teenage Thatcherite, an über-politics nerd who loved her for her utter lack of apology for who she was. I sensed in her, as others did, a final rebuke to the collectivist, egalitarian oppression of the individual produced by socialism and the stultifying privileges and caste identities of the class system. And part of that identity — the part no one ever truly gave her credit for — was her gender. She came from a small grocer's shop in a northern town and went on to educate herself in chemistry at Oxford, and then law. To put it mildly, those were not traditional decisions for a young woman with few means in the 1950s."

— From his blog, The Dish: http://dish.andrewsullivan.com/2013/04/08/thatcher-liberator/,8 April 2013

Acknowledgements

I thank first and foremost the Rt Hon John Bercow MP, Speaker of the House of Commons, for help and encouragement and Thomas Tweddle in his office. Lorraine Sutherland (Editor of the Official Report in the House of Commons), John Vice (Editor of Debates, House of Lords) and Liam Lawrence Smyth (Clerk of Journals, House of Commons) gave invaluable advice. The Rt Hon David Davis MP and I hatched the idea for this book together and I thank him for his *Introduction* and also his right hand Renate Sansom. As usual Christine Blundell did at least half of the real work needed to get this book into print; Susannah Hickling and Carroll Rodriguez also helped by tracking down many international comments.

Finally, I thank The Heritage Foundation, under whose umbrella I put this volume together, for its help, in particular Dr Edwin J Feulner Jr (founder and past president), Dr Matthew Spalding (Vice President), and Phillip N Truluck (Executive Vice President). Support from Maria and Meg Allen, Dan Peters, and Jim Whitaker is, as always, much appreciated.

4234934R00132

Printed in Great Britain
by Amazon.co.uk, Ltd.,
Marston Gate.